The Cosmic Game

SUNY Series in Transpersonal and Humanistic Psychology
Richard D. Mann, editor

The Cosmic Game

Explorations of the Frontiers
of Human Consciousness

Stanislav Grof

STATE UNIVERSITY OF NEW YORK PRESS

Cover Illustration: Plate 48 from Rawson, Philip, *Tantra: The Indian Cult of Ecstasy*, (London: Thames & Hudson, Ltd, 1973). Copyright © Thames & Hudson. Used by permission. From the Collection of Ajit Mookerjee, New Delhi.

Published by
State University of New York Press, Albany

© 1998 State University of New York

For information, address State University of New York Press, State University Plaza, Albany, N.Y., 12246

Production by Marilyn P. Semerad
Marketing by Dana E. Yanulavich

Library of Congress Cataloging-in-Publication Data

Grof, Stanislav, 1931–
    The cosmic game : explorations of the frontiers of human consciousness / Stanislav Grof.
        p.   cm. — (SUNY series in transpersonal and humanistic psychology)
    Includes bibliographical references and index.
    ISBN 0-7914-3875-9 (hardcover : alk. paper). — ISBN 0-7914-3876-7 (pbk. : alk. paper)
    1. Spiritual life. 2. Altered states of consciousness.
I. Title. II. Series.
BL625.G697   1998
200'.1'9—dc21   97-41502
                                                                      CIP

10 9 8 7 6 5 4 3 2 1

Contents

Experiential Holotropic Breathwork™ Workshops
and Training for Facilitators

Those readers who are interested in a personal experience of the Holotropic Breathwork or would like to participate in a training program for Holotropic Breathwork facilitators can obtain the necessary information from:

Cary Sparks
Director
Grof Transpersonal Training
20 Sunnyside Ave, #A 314
Mill Valley, California 94941

tel.: (415) 383-8779
fax.: (415) 383-0965
e-mail: gtt@dnai.com
website: www.holotropic.com

List of Illustrations

Acknowledgments

This book is an attempt to summarize the philosophical and spiritual insights from forty years of my personal and professional journey that involved exploration of uncharted frontiers of the human psyche. It has been a complex, difficult, and at times challenging pilgrimage that I could not have undertaken alone. Over the years, I have received invaluable help, inspiration, and encouragement from many people. Some of them have been my close friends, others important teachers, and most of them have played an important part in my life in both roles. I cannot acknowledge all of them individually, but some of them deserve special notice.

Angeles Arrien, an anthropologist and daughter of a "vision maker"—a spiritual teacher from the Basque mystical tradition—has been for many years a true friend and an important teacher. Drawing on forty years of her spiritual training, she has been a living example of how to integrate the feminine and masculine aspects of one's psyche and how to "walk the mystical path with practical feet."

Gregory Bateson, an original and seminal thinker, with whom I had the privilege of spending hundreds of hours in personal and professional discussions during the two and half years when we were both scholars-in-residence at the Esalen Institute in Big Sur, California, was for me an important teacher and a special friend. In our talks, he never wholeheartedly embraced the mystical realm. However, the relentless logic of his inquisititive mind produced an incisive critique of mechanistic thinking in science that provided a large opening for the transpersonal vision.

David Bohm's work has been one of the most important contributions to my efforts to establish connections between my own findings concerning the nature and dimensions of human consciousness, on the one hand, and the scientific worldview, on the other. I found his holographic model of the universe invaluable for my own theoretical formulations. The fact that Karl Pribram's model of the brain is also based on holographic principles has been particularly important for this bridging work.

Joseph Campbell, brilliant thinker, story teller, and master teacher, and for many years my dear friend, has taught me to understand the meaning of mythology and its function as a bridge to the realms of the sacred. He had a strong influence on my own thinking and his contributions to my personal life were equally profound. Today I consider mythology as understood by C. G. Jung and Joseph Campbell to be of critical importance for psychology, as well as for spirituality and religion.

Fritjof Capra's ground-breaking book *The Tao of Physics* was extremely influential in my own intellectual quest. By showing the convergence between quantum-relativistic physics and the Eastern spiritual philosophies, it gave me hope that spirituality and transpersonal psychology will one day become an integral part of a comprehensive scientific paradigm of the future. It helped me enormously to free myself from the straitjacket of my own academic training. Our friendship over the years has been a source of inspiration.

Brother David Steindl-Rast, a Benedictine monk and philosopher, has helped me to understand the difference between spirituality and religion. More specifically, he taught me to appreciate the mystical core of Christianity and the nature of Jesus' original message that in my early life was for me obscured by the complex and confusing history of the Christian Church.

Michael Harner, who has been able to integrate in a unique way his academic training as an anthropologist and his shamanic initiation in the Amazon, is one of my closest friends, as well as an important teacher. I have been able to learn from him, both theoretically and experientially, to deeply appreciate shamanism, humanity's oldest religion and healing art. This has been an important complement to my direct experiences with North American, Mexican, South American, and African shamans.

Albert Hofmann has had indirectly a more profound influence on my personal and professional life than any other single individual. His "serendipitous" discovery of the powerful psychedelic effects of LSD led to my first experience with this substance in 1956 when I was a beginning psychiatrist. This experiment has changed my personal and professional life and generated a profound interest in nonordinary states of consciousness.

Jack Kornfield, is a dear friend, colleague, spiritual teacher, and a true master of "skillful means" in the meditation hall, as well as in everyday life. He has been able to bring together and integrate in a remarkable way years of training as a Buddhist monk with his Western academic training in psychology. All of us who know him, friends and disciples alike, admire his compassion, wisdom, and extraordinary humor. In the two decades we have known each other, we have co-led many workshops and retreats. I have probably learned from him more about Buddhism and spirituality than from all the books I have read on these subjects.

Ervin Laszlo, the world's foremost representative of systems philosophy and the theory of general evolution, has been a very important influence in my professional life. His books—in which he succeeded in formulating the outlines of a unified science of matter, life, and mind—as well as personal discussions with him, provided for me the most satisfying conceptual framework for understanding my own experiences and observations. They made it possible to integrate my findings into a comprehensive worldview that unites spirituality and science.

Ralph Metzner, a psychologist and psychotherapist, who represents a rare combination of rigorous scholarship, concern for nature and the future of humanity, and an adventurous spirit,

Acknowledgments

has been since our first meeting thirty years ago an important friend and fellow seeker. He has been for me an important model for maintaining emotional balance and intellectual rigor in view of challenging and unsettling experiences and observations.

Ram Dass, another member of a close circle of special friends, has been one of my most important spiritual teachers. Representing a unique combination of jñāna, bhakti, karma, and rāja yoga, he has played in our culture the role of an archetypal spiritual seeker reporting with brutal honesty all the triumphs and failures of his spiritual quest. I do not remember a single time among our many meetings where he would not have enriched me with some unique insights and ideas.

Rupert Sheldrake has brought to my attention with unusual incisiveness and clarity the shortcomings of mainstream science. This helped me to be more open to new observations and trust my own judgment, even if my findings contradicted basic metaphysical assumptions of the conceptual frameworks I had been brought up with. I found his emphasis on the need to find adequate explanations for form, pattern, order, and meaning to be particularly important for my work.

Rick Tarnas, a psychologist, philosopher, and astrologer, has been one of my closest friends and a constant source of inspiration and new ideas. During the years we lived at the Esalen Institute in Big Sur, California, and more recently in the classes we have been jointly teaching at the California Institute of Integral Studies (CIIS), we have been exploring the extraordinary correlations between holotropic states of consciousness, archetypal psychology, and transit astrology. Through his meticulous research, Rick has helped me to deeply appreciate the grand design underlying creation.

Charles Tart has been for me an example of a brilliant and accomplished academician who has the courage, honesty, and integrity to stand uncompromisingly behind what he believes is true and to pursue unorthodox avenues in research, even if they are as controversial and misunderstood as parapsychology and spirituality. I admire him and have learned much from him.

Frances Vaughan and Roger Walsh are important pioneers and leaders in the field of transpersonal psychology. They are partners in life and work and I will thank them as a couple. They have been for me a source of continuing inspiration, support, and encouragement. In their lectures, seminars, and writings, as well as in their personal life, they have been modeling the possibility of integrating science, spirituality, and sane living. It has been wonderful to have them as friends and colleagues.

Ken Wilber has done more than any other single individual in terms of laying solid philosophical foundations for future reconciliation of science and spirituality. The series of his ground-breaking books has been a *tour de force,* offering an extraordinary synthesis of data drawn from a vast variety of areas and disciplines, Eastern and Western. Although we have occasionally disagreed about details, his work has been for me a rich source of information, stimulation, and conceptual challenge. I also greatly appreciate his critical comments on the present book.

I also feel deep gratitude to John Buchanan—for the inspiration, the humor he brought into our lives, and the generous support he has given my work over the years. Last but not least, I would like to express my high regard for Robert McDermott, president of the California Institute of Integral Studies (CIIS) for the extraordinary generosity and open-mindedness with which he supports and encourages free exchange of ideas in the controversial area of transpersonal psychology. I am also very grateful for the thoughtful and valuable comments he offered me after reading the manuscript of this book.

My special thanks go to the immediate members of my family, who have shared with me the excitement and the vicissitudes of my stormy personal and professional journey and have been a constant source of support and encouragement—my wife Christina, my brother Paul, and my late parents. Christina and I have jointly developed the holotropic breathwork that has been an important source of data for this book and have used it in our workshops and training all over the world. I feel deep gratitude for all she has contributed to the spiritual journey we have shared over the years. I would also like to express my appreciation to Cary and Tav Sparks, who have played an important role in my life by being close friends, as well as highly competent, dependable, and dedicated co-workers.

Many people whose contributions to this book were absolutely essential and critical will have to remain anonymous. I am referring here to thousands of individuals with whom I have worked over the years and who have discussed with me their experiences and insights from nonordinary states of consciousness. I feel great respect for their courage in exploring hidden dimensions of reality and gratitude for the openness and honesty with which they have shared with me their remarkable adventures. Without them this book could not have been written.

1
Introduction

The most beautiful experience we can have is the mysterious. . . . He to whom this emotion is a stranger, who can no longer pause to wonder and stand rapt in awe, is as good as dead.

—Albert Einstein

Use the light that dwells within you to regain your natural clarity of sight.

—Lao-tzu

This book addresses some of the most fundamental questions of existence that human beings have been asking since time immemorial. How did our universe come into being? Is the world we live in merely a product of mechanical processes involving inanimate, inert, and reactive matter? Do we have to assume the existence of superior cosmic intelligence responsible for the creation and evolution of the cosmos? Can material reality be explained solely in terms of natural laws or does it involve forces and principles that elude such descriptions?

How can we come to terms with such dilemmas as finiteness of time and space versus eternity and infinity? What is the source of order, form, and meaning in the universe? What is the relationship between life and matter, and between consciousness and the brain? Many of the issues that we will explore in this book have great relevance for everyday existence. How should we understand the apparent conflict between good and evil, the mystery of karma and reincarnation, and the problem of the meaning of human life?

These are not questions that are usually asked in the context of psychiatric practice or psychological research. And yet, in my work as a psychiatrist, these issues emerged quite spontaneously and with extraordinary urgency in the minds of many of the people with whom I have worked. The reason for this is the unusual field of study that has been the main focus of my interest during the forty years of my professional life—research of non-ordinary states of consciousness.

This interest began quite unexpectedly and in a very dramatic way in 1956, only a few months after my graduation from medical school, when I volunteered for an experiment with LSD in the Psychiatric Department of the School of Medicine in Prague, Czechoslovakia. This experience profoundly influenced my personal and professional life and provided the inspiration for my lifelong commitment to consciousness research.

Although I have been interested in the entire spectrum of nonordinary states of consciousness, I have had most personal experience with psychedelic research, with therapeutic work involving individuals undergoing spontaneous psychospiritual crises (spiritual emergencies), and with holotropic breathwork, a method that I have developed jointly with my wife Christina. In psychedelic therapy the nonordinary states of consciousness are induced by chemical means; in spiritual emergencies they develop spontaneously for unknown reasons in the middle of everyday life; and in holotropic breathwork they are facilitated by a combination of faster breathing, evocative music, and a specific form of focused body work. In this book, I will be drawing on all these three areas, since the insights from all of them are very similar, if not identical.

Consciousness Research and Perennial Philosophy

In my previous publications, I have described the important implications of systematic study of nonordinary states of consciousness for the understanding of emotional and psychosomatic disorders and for psychotherapy (Grof 1985, 1992). This book has a much larger and general focus: it explores the extraordinary philosophical, metaphysical, and spiritual insights that have emerged in the course of this work. The experiences and observations from this research have revealed important aspects and dimensions of reality that are usually hidden from our everyday awareness.

Throughout centuries, these experiences and the realms of existence they disclose have been described in the context of spiritual philosophies and mystical traditions, such as Vedānta, Hīnayāna and Mahāyāna Buddhism, Taoism, Sufism, Gnosticism, Christian mysticism, Cabala, and many other sophisticated spiritual systems. The findings of my research and contemporary consciousness research in general essentially confirm and support the position of these ancient teachings. They are thus in radical conflict with the most fundamental assumptions of materialistic science concerning consciousness, human nature, and the nature of reality. They clearly indicate that consciousness is not a product of the brain, but a primary principle of existence, and that it plays a critical role in the creation of the phenomenal world.

This research also radically changes our conception of the human psyche. It shows that, in its farthest reaches, the psyche of each of us is essentially commensurate with all of existence and ultimately identical with the cosmic creative principle itself. This conclusion, while seriously challenging the worldview of modern technological societies, is in far-reaching agreement with the image of reality found in the great spiritual and mystical traditions of the world, which the Anglo-American writer and philosopher Aldous Huxley referred to as the "perennial philosophy" (Huxley 1945).

Modern consciousness research has generated important data that support the basic tenets of the perennial philosophy. It has revealed a grand purposeful design underlying all of creation and has shown that all of existence is permeated by superior intelligence. In the light of these new discoveries, spirituality is affirmed as an important and legitimate endeavor in human life, since it reflects a critical dimension of the human psyche and of the universal scheme of things. The mystical traditions and spiritual philosophies of the past have often been dismissed and even ridiculed for being "irrational" and "unscientific". This is an uninformed judgment that is unwarranted and unjustified. Many of the great spiritual systems are products of centuries of in-depth exploration of the human psyche and consciousness that in many ways resembles scientific research.

These systems offer detailed instructions concerning the methods of inducing spiritual experiences on which they base their philosophical speculations. They have systematically col-lected data drawn from these experiences and subjected them to collective consensus validation, usually over a period of many centuries. These are exactly the stages necessary for achieving valid and reliable knowledge in any area of scientific endeavor (Smith 1976; Wilber 1997). It is very exciting that the claims of various schools of perennial philosophy can now be supported by data from modern consciousness research.

The approaches to self-exploration that make this modern validation possible, as they are described in this book, do not require the same degree of commitment and personal sacrifice as the ancient spiritual practices. They are more accessible and practical for Westerners who are trapped in the complexity of modern life. The use of psychedelics has been compromised by widespread unsupervised experimentation and is at present se-riously barred by a host of administrative and legal restrictions. However, holotropic breathwork is a method that is available for all those interested in exploring the validity of the insights de-scribed in this book. The experiences from our workshops con-ducted all over the world and the feedback from several hundred people who have completed our training and facilitate holotropic breathwork sessions themselves have convinced me that the observations I have described in this book are fully replicable.

Holotropic States of Consciousness

Before we begin to explore the spiritual and philosophical in-sights from my work, I would like to clarify in which sense I will be using in this book the term *nonordinary states of conscious-ness*. My primary interest is to focus on experiences that represent a useful source of data about the human psyche and the nature of reality, particularly those that reveal various aspects of the spiritual dimension of existence. I would also like to examine the healing, transformative, and evolutionary potential of these experiences. For this purpose, the term *nonordinary states of consciousness* is too general, since it includes a wide range of conditions that are not interesting or relevant from this point of view.

Consciousness can be profoundly changed by a variety of pathological processes—by cerebral traumas, by intoxications with poisons, by infections, or by degenerative and circulatory processes in the brain. Such conditions can certainly result in profound mental changes that would be included in the category of nonordinary states of consciousness. However, they cause "trivial deliria" or "organic psychoses," states that are very important clinically, but are not relevant for our discussion. People suffering from delirious states are typically disoriented. They might be confused to such a degree that they do not know who and where they are and what month or year it is. They typically show a disturbance of intellectual functions and have subsequent amnesia for the experiences they have had.

I will, therefore, narrow our discussion to a large and important subgroup of nonordinary states of consciousnes for which contemporary psychiatry does not have a specific term. Because I am convinced that they deserve to be distinguished from the rest and placed into a special category, I have coined for them the name *holotropic* (Grof 1992). This composite word literally means "oriented toward wholeness" or "moving in the direction of wholeness" (from the Greek *holos* = whole, and *trepein* = moving toward or in the direction of something). The full meaning of this term and the justification for its use will become clear later in this book. It suggests that in our everyday state of consciousness we are not really whole; we are fragmented and identify with only a small fraction of who we really are.

Holotropic states are characterized by a specific transformation of consciousness associated with perceptual changes in all sensory areas, intense and often unusual emotions, and profound alterations in the thought processes. They are also usually

accompanied by a variety of intense psychosomatic manifestations and unconventional forms of behavior. Consciousness is
changed qualitatively in a very profound and fundamental way
but, unlike in the delirant conditions, it is not grossly impaired.
In holotropic states, we experience intrusion of other dimensions
of existence that can be very intense and even overwhelming.
However, at the same time, we typically remain fully oriented
and do not completely lose touch with everyday reality. We
experience simultaneously two very different realities.

Extraordinary changes in sensory perception represent a
very important and characteristic aspect of holotropic states. With
the eyes open, we typically experience profound changes in the
shapes and colors of the environment. When we close our eyes,
we can be flooded with images drawn from our personal history
and from the collective unconscious. We can also have visions
portraying various aspects of nature, of the cosmos, or of the
mythological realms. This can be accompanied by a wide range
of experiences engaging other senses—various sounds, physical
sensations, smells, and tastes.

The emotions associated with holotropic states cover a very
broad spectrum that extends far beyond the limits of our everyday experience. They range from feelings of ecstatic rapture,
heavenly bliss, and "peace that passeth all understanding" to
episodes of abysmal terror, overpowering anger, utter despair,
consuming guilt, and other forms of extreme emotional suffering.
The intensity of these agonizing experiences can match the
descriptions of the tortures of hell in some of the great religions
of the world. The physical sensations that accompany these states
are similarly polarized. Depending on the content of the experience, it can be a sense of extraordinary health and well-being,
optimal physiological functioning, and orgastic sexual sensations
of enormous intensity, but also extreme discomfort, such as
excruciating pains, pressures, nausea, or feelings of suffocation.

A particularly interesting aspect of holotropic states is their
effect on the thought processes. The intellect is not impaired, but
it operates in a way that is significantly different from its everyday functioning. While we might not be able to rely in these
states on our judgment in ordinary practical matters, we can be

literally flooded with remarkable new information on a variety of subjects. We can reach profound psychological insights concerning our personal history, unconscious dynamics, emotional difficulties, and interpersonal problems. We can also experience extraordinary revelations concerning various aspects of nature and the cosmos that transcend our educational and intellectual background. By far the most interesting insights that become available in holotropic states revolve around philosophical, metaphysical, and spiritual issues. Exploration of these insights is the main focus of this book.

Philosophical and Spiritual Insights from Holotropic States

The content of holotropic states of consciousness is often philosophical and mystical. In these episodes, we can experience sequences of psychospiritual death and rebirth or feelings of oneness with other people, nature, the universe, and God. We might uncover what seem to be memories from other incarnations, encounter powerful archetypal beings, communicate with discarnate entities, and visit numerous mythological domains. The rich spectrum of these states also includes out-of-body experiences during which the disembodied consciousness maintains the capacity of optical perception and can accurately observe from unusual angles and distances the events in the immediate environment of the body, as well as in various remote locations.

Holotropic experiences can be induced by a variety of ancient and aboriginal techniques, "technologies of the sacred." These procedures combine in various ways drumming, rattling, sounds of bells or gongs, chanting, rhythmic dancing, changes of breathing, and cultivation of special forms of awareness. They might include extended social and sensory isolation, fasting, sleep deprivation, dehydration, and even drastic physical interventions, such as bloodletting, powerful laxatives and purgatives, and infliction of severe pain. A particularly effective technology of the sacred has been ritual use of psychedelic plants and substances.

These mind-altering techniques have played a critical role in the ritual and spiritual history of humanity. Induction of holotropic states has been absolutely essential for shamanism, rites of passage, and other ceremonies of native cultures. It also represented the key element of the ancient mysteries of death and rebirth that were conducted in different parts of the world and particularly flourished in the Mediterranean area. Holotropic experiences have been equally important for various mystical branches of the great religions of the world. These esoteric traditions have developed a variety of technologies of the sacred—specific methods of inducing such experiences. Here belong various forms of yoga, meditation and concentration techniques, multivocal chanting, whirling of the dervishes, ascetic practices, the Christian hesychasm or "Jesus prayer," and many others.

In modern times, the spectrum of mind-altering techniques has been considerably enriched. The clinical approaches include the use of pure alkaloids from psychedelic plants or synthetic psychedelic substances, as well as powerful forms of experiential psychotherapy, such as hypnosis, primal therapy, rebirthing, and holotropic breathwork. The most popular of the laboratory methods for inducing holotropic states has been sensory deprivation, an approach based on various degrees of reduction of sensory stimuli. Another well-known method is biofeedback, which makes it possible to use the information about the changes in one's brain waves as a guideline to specific states of consciousness. Many special electronic devices use the principle of "entrainment" or "driving" of the brainwaves by various acoustic and optical stimuli.

It is important to emphasize that episodes of holotropic states of varying depth and duration can also occur spontaneously, without any specific identifiable cause, and often against the will of the people involved. Since modern psychiatry does not differentiate between mystical or spiritual states and psychotic episodes, people experiencing these states are often diagnosed as mentally ill, hospitalized, and subjected to routine suppressive pharmacological treatment. My wife Christina and I have suggested that many of these states are actually psychospiritual crises or spiritual emergencies. If they are properly understood and individuals undergoing them are supported by experienced facilitators, episodes of this kind can result in psychosomatic healing, spiritual opening, positive personality transformation, and consciousness evolution (Grof and Grof 1990).

Ancient Wisdom and Modern Science

As we have seen from the above description, holotropic experiences are the common denominator in many procedures that have throughout centuries shaped the ritual, spiritual, and cultural life of many human groups. They have been the main source of cosmologies, mythologies, philosophies, and religious systems describing the spiritual nature of the cosmos and of existence. They are the key for understanding the spiritual life of humanity from shamanism and sacred ceremonies of aboriginal tribes to the great religions of the world. But, most important, they provide invaluable practical guidelines for a rich and satisfying life strategy that makes it possible to realize to the fullest our creative potential. For all these reasons, it is important that Western scientists free themselves from their materialistic prejudices and subject holotropic states to unbiased systematic research.

I have been deeply interested in all the categories of holotropic states of consciousness mentioned above and have had important personal experiences in many of them. However, as I have mentioned earlier, most of my professional work has been in the areas of psychedelic therapy, holotropic breathwork, and "spiritual emergency." Although the experiences observed in these three situations differ in terms of the triggers that initiate them, they seem to be remarkably similar in terms of their experiential content and of the spiritual and philosophical insights that they convey.

During my professional career, I have personally conducted over four thousand psychedelic sessions with such substances as LSD, psilocybine, mescaline, dipropyl-tryptamine (DPT), and methylene-dioxy-amphetamine (MDA), and had access to over two thousand sessions conducted by my colleagues. A significant proportion of these sessions involved psychiatric patients suffering from various forms of emotional and psychosomatic disorders, such as depression, psychoneurosis, psychosomatic disorders, alcoholism, and narcotic drug addiction.

Another large group consisted of patients suffering from various forms of cancer, most of them terminal. In this study, the objective was not only to relieve the emotional distress and severe physical pain associated with this illness, but also to offer these patients an opportunity to achieve mystical states in order to alleviate their fear of death, change their attitude toward it, and transform their experience of dying. The remaining subjects were "normal volunteers," such as psychiatrists, psychologists, social workers, clergy, artists, and scientists from various disciplines, who volunteered for psychedelic sessions because they sought understanding and insight.

The breathing sessions were conducted in the context of a long-term training program of professionals and of experiential workshops with a broad cross-section of the general population. Over the years, my wife Christina and I have supervised over thirty thousand holotropic sessions, mostly carried out in groups, only exceptionally on an individual basis. Besides the experimentation with psychedelics and with the holotropic breathwork, I have also worked with many individuals undergoing spontaneous psychospiritual crises. This occurred occasionally as part of my personal and professional life and was not carried out systematically as a specific project.

In writing this book, I used the records that I had amassed during more than forty years of work in the field of consciousness studies. I have focused specifically on those parts of the records that described experiences and observations related to basic ontological and cosmological questions. To my surprise, what emerged from these accounts of holotropic states was a comprehensive and logically consistent alternative to the understanding of human nature and of existence that has been formulated by materialistic science and that represents the official ideology of the Western industrial civilization.

People who experience holotropic states and integrate them effectively do not develop idiosyncratic delusional worldviews representing disjointed distortions of "objective reality." They discover various partial aspects of a grand vision of a universe that is created and permeated by superior cosmic intelligence. In the last analysis, this ensouled cosmos is commensurate with their own psyche and consciousness. These insights show a remarkable similarity to the understanding of reality that has repeatedly emerged, often quite independently, throughout history in different parts of the world. In many variations, this vision of reality has been shared by all the people who have had the opportunity to complement their everyday experience of material reality with insights from holotropic states of consciousness.

This finding brings good news to the millions of Westerners and people in technologized societies who have had various forms of holotropic experiences and were unable to integrate them with the belief system of their mainstream cultures. Because of this discrepancy, many of them questioned their own sanity or had their sanity questioned by others, including the mental health professionals from whom they sought advice or to whom they were brought against their will. The study of holotropic states vindicates these people and reveals the shortcomings of contemporary psychiatry. It shows an urgent need for a radical revision and revisioning of our understanding of human nature and of the nature of reality.

As the revolutionary advances of various disciplines of modern science continue to lift the spell of the outdated materialistic worldview, we begin to see the outlines of a new comprehensive understanding of ourselves, nature, and the universe. It is increasingly clear that this emerging alternative approach to existence will integrate science and spirituality and introduce important elements of the ancient wisdom into our technological world. Even at present, we have much more than just a disjointed mosaic of revolutionary theories and a vague outline of such a vision. Ervin Laszlo has already provided a brilliant synthesis of the most important theoretical breakthroughs in various fields of modern science (Laszlo 1993). Ken Wilber has formulated an extraordinary interdisciplinary framework that provides the necessary philosophical foundations for such integral understanding of reality (Wilber 1995, 1996, 1997).

Clearly, when this new vision of the cosmos is completed, it will not be a simple return to prescientific understanding of reality, but an overarching creative synthesis of the best of the past and the present. A worldview preserving all the achievments of modern science and, at the same time, reintroducing into the Western civilization the spiritual values that it has lost, could have profound influence on our individual, as well as collective life. I firmly believe that the experiences and observations from holotropic states explored in this book will be an integral part of this exciting new image of reality and of human nature that is now painfully being born.

2
Cosmos, Consciousness, and Spirit

As we progress and awaken to the soul in us and things, we shall realize that there is consciousness also in the plant, in the metal, in the atom, in electricity, in every thing that belongs to physical nature.

—Śri Aurobindo, *The Synthesis of Yoga*

The difference between most people and myself is that for me the 'dividing walls' are transparent.

—C. G. Jung, *Memories, Dreams, Reflections*

The Worldview of Materialistic Science

According to Western science, the universe is an immensely complex assembly of material particles that has essentially created itself. Life, consciousness, and intelligence are insignificant and more or less accidental latecomers on the cosmic scene. These three aspects of existence allegedly appeared in a negligible portion of an immense cosmos after billions of years of evolution of matter. Life owes its origin to random chemical processes in the primeval ocean that gathered atoms and inorganic molecules into organic compounds. The organic material then acquired during further evolution the capacity for self-preservation, reproduction, and cellular organization. The unicellular organisms assembled into larger and larger multicellular life forms and eventually developed into the rich panoply of species inhabiting this earth, including *Homo sapiens*.

We are told that consciousness emerged in late stages of this evolution out of the complexity of the physiological processes in the central nervous system. It is a product of the brain and, as such, it is confined to the inside of our skull. From this perspective, consciousness and intelligence are functions that are limited to human beings and higher animals. They certainly do not and cannot exist independently of biological systems. According to this way of understanding reality, the content of our psyche is more or less limited to the information we have received through our sensory organs from the external world since the time we were born.

Here Western scientists basically agree with the old saying of the British empiricist school of philosophy: "There is nothing in the intellect that was not previously in a sense organ." This position, first articulated by John Locke in the eighteenth century, naturally excludes the possibility of extrasensory perception (ESP)—access to information of any kind that is not mediated by the senses, such as telepathy, clairvoyance, or out-of-body experiences with accurate perception of remote locations.

In addition, the nature and extent of our sensory input is determined by the physical characteristics of the environment and by the physiological properties and constraints of our senses. For example, we cannot see objects if we are separated from them by a solid wall. We lose from our view a ship that passes beyond the horizon, and we are unable to observe the other side of the moon. Similarly, we cannot hear the sounds if the acoustic waves created by an external event do not reach our ears with sufficient intensity. When we are in San Francisco, we cannot see and hear what our friends are doing in New York City, unless, of course, this perception is mediated by some modern technological inventions, such as television or telephone.

Conceptual Challenges from Modern Consciousness Research

The experiences in nonordinary states of consciousness seriously challenge such narrow understanding of the potential of the human psyche and of the limits of our perception. What we can experience in these states is not limited to memories from our life after we were born and to the Freudian individual unconscious, as materialistic scientists have taught us to believe. Holotropic experiences reach far beyond the boundaries of what the Anglo-American writer and philosopher Alan Watts facetiously called "the skin-encapsulated ego." They can take us into vast territories of the psyche as yet uncharted by Western psychologists and psychiatrists. In an effort to describe and classify all the phenomena that become available in holotropic states, I have sketched a new map of human experience that expands the conventional understanding of the psyche. In this context, I will only briefly outline the basic features of this new cartography. A more detailed description can be found in my earlier books (Grof 1975, 1988).

To account for all the experiences that can occur in holotropic states, I had to radically expand the current Western understanding of the psyche by adding two large domains. The first of these is a repository of intense physical sensations and emotions linked to the trauma of birth, such as extreme physical pains in various parts of the body, feelings of suffocation, experience of vital anxiety, hopelessness, and intense rage. In addition, this domain also contains a rich spectrum of corresponding symbolic images revolving around the issues of birth, death, sex, and violence. I refer to this level of the psyche as *perinatal* because of its association with biological birth (from the Greek *peri* = around or near, and the Latin *natalis* = pertaining to chilbirth). I will return to this topic later in the chapter exploring the spiritual dimensions of birth, sex, and death.

The second additional domain of the psyche included in my cartography can be referred to as *transpersonal,* since its basic characteristic is the experience of transcending the usual personal limitations of the body and the ego. Transpersonal experiences vastly expand the sense of personal identity by including elements of the external world and other dimensions of reality. One important category of transpersonal experiences involves, for example, authentic experiential identification with other people, animals, plants, and various other aspects of nature and the cosmos.

Another large group of transpersonal phenomena can be described in terms of what the Swiss psychiatrist C. G. Jung (1959) called the collective unconscious. This vast repository of ancestral, racial, and collective memories contains the entire historical and cultural heritage of humanity. It also harbors primordial organizing principles that Jung called archetypes. According to him, the archetypes govern the processes in our psyche, as well as the events in the world at large. They also are the creative force behind the infinitely rich imaginal world of the psyche with its pantheons of mythological realms and beings. In holotropic states, the contents of the collective unconscious become available for conscious experience.

Careful study of the perinatal and transpersonal experiences shows that the boundaries between the individual human psyche and the rest of the cosmos are ultimately arbitrary and can be transcended. This work brings strong evidence suggesting that, in the last analysis, each of us is commensurate with the totality of existence. What it means practically is that anything that we would, in our everyday state of consciousness, perceive as an object, can be also encountered as a corresponding subjective experience when we are in a holotropic state. In addition to all the elements of the material world throughout the entire range of space-time, we can also experience various aspects of other dimensions of reality, such as archetypal beings and mythological domains of the collective unconscious.

In holotropic states, we can experience in remarkable detail all the stages of our biological birth, memories of prenatal existence, and even a cellular record of our conception. Transpersonal experiences can bring forth episodes from the lives of our immediate or remote ancestors or take us into the realm of the racial and collective unconscious. They can provide access to episodes that appear to be memories from previous incarnations, or even vestiges from the lives of our animal ancestors. We might experience full conscious identification with other people, groups of people, animals, plants, and even inorganic objects and processes. During such experiences, we can gain entirely new accurate information about various aspects of the universe, including the data that we could not have possibly acquired in our present lifetime through the ordinary channels.

When we have experienced to sufficient depth these dimensions that are hidden to our everyday perception, we typically undergo profound changes in our understanding of existence and of the nature of reality. The most fundamental metaphysical insight we obtain is the realization that the universe is not an autonomous system that has evolved as a result of mechanical interplay of material particles. We find it impossible to take seriously the basic assumption of materialistic science, which asserts that the history of the universe is merely the history of evolving matter. We have directly experienced the divine, sacred, or numinous dimensions of existence in a very profound and compelling way.

The Ensouled Universe

Following powerful transpersonal experiences, our worldview typically expands to include some elements of the cosmologies of various native peoples and ancient cultures. This development is completely independent of our intelligence, educational background, or profession. Authentic and convincing experiences of conscious identification with animals, plants, and even inorganic materials and processes make it easy to understand the beliefs of animistic cultures that see the entire universe as being ensouled. From their perspective, not only all the animals, but also the trees, the rivers, the mountains, the sun, the moon, and the stars appear to be sentient beings.

The following experience shows how it is possible in holotropic states of consciousness to experience inorganic objects as divine entities. It involves John, an intelligent and educated American, who had a powerful experience of loss of his everyday identity and conscious identification with a granite mountain while camping with his friends at a high altitude in Sierra Nevada.

I was resting on a large flat slab of granite with my feet immersed in a pristine creek cascading down the mountain. I was basking in the sun, absorbing its rays with my whole being. As I was getting more and more relaxed, I felt deep peace, deeper than I could ever imagine. Time was progressively slowing down until it finally seemed to stop. I felt the touch of eternity.

Gradually, I lost the sense of boundaries and merged with the granite mountain. All my inner turmoil and chatter quieted down and was replaced with absolute stillness. I felt that I had arrived. I was in a state of ultimate rest where all my desires and needs were satisfied and all questions answered. Suddenly I realized that this profound unfathomable peace had something to do with the nature of granite. As incredible as it might seem, I felt that I became the consciousness of granite.

I suddenly understood why the Egyptians made granite sculptures of deities and why the Hindus saw the Himalayas as the reclining figure of Shiva. It was the imperturbable state of consciousness that they worshipped. It takes tens of millions of years before even the surface of granite is broken by the assaults of weather. During that time the mercurial organic world undergoes countless changes: species originate, exist, and get extinct; dynasties are founded, rule, and are replaced by others; and thousands of generations play out their silly dramas. The granite mountain stands there like a majestic witness, like a deity, immovable and untouched by anything that happens.

The World of Deities and Demons

Holotropic states of consciousness, can also provide deep insights into the worldview of the cultures that believe that the cosmos is populated by mythological beings and that it is governed by various blissful and wrathful deities. In these states, we can gain direct experiential access to the world of gods, demons, legendary heroes, suprahuman entities, and spirit guides. We can visit the domain of mythological realities, fantastic landscapes, and abodes of the Beyond. The imagery of such experiences can be drawn from the collective unconscious and can feature mythological figures and themes from any culture in the entire history of humanity. Deep personal experiences of this realm help us realize that the images of the cosmos found in pre-industrial societies are not based on superstition or primitive "magical thinking," but on direct experiences of alternate realities.

A particularly convincing proof of the authenticity of these experiences is the fact that, like other transpersonal phenomena, they can bring us new and accurate information about various archetypal beings and realms. The nature, scope, and quality of this information often by far surpasses our previous intellectual knowledge concerning the respective mythologies. Observations of this kind led C. G. Jung to the assumption that, besides the individual unconscious as described by Sigmund Freud, we also have a collective unconscious that connects us with the entire cultural heritage of all humanity.

I will describe here as an illustration one of the most interesting experiences of this kind I have observed during the years of my work with holotropic states of consciousness. It involved Otto, one of my clients in Prague, whom I treated for depression and pathological fear of death (thanatophobia). In one of his psychedelic sessions, he experienced a powerful sequence of psychospiritual death and rebirth. As the experience was culminating, he had a vision of an ominous entrance into the underworld guarded by a terrifying pig-goddess. At this point, he suddenly felt an urgent need to draw a specific geometrical design.

Although I generally asked my clients to stay during their sessions in a reclining position with the eyes closed and keep the experiences internalized, at this point Otto opened his eyes, sat up, and urgently asked me to bring him some sheets of paper and drawing utensils. He drew an entire series of complex abstract patterns and, with great dissatisfaction and despair, he kept impulsively tearing and crumpling these intricate designs as soon as he finished them. He was very dissatisfied with his drawings and was getting increasingly frustrated, because he was not able to "get it right." When I asked him what he was trying to do, he was not able to explain it to me. He said that he simply felt an irresistible compulsion to draw these geometrical patterns and was convinced that drawing the right kind of design was somehow a necessary condition for a successful completion of his session.

The theme clearly had a strong emotional charge for Otto and it seemed important to understand it. At that time, I was still under a strong influence of my Freudian training and I tried my best to identify the unconscious motives for this strange behavior by using the method of free associations. We spent much time on this task, but without much success. The entire sequence simply did not make any sense. Eventually, the process moved to other areas and I stopped thinking about this situation. The entire episode had remained for me completely mysterious until many years later, when I moved to the United States.

During my stay in Baltimore, a friend of mine suggested that Joseph Campbell might be interested in the implications of my research for mythology and offered to arrange a meeting with him. After a few initial encounters, we became good friends and he played a very important role in my personal and professional life. Joseph has been considered by many to be the greatest mythologist of the twentieth century and possibly of all times. His intellect was remarkable and his knowledge of world mythology truly encyclopedic. He had a keen interest in the research of nonordinary states of consciousness, which he considered to be very relevant for the study of mythology (Campbell 1972). We had many fascinating discussions over the years, during which I shared with him various observations of obscure archetypal experiences from my work that I was not able to understand. In most instances, Joseph had no difficulties identifying the cultural sources of the symbolism involved.

During one of these discussions, I remembered the above episode and shared it with him. "How fascinating," said Joseph without any hesitation, "it was clearly the Cosmic Mother Night of Death, the Devouring Mother Goddess of the Malekulans in New Guinea." He then continued to tell me that the Malekulans believed they would encounter this deity during the Journey of the Dead. She had the form of a frightening female figure with distinct pig features. According to the Malekulan tradition, she sat at the entrance into the underworld and guarded an intricate sacred labyrinthine design.

The Malekulans had an elaborate system of rituals that involved breeding and sacrificing pigs. This complex ritual activity was aimed at overcoming the dependency on their human mothers and eventually on the Devouring Mother Goddess. The Malekulans spent an enormous amount of time practicing the art of the labyrinth drawing, since its mastery was considered essential for a successful journey to the Beyond. Joseph, with his lexical knowledge, was able to solve an important part of this puzzle that I had come across during my research. The remaining question, that even he was not able to answer, was why my client had to encounter specifically this Malekulan deity at that particular time of his therapy. However, the task of mastering the posthumous journey certainly made good sense for somebody whose main symptom was pathological fear of death.

C. G. Jung and the Universal Archetypes

In holotropic states we discover that our psyche has access to entire pantheons of mythological figures, as well as domains that they inhabit. According to C. G. Jung, these are manifestations of primordial universal patterns that represent intrinsic constituents of the collective unconscious. The archetypal figures fall into two distinct categories. The first one includes blissful and wrathful beings embodying various specific universal roles and functions. The most famous of them are the Great Mother Goddess, the Terrible Mother Goddess, the Wise Old Man, the Eternal Youth (Puer Eternus and Puella Eterna), the Lovers, the Grim Reaper, and the Trickster. Jung also discovered that men harbor in their unconscious a generalized representation of the feminine principle that he called Anima. Her counterpart, the generalized representation of the masculine principle in the unconscious of women, is the Animus. The unconscious representation of the dark, destructive aspect of human personality is in Jungian psychology called the Shadow.

In holotropic states, all these principles can come to life as complex protean appearances condensing in a holographic fashion countless specific instances of what they represent. I will use here as an example my own experience of an encounter with the world of the archetypes.

In the final sequence of the session, I had a vision of a large brilliantly lit stage that was located somewhere beyond time and space. It had a beautiful ornate curtain decorated with intricate patterns that seemed to contain the entire history of the world. I intuitively understood that I was visiting the Theater of the Cosmic Drama, featuring the forces that shape human history. I began to witness a magnificent parade of mysterious figures who entered the stage, presented themselves, and slowly departed.

I realized that what I was seeing were personified universal principles, archetypes, that through a complex interplay create the illusion of the phenomenal world, the divine play that the Hindus call *līlā*. They were protean personages condensing many identities, many functions, and even many scenes. As I was watching them, they kept changing their forms in extremely intricate holographic interpenetration, being one and many at the same time. I was aware that they had many different facets, levels, and dimensions of meaning, but was not able to focus on anything in particular. Each of these figures seemed to represent simultaneously the essence of his or her function, as well as all the concrete manifestations of the principle they represented.

There was Māyā, the magical ethereal figure symbolizing the world illusion, Anima, embodying the eternal Female, the Warrior, a Mars-like personification of war and aggression, the Lovers, representing all the sexual dramas and romances throughout ages, the royal figure of the Ruler or Emperor, the withdrawn Hermit, the facetious and elusive Trickster, and many others. As they were passing across the stage, they bowed in my direction, as if expecting appreciation for their stellar performance in the divine play of the universe.

The archetypal figures of the second category represent various deities and demons related to specific cultures, geographical areas, and historical periods. For example, instead of a generalized universal image of the Great Mother Goddess, we can experience one of her concrete culture-bound forms, such as the Virgin Mary, the Hindu goddesses Lakshmī and Pārvatī, the Egyptian Isis, the Greek Hera, and many others. Similarly, specific examples of the Terrible Mother Goddess could be, besides the Malekulan pig-goddess described in the above example, the Indian Kālī, the Pre-Columbian serpent-headed Coatlicue, or the Egyptian lion-headed Sekhmet. It is important to emphasize that these images do not have to be limited to our own racial and cultural heritage. They can be drawn from the mythology of any human group, even those we have never heard about.

Particularly frequent in my work have been encounters or even identification with various deities from different cultures who were killed by others or sacrificed themselves and later came back to life. These figures representing death and resurrection tend to emerge spontaneously when the process of inner self-exploration reaches the perinatal level and takes the form of psychospiritual rebirth. At this point, many people have, for example, visions of crucifixion or experience an agonizing identification with Jesus Christ on the Cross. The emergence of this motif in individuals with a Euro-American background seems to make sense, because of the important role Christianity has over the centuries played in Western culture.

However, we have also seen many powerful experiences of identification with Jesus during our holotropic breathwork seminars in Japan and India. They occurred in individuals whose background was Buddhist, Shinto, or Hindu. Conversely, many Anglo-Saxons, Slavs, and Jews identified during their psychedelic or holotropic breathwork sessions with Shiva or Buddha, the Egyptian resurrected god Osiris, the Sumerian goddess Inanna, or the Greek deities Persephone, Dionysus, Attis, and Adonis. Occasional identifications with the Aztec deity of death and rebirth, Quetzalcoatl or the Plumed Serpent, or one of the Hero Twins from the Mayan Popol Vuh, were even more surprising, since these deities appear in mythologies not generally known in the West.

The encounters with these archetypal figures were very impressive and often brought new and detailed information that was independent of the subjects' racial, cultural, and educational background and previous intellectual knowledge of the respective mythologies. Depending on the nature of the deities involved, these experiences were accompanied by extremely intense emotions ranging from ecstatic rapture to paralyzing metaphysical terror. People who experienced these encounters usually viewed these archetypal figures with great awe and respect, as beings that belonged to a superior order, were endowed with extraordinary energies and power, and had the capacity to shape events in our material world. These subjects thus shared the attitude of many pre-industrial cultures that have believed in the existence of deities and demons.

However, none of these individuals perceived their experiences of archetypal figures to be encounters with the supreme principle in the universe, nor did they claim to have gained an ultimate understanding of existence. They experienced these deities to be creations of a higher power that transcended them. This insight echoes Joseph Campbell's idea that the deities should be "transparent to the transcendent." They should function as a bridge to the divine source, but not be confused with it. When we are involved in systematic self-exploration or spiritual practice, it is important to avoid the pitfall of making a particular deity opaque and seeing it as the ultimate cosmic force rather than a window into the Absolute.

Mistaking a specific archetypal image for the ultimate source of creation leads to idolatry, a divisive and dangerous mistake widespread in the histories of religions and cultures. It might unite the people who share the same belief, but sets this group against others who have chosen a different representation of the divine. They might then try to convert others or conquer and eliminate them. By contrast, genuine religion is universal, all-inclusive, and all-encompassing. It has to transcend specific culture-bound archetypal images and focus on the ultimate source of all forms. The most important question in the world of religion is thus the nature of the supreme principle in the universe. In the next chapter, we will explore the insights from holotropic states of consciousness regarding this subject.

3
The Cosmic Creative Principle

O landless void, O skyless void,
O nebulous, purposeless space,
Eternal and timeless,
Become the world, extend!

—Tahitian creation tale

What is soundless, touchless, formless, imperishable,
Likewise tasteless, constant, odorless,
Without beginning, without end, higher than the great,
   stable—
By discerning That, one is liberated from the mouth of
   Death.

—Katha Upanishad

Absolute Consciousness

After we have had direct experiences of the spiritual dimensions
of reality, the idea that the universe, life, and consciousness
could have developed without the participation of superior creative intelligence appears to us absurd, naïve, and untenable.
However, as we have seen, the experiences of nature as ensouled
and the encounters with archetypal figures are not in and of
themselves sufficient to satisfy fully our spiritual craving. I therefore searched in the reports of the people with whom I had
worked for states of consciousness that were perceived as reaching the ultimate frontiers of the human spirit. I was trying to find
out what experiences would convey the sense of encountering
the supreme principle in the universe.

25

People who had an experience of the Absolute that fully satisfied their spiritual longing typically did not see any specific figurative images. When they felt that they attained the goal of their mystical and philosophical quest, their descriptions of the supreme principle were highly abstract and strikingly similar. Those who reported such an ultimate revelation showed quite remarkable agreement in describing the experiential characteristics of this state. They reported that the experience of the Supreme involved transcendence of all the limitations of the analytical mind, all rational categories, and all the constraints of ordinary logic.

This experience was not bound by the usual categories of three-dimensional space and linear time as we know them from everyday life. It also contained all conceivable polarities in an inseparable amalgam and thus transcended dualities of any kind. Time after time, people compared the Absolute to a radiant source of light of unimaginable intensity, though they emphasized that it also differed in some significant aspects from any forms of light that we know in the material world. To describe the Absolute as light entirely misses some of its essential characteristics, particularly the fact that it also is an immense and unfathomable field of consciousness endowed with infinite intelligence and creative power.

The supreme cosmic principle can be experienced in two different ways. Sometimes, all personal boundaries dissolve or are drastically obliterated and we completely merge with the divine source, becoming one with it and indistinguishable from it. Other times, we maintain the sense of separate identity, assuming the role of an astonished observer who is witnessing as if from the outside the *mysterium tremendum* of existence. Or, like some mystics, we might feel the ecstasy of an enraptured lover experiencing the encounter with the Beloved. Spiritual literature of all ages abounds in descriptions of both types of experiences of the Divine.

"Just as a moth flies into the flame and becomes one with it," say the Sufis, "so do we merge with the Divine." Śri Ramana Maharshi, the Indian saint and visionary, describes in one of his spiritual poems "a sugar doll who went to the ocean for a swim and completely dissolved." By contrast, the Spanish mystic St.

Teresa of Avila and Rūmī, the great Persian transcendental poet, refer to God as the Beloved. Similarly, the bhaktas, Indian representatives of the yoga of devotion, prefer to maintain a sense of separateness from and a relationship with the Divine. They do not want to become Śri Ramana's sugar doll who completely loses her identity in the cosmic ocean. The great Indian saint and mystic Śri Ramakrishna once exclaimed emphatically: "I want to taste sugar, not to become sugar."

People who have had the experience of the supreme principle described above know that they have encountered God. However, most of them feel that the term *God* does not adequately capture the depth of their experience, since it has been distorted, trivialized, and discredited by mainstream religions and cultures. Even the names like Absolute Consciousness or Universal Mind that are often used to describe this experience seem to be hopelessly inadequate to convey the immensity and shattering impact of such an encounter. Some people consider silence to be the most appropriate reaction to the experience of the Absolute. For them, it is obvious that "those who know do not speak and those who speak do not know."

The supreme principle can be directly experienced in holotropic states of consciousness, but it eludes any attempts at adequate description or explanation. The language that we use to communicate about matters of daily life simply is not adequate for this task. Individuals who have had this experience seem to agree that it is ineffable. Words and the structure of our language are painfully inappropriate tools to describe its nature and dimensions, particularly to those who have not had it.

With all these reservations, I include the following report written by Robert, a thirty-seven-year-old psychiatrist, who in his session had the experience of what he considered to be the ultimate reality:

> The beginning of the experience was very sudden and dramatic. I was hit by a cosmic thunderbolt of immense power that instantly shattered and dissolved my everyday reality. I completely lost contact with the surrounding world; it disappeared as if by magic. The

awareness of my everyday existence, my life, and my name faintly echoed like dreamlike images on the far periphery of my consciousness. Robert . . . California . . . United States . . . planet Earth . . . I tried hard to remind myself of the existence of these realities, but they suddenly did not make any sense. Equally absent were any archetypal visions of deities, demons, and mythological domains that were so predominant in my previous experiences.

At that time, my only reality was a mass of swirling energy of immense proportions that seemed to contain all of Existence in an entirely abstract form. It had the brightness of myriads of suns, yet it was not on the same continuum with any light I knew from everyday life. It seemed to be pure consciousness, intelligence, and creative energy transcending all polarities. It was infinite and finite, divine and demonic, terrifying and ecstatic, creative and destructive . . . all of that and much more. I had no concept, no categories for what I was witnessing. I could not maintain a sense of separate existence in the face of such a force. My ordinary identity was shattered and dissolved; I became one with the Source. Time lost any meaning whatsoever.

In retrospect, I believe I must have experienced the Dharmakaya, the Primary Clear Light, that according to the Tibetan Book of the Dead, the *Bardo Thödol*, appears at the moment of death.

Robert's encounter with the Supreme lasted approximately twenty minutes of clocktime, although during the entire duration of his experience time did not exist for him as a meaningful dimension. While this was happening, he had no contact with the environment and was not able to communicate verbally. Then he slowly began experiencing a gradual return to ordinary reality, concerning which he wrote:

After what seemed like eternity, concrete dreamlike images and concepts began to form in my experiential field. I started to feel that something like the earth with large continents and specific countries might actually exist somewhere, but it all seemed very distant and unreal. Gradually, this crystallized further into the images of United States and California. Later, I connected with my everyday identity and started to experience fleeting images of my present life. At first, the contact with this reality was extremely faint. For some time, I thought that I was dying and that I was experiencing the bardo, the intermediate state between the present life and the next incarnation, as it is described in the Tibetan texts.

As I was regaining contact with ordinary reality, I reached a point where I knew that I would survive this experience. I was lying on the couch feeling ecstatic and awed by what had been revealed to me. Against this background, I was experiencing various dramatic situations happening in different parts of the world throughout centuries. They seemed to be scenes from my previous incarnations, many of them dangerous and painful. Various groups of muscles in my body were twitching and shaking, as my body was hurting and dying in these different contexts. However, as my karmic history was being played out in my body, I was in a state of profound bliss, completely detached from these dramas.

For many days afterwards, it was very easy for me to reach in my meditations a state of peace and serenity. I am sure that this experience will have a lasting influence on my life. It seems impossible to experience something like this and not be profoundly touched and transformed by it.

The Pregnant Void

The encounter with Absolute Consciousness or identification with it is not the only way to experience the supreme principle in the cosmos or the ultimate reality. The second type of experience that seems to satisfy those who search for ultimate answers is particularly surprising, since it has no specific content. It is the identification with Cosmic Emptiness and Nothingness described in the mystical literature as the Void. It is important to emphasize that not every experience of emptiness that we can encounter in nonordinary states qualifies as the Void. People very often use this term to describe an unpleasant sense of lack of feeling, initiative, or meaning. To deserve the name Void, this state has to meet very specific criteria.

When we encounter the Void, we feel that it is primordial emptiness of cosmic proportions and relevance. We become pure consciousness aware of this absolute nothingness; however, at the same time, we have a strange paradoxical sense of its essential fullness. This cosmic vacuum is also a plenum, since nothing seems to be missing in it. While it does not contain anything in a concrete manifest form, it seems to comprise all of existence in a potential form. In this paradoxical way, we can transcend the usual dichotomy between emptiness and form, or existence and nonexistence. However, the possibility of such a resolution cannot be adequately conveyed in words; it has to be experienced to be understood.

The Void transcends the usual categories of time and space. It is unchangeable, and lies beyond all dichotomies and polarities, such as light and darkness, good and evil, stability and motion, microcosm and macrocosm, agony and ecstasy, singularity and plurality, form and emptiness, and even existence and nonexistence. Some people call it Supracosmic and Metacosmic, indicating that this primordial emptiness and nothingness appears to be the principle that underlies the phenomenal world as we know it and, at the same time, is supraordinated to it. This metaphysical vacuum, pregnant with potential for everything there is, appears to be the cradle of all being, the ultimate source of existence. The creation of all phenomenal worlds is then the realization and concretization of its pre-existing potentialities.

When we experience the Void, we have a sense that while it is the source of all existence, it also contains all creation within itself. Another way of expressing it is to say that it is all of existence, since nothing exists outside of its realm. In terms of our usual concepts and logical norms, this seems to involve some basic contradictions. It would certainly seem absurd to think about emptiness as containing the world of phenomena, the essential characteristic of which seems to be that they have specific forms. Similarly, common sense is telling us that the creative principle and its creation cannot be the same, that they have to be different from each other. The extraordinary nature of the Void transcends these paradoxes.

The following example is the description of an experience of the Cosmic Void of Christopher Bache, a philosopher of religion, who has been involved for many years in a systematic spiritual quest:

> Suddenly an enormous Void opened up inside this world. Visually, It took the form of a warping of my visual field, as if a giant, invisible bowl had been inserted into my seeing and was bending all the lines out to the outer edges of the picture. Nothing was torn or disrupted, but everything was being stretched and stopped to reveal this underlying reality. It was as if God suddenly paused between inhaling and exhaling, and the entire universe was suddenly suspended, not dissolved but held in its place for an eternity. It was a gaping, yawning opening in existence.
>
> At first this sensation took my breath away, both literally and figuratively, and I waited in suspension for movement to be restored. But movement was not restored. I was fully conscious, but absolutely suspended. And this suspension went on and on and on. I could not believe how long it lasted. As I soaked in this experience I realized that this was the Void out of which all form springs. This was the living Stillness out of which all movement flows. This contentless experience of concentrated consciousness that was pre-form and outside-form had to be what Eastern philosophers called śunyatā. When slowly movement resumed and the forms congealed, in the wake of the Void came an

exquisite sense of "suchness." Fresh from the Void, I touched the edges of experiencing existence "just as it is."

On several occasions, people who experienced both the Absolute Consciousness and the Void had the insight that these two states are essentially identical and interchangeable, in spite of the fact that they can be experientially distinguished from each other and that they might appear conceptually and logically incompatible. These individuals claimed to have witnessed the emergence of creative Cosmic Consciousness from the Void or, conversely, its return into the Void and disappearance. Others experienced these two aspects of the Absolute simultaneously, identifying with the Cosmic Consciousness and, at the same time, recognizing its essential voidness.

The experience of the Void as the source of creation can also be associated with the recognition of the fundamental emptiness of the material world. The realization of the voidness of everyday reality is the core message of one of the most important spiritual texts of Mahāyāna Buddhism, the Prajñaparamitā Hridaya Sūtra or Heart of Perfect Wisdom Sūtra. In the text Avalokiteshvara addresses Buddha's disciple Shāriputra: "The nature of form is emptiness, the nature of emptiness is form. Form is not different from emptiness, emptiness is not different from form. . . . Feelings, perceptions, mental formations, and consciousness are also like this."

It is interesting that the concept of the vacuum that is a plenum and of the "pregnant void" also exists in modern physics. A statement by Paul Dirac, one of the founders of quantum physics and the "father" of antimatter, describes it in these words: "All matter is created out of some imperceptible substratum and . . . the creation of matter leaves behind it a 'hole' in this substratum which appears as antimatter. Now, this substratum itself is not accurately decribed as material, since it uniformly fills all space and is undetectable by any observation. But it is a peculiarly material form of nothingness, out of which matter is created." The late American physicist Heinz Pagels is even more explicit: "The view of the new physics suggests: 'The vacuum is all of physics.' Everything that ever existed or can exist is already there in the nothingness of space . . . that nothingness contains all being" (Pagels 1990).

In their experiments, involving acceleration of elementary particles to high velocities and their collisions, physicists have observed creation of new subatomic particles emerging from what they call the "dynamic vacuum" and their disappearance back into this matrix. Of course, the similarity is only partial and does not go very far. The problem of cosmic creation is not limited to the origin of the fundamental building blocks of matter. It has important aspects that are outside of the reach of physicists, such as the problem of the origin of forms, order, laws, and meaning. The Void that we can experience in holotropic states seems to be responsible for all the aspects of creation, not just the raw material for the phenomenal world.

In our daily life, everything that happens involves complex chains of causes and effects. The assumption of strict linear causality is a necessary prerequisite for traditional Western science. Another fundamental characteristic of material reality is that all processes in our world follow the law of conservation of energy. Energy cannot be created or destroyed, it can only be transformed into other forms of energy. This way of thinking appears to be adequate for most of the events in the macroworld. However, it breaks down when we trace the chains of causes and effects back to the beginnings of the universe. When we apply it to the process of cosmic creation, we are confronted with formidable problems: If everything is causally determined, what is the original cause, the cause of causes, the Prime Mover? If energy has to be conserved, where did it come from in the first place? And what about the origin of matter, space, and time?

The current cosmogenetic theory of the Big Bang, suggesting that matter, time, and space were simultaneously created out of a dimensionless "singularity" some 15 billion years ago, can hardly be accepted as an adequate rational explanation of the deepest mystery of existence. And we generally cannot imagine that a satisfactory answer could be anything else but rational. The solution to these problems provided by transcendental experiences is of an entirely different nature and order. Experiencing Absolute Consciousness, the Void, and their mutual relationship makes it possible to transcend the baffling paradoxes that plague scientists theorizing about a material universe governed by causality and mechanical laws. Holotropic states can provide satisfactory answers to these questions and paradoxes; however, these answers are not logical, but experiential and transrational in nature.

When we experience the transition from the Void to Absolute Consciousness or vice versa, we do not have the feeling of absurdity that we would have in the usual state of consciousness, while considering the possibility of something originating out of nothing or, conversely, disappearing into nothingness without traces. On the contrary, there is a sense of self-evidence, simplicity, and naturalness about this process. The experiential insights in this regard are accompanied with the feeling of sudden clarification or an "aha" reaction. Since on this level the material world is seen as an expression of Absolute Consciousness and the latter, in turn, appears to be interchangeable with the Void, transcendental experiences of this kind provide an unexpected solution for some of the most difficult and taxing problems that beset the rational mind.

The insights of people who have experienced holotropic states of consciousness concerning the source of existence are strikingly similar to those found in perennial philosophy. I have already mentioned the description of cosmic emptiness from the Prajñāpāramitā Sūtra. Here is a passage from the ancient *Tao Te Ching* by the Chinese sage Lao-tzu (1988):

There was something formless and perfect
before the universe was born.
It is serene. Empty.
Solitary. Unchanging.
Infinite. Eternally present.
It is the mother of the universe.
For lack of a better name,
I call it the Tao.
It flows through all things,
inside and outside, and returns
to the origin of things.

Rūmī, the thirteenth-century Persian visionary and mystical poet, describes the source of creation in these words: "Nonexistence is eagerly bubbling in the expectation of being given existence. . . . For the mine and treasure-house of God's making is naught but nonexistence coming into manifestation." And here, for comparison, are two passages from the Jewish mystical tradition. The thirteenth-century Cabalist Azriel of Gerona says the following: "You may be asked: 'How did God bring forth being from nothingness? Is there not an immense difference between being and nothingness?' Answer as follows: 'Being is in nothingness in the mode of nothingness, and nothingness is in being in the form of being.' Nothingness is being and being is nothingness." And the fourteenth-century Cabalist David Ben Abraham he-Lavan writes: "Ayin, Nothingness, is more existent than all the being of the world. But since it is simple, and every simple thing is complex compared with its simplicity, it is called Ayin." And, according to the Christian mystic Meister Eckhart, "God's nothingness fills the entire world; his something is nowhere."

Words for the Ineffable

Illuminating insights into ultimate realities experienced in mystical states cannot be adequately described in our everyday language. Lao-tzu was well aware of it and put it very succinctly: "The tao that can be told is not the eternal Tao. The name that can be named is not the eternal Name." Any descriptions and definitions have to rely on words that have been developed to denote objects and activities in the material world as it is experienced in daily life. For this reason, ordinary language proves to be inappropriate and inadequate when we want to communicate about the experiences and insights encountered in various holotropic states of consciousness. This is particularly true when our experiences focus on the ultimate problems of existence, such as the Void, Absolute Consciousness, and creation.

Those who are familiar with the Eastern spiritual philosophies, often resort to words from various Asian languages when
describing their spiritual experiences and insights. They use
Sanskrit, Tibetan, Chinese, or Japanese terms like *samādhi* (union
with God), *śunyatā* (Void), *kundalinī* (Serpent Power), *bardo*
(intermediate state after death), *anatta* (no-self), *satori* (enlightenment experience), *nirvāṇa, ch'i* or *ki energy*, and *the Tao* for
high transcendental states or, conversely, *saṃsara* (the world of
birth and death), *māyā* (world illusion), *avidyā* (ignorance), and
the like when referring to everyday reality. These languages
were developed in cultures with high sophistication in regard to
holotropic states and spiritual realities. Unlike the Western languages, they contain many technical terms specifically describing
nuances of the mystical experiences and related issues. Ultimately even these words can be fully understood only by those
who have had the corresponding experiences.

Poetry, although still a highly imperfect tool, seems to be a
more adequate and appropriate means for conveying the essence
of spiritual experiences and for communicating about transcendental realities. For this reason, many of the great visionaries and
religious teachers resorted to poetry while sharing their metaphysical insights. Many people with whom I have worked re-
called and quoted passages from various transcendental poets. I
have often heard them say that, after their own mystical experience, visionary poems that they previously had not compre-
hended or related to, suddenly became clear and illumined with
new meaning.

Particularly popular among the people involved in spiritual
quest seem to be transcendental poets from the Middle East,
such as the mystics Omar Khayyām, Rūmī, and Kahlil Jibran, and
the Indian visionaries Kabīr, Princess Mira Bai, and Śri Aurobindo.
I have chosen here as an example a poem by Kabīr, a fifteenth-
century Indian sage, son of a Moslem weaver in Benares. In his
long life that lasted 120 years, Kabīr drew on the best of the
Hindu and of the Sufi tradition and expressed his spiritual wisdom in ecstatic verses. The following poem echoes the parallels
between the natural cycle of water and the creative process
described in the following section of this book.

I have been thinking of the difference
between water
and the waves on it. Rising,
water's still water, falling back,
it is water, will you give me a hint
how to tell them apart?

Because someone has made up the word
"wave," do I have to distinguish it
from water?

There is a Secret One inside us;
the planets in all the galaxies
pass through his hands like beads.

That is a string of beads one should look at with
luminous eyes.

We have also our own rich Western tradition of visionary
poetry, represented by William Blake, D. H. Lawrence, Rainer
Maria Rilke, Walt Whitman, William Butler Yeats, and others.
People who have experienced mystical states often refer to these
poets and recite passages from their work. Here is as an example
William Blake's often quoted poem capturing the mystery of the
immanent divine:

To see a World in a Grain of Sand
And a Heaven in a Wild Flower,
Hold Infinity in the palm of your hand
And Eternity in an hour.

The Beyond Within

In systematic spiritual practice involving holotropic states of
consciousness, we can repeatedly transcend the ordinary boundaries of the body-ego and identify with other people, animals,
plants, or inorganic aspects of nature and also with various

archetypal beings. We discover in this process that any boundaries in the material universe and in other realities are ultimately
arbitrary and negotiable. By shedding the limitations of the rational mind and the straitjacket of commonsense and everyday
logic, we can break through the many separating barriers, expand our consciousness to unimaginable proportions, and eventually experience union and identity with the transcendental source
of all being.

When we reach experiential identification with Absolute
Consciousness, we realize that our own being is ultimately commensurate with the entire cosmic network, with all of existence.
The recognition of our own divine nature, our identity with the
cosmic source, is the most important discovery we can make
during the process of deep self-exploration. This is the essence
of the famous statement found in the ancient Indian scriptures,
the Upanishads: "Tat tvam asi." The literal translation of this
sentence is "Thou are That," meaning "You are of divine nature,"
or "you are Godhead." It reveals that our everyday identification
with the "skin-encapsulated ego," embodied individual consciousness, or "name and form" (*nāmarūpa*) is an illusion and
that our true nature is that of cosmic creative energy (Ātman-
Brahman).

This revelation concerning the identity of the individual
with the divine is the ultimate secret that lies at the core of all
great spiritual traditions, although it might be expressed in somewhat different ways. I have already mentioned that in Hinduism
Ātman, the individual consciousness, and Brahman, the universal
consciousness, are one. The followers of Siddha Yoga hear in
many variations the basic tenet of their school: "God dwells
within you as you." In Buddhist scriptures, we can read: "Look
within, you are the Buddha." In the Confucian tradition, we are
told that "Heaven, earth, and human are one body."

The same message can be found in the words of Jesus
Christ: "Father, you and I are one." And St. Gregory Palamas, one
the greatest theologians of the Christian Orthodox Church, de-
clared: "For the kingdom of heaven, nay rather, the King of
Heaven . . . is within us." Similarly, the great Jewish sage and
Cabalist Avraham ben Shemu'el Abulafia taught that "He and we

are one." According to Mohammed, "whoso knoweth himself knoweth his Lord." Mansūr al-Hallāj, the Sufi ecstatic and poet known as "the martyr of mystical love," described it in this way: "I saw my Lord with the Eye of the Heart. I said: 'Who art thou?' He answered: 'Thou.' " Al-Hallāj was imprisoned and sentenced to death for his statement: "Ana'l Haqq—I am God, the Absolute Truth, the True Reality."

The Divine and Its Creation

We can now summarize the insights from holotropic states of consciousness concerning the creative principle, the nature of reality, and our own nature. As we have seen, these insights echo the message of the great spiritual traditions of the world. They suggest that the world of solid matter—featuring three-dimensional space, linear time, and unrelenting causality, as we experience it in our ordinary states of consciousness—does not have an independent existence of its own. Rather than being the only true reality, as it is portrayed by materialistic science, it is a creation of Absolute Consciousness.

In the light of these insights, the material world of our everyday life, including our own body, is an intricate tissue of misperceptions and misreadings. It is a playful and somewhat arbitrary product of the cosmic creative principle, an infinitely sophisticated "virtual reality," a divine play created by Absolute Consciousness and the Cosmic Void. Our universe that appears to contain countless myriads of separate entities and elements, is in its deepest nature just one being of immense proportions and unimaginable complexity.

The same is true about all the other dimensions and do-mains of existence that we can discover in holotropic states of consciousness. Since there are no absolute boundaries between the individual psyche, any part of creation, and the cosmic cre-ative principle itself, each of us is ultimately identical with the divine source of creation. We thus are, collectively and individu-ally, both the playwrights and actors in this cosmic drama. Since in our true nature we are identical with the cosmic creative principle, we cannot assuage our cravings by pursuits in the material world, no matter what their nature and scope. Nothing short of the experience of mystical unity with the divine source will quench our deepest longing.

4
The Process of Creation

As, from a well-blazing fire, sparks
By the thousand issue forth of like form,
So from the Imperishable, my friend, beings manifold
Are produced, and thither also go.

—*Mundaka Upanishad*

Even though you tie a hundred knots
The string remains one.

—Rūmī

The Mystery of the Creative Impulse

The realization that all the phenomenal worlds, including our material plane, are virtual realities created by Absolute Consciousness leads to some very interesting questions. The merging and union with the cosmic creative principle, as it was described in the previous chapter, is certainly an extraordinary and very desirable experience from the point of view of an individual human being. Many spiritual traditions consider reaching this state to be the ultimate goal of the spiritual quest. Those who actually attain the union with the Universal Mind realize that the situation is much more complicated.

They discover that what they once considered to be the goal of the spiritual journey is also the source of creation. It becomes clear to them that, in order to create the phenomenal worlds, the Divine has to abandon its original state of pristine undifferentiated unity. Considering how fantastic the experience of identification with Absolute Consciousness is from the human perspective, it seems strange that the creative principle should seek an alternative, or at least a complement, to a simple experience of itself. This naturally leads to the question about the nature of the forces that compel Absolute Consciousness to relinquish its primordial state and to engage in the process of creating experiential realities like the world we live in. What could possibly motivate the Divine to seek separation, pain, struggle, incompleteness, and impermanence, in short, precisely the states from which we are trying to escape when we embark on the spiritual journey?

People who achieve in their inner exploration the identification with Absolute Consciousness often experience fascinating insights into the dynamics of creation. Before we start examining these revelations, it is important to remember that holotropic states in general, and those that involve transcendental levels of awareness in particular, do not lend themselves well to verbal descriptions. As we review these reports, we might find them interesting and intellectually stimulating or feel inspired by them, but we should not expect logical explanations that would fully satisfy our rational mind. Because of the inherent limitations of our intellectual faculties, the human attempts to understand the "reasons" or "motives" for creation will never be completely satisfactory. Reason is an inadequate instrument for the analysis of transcendental dimensions of existence and of principles that operate on a very high metaphysical level. Ultimately, true understanding in these matters is possible only through direct personal experience.

Individuals describing their experiences of identification with the Divine are not able to avoid anthropocentric perspectives and to overcome the limitations of language. Thus the creative impulse of Absolute Consciousness is often described in terms of certain psychological states that we know from our everyday life, such as love, longing, or loneliness. Their authors usually capitalize the first letters of such words to indicate that they mean transcendental analogs, or "higher octaves," of such feelings rather than states that are directly comparable to those that we know from our everyday life. This is a practice well known from the writings of psychiatric patients who have experienced unusual revelations concerning transcendental issues and struggle to describe what happened to them.

The reports of people who in their holotropic states of consciousness have had insights into the "motivation" of the divine creative principle to generate experiential worlds contain some interesting contradictions. One important category of these insights emphasizes the fantastic resources and inconceivable capacities of Absolute Consciousness. Another group of revelations suggests that, in the process of creation, Absolute Consciousness seeks something that it lacks and misses in its original pristine state. From an ordinary perspective, these two categories of insights appear to contradict each other. In holotropic states, this conflict disappears and they can easily coexist.

Divine Cornucopia

The impulse to create is often described as an elemental force that reflects the unimaginable inner richness and abundance of the Divine. The creative cosmic source is so immense and overflowing with limitless possibilities that it cannot contain itself and has to express its full hidden potential. The experience of this quality of Absolute Consciousness is sometimes likened to a close-up view of the thermonuclear processes in the sun, the life-giving principle and source of energy for our planet. People who have this experience realize that the sun is the most immediate expression of the divine that we can experience in the material world and they understand why some cultures worshipped the sun as God.

However, they usually emphasize that this similarity should not be taken too literally, since there are also important differences between the sun as an astronomical body and the Cosmic Sun, the creative principle responsible for creation. The physical sun only contributes the energy necessary for the life processes, while the divine source also provides the Logos for creation—its order, forms, and meaning. Yet, in our everyday life, observing the sun seems to be the closest approximation to the experience of the divine source of creation as it reveals itself to us in holotropic states.

Other descriptions stress the immense desire of the Universal Mind to get to know itself and to explore and experience its full potential. This can only be done by exteriorization and manifestation of all its latent possibilities in the form of a concrete creative act. It requires polarization into subject and object, the dichotomy of the observer and the observed. These insights are reminiscent of the way creation is explained in certain Cabalistic texts, according to which there once was a state of previous nonexistence, in which "Face did not gaze upon Face." The reason for creation was that "God wished to behold God." Similarly, the great Persian mystic Jalāluddīn Rūmī wrote: "I was a Hidden Treasure, so I wanted to be known. . . . I created the whole of the universe, and the goal in all of it is to make Myself manifest" (Hines 1996).

Additional important dimensions of the creative process that are often emphasized are the playfulness, self-delectation, and cosmic humor of the Creator. These are elements that have best been described in ancient Hindu texts that talk about the universe and existence as *līlā,* or Divine Play. According to this view, creation is an intricate, infinitely complex cosmic game that the Godhead, Brahman, creates from himself and within himself. He is the playwright who conceived the game, as well as its producer, director, and also all the actors who play the countless myriads of the roles involved. This cosmic game of games is played in many dimensions, on many levels, and on unimaginable scales.

Creation can also be viewed as a colossal experiment that expresses the immense curiosity of Absolute Consciousness, a passion that is analogous to the infatuation of a scientist who dedicates his or her life to exploration and research. However, the cosmic experiment is naturally infinitely more complex than anything that collective effort of all of the scientists of the world could possibly conceive of. All the fascinating discoveries of science that extend far into the microworld and into the remote regions of the universe just barely scratch the surface of the unfathomable enigma of existence. Science, as we know it, only explores in increasingly refined ways the nature and content of the final products of creation, but does not reveal anything about the mysterious process that underlies it and brings it forth.

The question that repeatedly emerges in nonordinary states is the degree of control that the Divine has in the process of creation. It is a problem that Albert Einstein often struggled with. Here it is stated in his own words: "What really interests me is whether God had any choice in the creation of the world." The answers of the people who have reached this level of insight are not unanimous. Sometimes it appears that Absolute Consciousness is fully in charge of creation in its totality and in all its details. In this case, any surprises in the cosmic game occur only to individual protagonists. They are due to sudden lifting of their veil of ignorance that reveals significant aspects of divine knowledge that were previously hidden from them.

Occasionally, people experiencing holotropic states become aware of a significant alternative to this scenario. They see that it might be possible that only the basic parameters of creation are clearly defined, but the final outcome in detail remains unpredictable even for the Divine. This latter model of the cosmic game can be compared to a kaleidoscope or a chess game. The inventor of the kaleidoscope obviously realized that rotating a tube containing specially arranged mirrors and colorful pieces of glass would produce arrays of beautiful dynamic images. However, he or she could not possibly have foreseen all the specific constellations and combinations that would arise in the process of the use of this device.

Similarly, the inventor of chess could see the general potential of a game played on a board of sixty-four black and white squares with figures of specifically defined roles and movements. Yet it would have been absolutely out of question to anticipate all the infinite possibilities of specific situations that playing chess would eventually lead to. Naturally, the complexity of creation is infinitely greater than that of the kaleidoscope or the chess game. Although the intelligence of Absolute Consciousness is immense, it is conceivable that the unfolding of the cosmic drama can be beyond its control and can provide genuine surprises.

This is closely related to the question of our own role in the cosmic drama. If the universal script is written by the Divine in all the details, this does not leave us as individual players any possibility of active creative participation. The best we can do is to awaken to the fact that in the past our life has been inauthentic because we were misinformed about critical aspects of existence and about our own nature. However, if certain developments are unpredictable even for the Divine, various undesirable trends, such as the current global crisis, might require our assistance. In that case, we could actually become truly active players and valuable partners of Absolute Consciousness in the divine play.

Some people who have experienced insights into the "motives" for creation also emphasize its esthetic side. In our everyday life, we are often struck by the inherent beauty of the universe and nature, as well as those aspects of creation that are mediated by human activity, such as exquisite art and architecture. In holotropic states the ability to appreciate the esthetic side of all the different aspects of life and existence is greatly enhanced. When the "doors of perception are cleansed," to use William Blake's expression, it is difficult to miss the astonishing beauty of creation. From this perspective, the universe we live in and all the experiential realities in other dimensions also appear to be ultimate works of art and the impulse to create them can be likened to the inspiration and creative passion of a supreme artist.

Divine Longing

As I mentioned earlier, sometimes the insights concerning the forces underlying creation reveal "motives" that are of a different kind and even seem to be in conflict with the ones described above. They do not reflect overflowing abundance, richness, ultimate self-sufficiency, and mastery of the cosmic creative principle, but a certain sense of deficiency, need, or want. For example, it is possible to discover that, in spite of the immensity and perfection of its state of being, Absolute Consciousness realizes that it is alone. This Loneliness finds its expression in an abysmal yearning for partnership, communication, and sharing—a kind of Divine Longing. The most powerful force behind creation is then described as the need of the creative principle to give and receive Love.

Another critical dimension of the creative process that has occasionally been reported in this category seems to be the primordial craving of the divine source for the experience of the tangible material world. According to these insights, Spirit has a profound desire to experience what is opposite and contrary to its own nature. It wants to explore all the qualities that in its pristine nature it does not have and to become everything that it is not. Being eternal, infinite, unlimited, and ethereal, it longs for the ephemeral, impermanent, limited by time and space, solid, and corporeal. This dynamic relation between spirit and matter was portrayed in the Aztec mythology as the tension between two deities—Tezcatlipoca (Smoking Mirror) symbolizing matter and Quetzalcoatl (Plumed Serpent) representing spirit. A beautiful illustration of this cosmic dance between Quetzalcoatl and Tezcatlipoca can be found in the Aztec screenfold known as Codex Borbonicus.

The understanding of the active role of consciousness in creation is not necessarily limited to religion, philosophy, and mythology. According to modern physicists, the act of conscious observation changes probability of certain events into actuality and thus participates in the creation of material reality. In one of his lectures exploring the philosophical and spiritual implications of quantum-relativistic physics, physicist Fred Alan Wolf referred to the active role that consciousness plays in the creation of the material world. He speculated about the mechanisms underlying this process and suggested that the ultimate reason for creation of the material world might be the addiction of consciousness and spirit to the experience of matter. In everyday life, this craving of spirit for matter might be the deepest root of all our human attachments and addictions.

Another important "motive" for creation that is occasionally mentioned is the element of monotony. However immense and glorious the experience of the Divine might appear from the human perspective, for the Divine it is always the same and, in that sense, monotonous. Creation can then be seen as a titanic effort expressing a transcendental longing for change, action,

Figure 1. Quetzalcoatl and Tezcatlipoca. The legends of ancient Mexico assert that the worlds of matter and spirit are coexistent and each has something that the other needs. In this painting from the Aztec Codex Borbonicus, the dynamic tension between Spirit and Matter is represented as the complementary cosmic dance of Quetzalcoatl (in his form of Ehecatl, god of wind and breath) and Tezcatlipoca, the Smoking Mirror.

Source: Stanislav Grof, Books of the Dead. *Thames & Hudson, London, 1996, p. 93. Reprinted with permission of the Bibliothèque de l'Assemblée Nationale, 126 Rue de l'Université, 75007 Paris.*

movement, drama, and surprise. The countless experiential realities in many different dimensions and on many different levels offer infinite number of opportunities for adventures in consciousness and divine self-entertainment. The extreme forms of descriptions portraying creation as an act aimed at overcoming the monotony of undifferentiated Absolute Consciousness even refer to Cosmic Boredom. This again echoes passages from medieval Cabalistic texts that describe that one of the reasons God created the universe was to overcome boredom.

The creation of various phenomenal worlds also makes it possible for Absolute Consciousness to escape from the intolerable Eternal Here and Now into the comforting and predictable experience of linear time, limited space, and impermanence. This would then be the polar opposite and negative mirror image of the human fear of death and impermanence that underlies our deep craving for immortality and transcendence. For people who have had this experience, the threat of extinction of consciousness can be permanently replaced by the awareness that ultimately there is no way out of consciousness.

All those who have been fortunate to experience such profound insights into the cosmic laboratory of creation seem to agree that anything that can be said about this level of reality cannot possibly do justice to what they have witnessed. The monumental impulse of unimaginable proportions that is reponsible for creating the worlds of phenomena seems to contain all the above elements, however contradictory and paradoxical they might appear to our everyday sensibility and commonsense, and many more. It is clear that, in spite of all our efforts to comprehend and describe creation, the nature of the creative principle and of the process of creation remains shrouded in unfathomable mystery.

Dynamics of the Creative Process

Besides the revelations concerning the "reasons" for creation (the "why" of creation), the experiences in holotropic states often bring illuminating insights into the specific dynamics and mechanisms of the creative process (the "how" of creation). These are related to the "technology of consciousness" that generates experiences with different sensory characteristics and by orchestrating them in a systematic and coherent way creates virtual realities. Although the descriptions of these insights vary in terms of details, language, and metaphors used to illustrate them, they typically distinguish two interrelated and mutually complementary processes that are involved in creating the worlds of phenomena.

The first of these is the activity that splits the original undifferentiated unity of Absolute Consciousness into an increasing number of derived units of consciousness. The Universal Mind engages in a creative play that involves complicated sequences of divisions, fragmentations, and differentiations. This finally results in experiential worlds that contain countless separate entities that are endowed with specific forms of consciousness and possess selective self-awareness. There seems to be general agreement that these come into being by multiple divisions and subdivisions of the originally undivided field of cosmic consciousness. The Divine thus does not create something outside of itself, but by transformations within the field of its own being.

The second important element in the process of creation is a unique form of "partitioning," or of isolating "cosmic screenwork," through which the filial conscious entities progressively and increasingly lose contact with their original source and the awareness of their pristine nature. They also develop a sense of individual identity and absolute separateness from each other. In the final stages of this process, intangible but relatively impermeable screens exist between these split-off units and also between each of them and the original undifferentiated pool of Absolute Consciousness. It is important to emphasize that this sense of separation is purely subjective and ultimately illusory. On a deeper level, the undivided and undifferentiated unity continues to underlie all of creation.

The terms "partitioning" and "cosmic screenwork" are not quite appropriate in this context, since they suggest mechanical separation of elements and breaking of the whole into its parts. Such concrete images are much more suitable for crafts dealing with various materials, such as masonry or carpentry, than for the dynamics I am referring to. This is why many people borrow the terminology from psychology and compare this process with such mechanisms as forgetting, repression, or dissociation. We are talking here about the phenomenon that the writer and philosopher Alan Watts called "the taboo against knowing who you are." According to the insights from various holotropic states, the split-off units of consciousness are not necessarily only humans and animals, but also plants and elements of the inorganic world, discarnate entities, and archetypal beings.

The relationship between Absolute Consciousness and its parts is unique and complex and cannot be understood in terms of conventional thinking and ordinary logic. Our common sense is telling us that a part cannot simultaneously be the whole and that the whole, being an assembly of its parts, has to be larger than any of its components. And because the whole is an assembly of its constituents, we should be able to understand it by studying its parts. Until recently, this has been one of the fundamental assumptions of Western science. In addition, the parts should have a specific location in the context of the whole and occupy a certain portion of its overall size. While all that has just been said about the relationship of the whole to its parts seems to be true and self-evident in our everyday life, none of these characteristics and limitations apply in an absolute sense to the cosmic game.

In the universal fabric, separate units of consciousness, in spite of their individuality and specific differences, remain on another level essentially identical with their source and with each other. They have a paradoxical nature, being wholes and parts at the same time. Essential information about each of them is distributed in the entire cosmic field and they, in turn, have potential access to the information about all of creation. This is most obvious in regard to human beings where we have direct evidence of these relationships in the form of an entire spectrum of transpersonal experiences.

In transpersonal states, we have the potential to experience ourselves as anything that is part of creation, as well as the creative principle itself. The same is true for other people who can experience themselves as anything and anybody else, including ourselves. In this sense, each human being is not only a small constituent part of the universe, but also the entire field of creation. Similar interconnectedness seems to exist in the animal and botanical kingdom and even in the inorganic world. Observations concerning the evolution of species and the paradoxes in quantum physics certainly point in that direction.

This situation is reminiscent of the descriptions found in the ancient Indian spiritual systems, particularly in Jainism and in Avatamsaka Buddhism. According to Jain cosmology, the world of creation is an infinitely complex system of deluded units of consciousness, or *jīvas,* trapped in different aspects and stages of the cosmic process. Their pristine nature is contaminated by their entanglement in material reality and, particularly, in biological processes. The Jains associate these *jīvas* not only with organic life forms, but also with inorganic objects and processes. Each *jīva,* in spite of its seeming separateness, remains connected with all the other *jīvas* and contains the knowledge about all of them.

The Avatamsaka Sūtra uses a poetic image to illustrate the interconnectedness of all things. It is the famous necklace of the Vedic god Indra: "In the heaven of Indra, there is said to be a network of pearls, so arranged that if you look at one, you see all the others reflected in it. In the same way, each object in the world is not merely itself, but involves every other object and, in fact, is everything else." Similar concepts can be found in the Hwa Yen school of Buddhist thought, the Chinese version of the same teaching. Hwa Yen is a holistic view of the universe that embodies one of the most profound insights the human mind has ever attained. The essence of this philosophy can be succinctly expressed in a few words: "One in One, One in Many, Many in One, Many in Many." The concept of mutual cosmic interpenetration characteristic for this school is beautifully exemplified in the following story:

The Empress Wu, who had difficulties understanding the complexity of Hwa Yen philosophy, asked Fa Tsang, one of the founders of the school, to give her a simple practical demonstration of cosmic inter-relatedness. Fa Tsang took her to a large hall, the entire interior of which—the walls, ceiling, and floor—was covered with mirrors. He first lit a candle in the center of this hall and suspended it from the ceiling. In the next moment, they were surrounded by myriads of glowing candles of different sizes reaching to infinity. This was Fa Tsang's way of illustrating the relationship of the One to the many.

He then placed in the center of the hall a small crystal with many facets. Everything around the crystal, including all the countless images of candles, was now collected and reflected in the small interior of the brilliant stone. In this way, Fa Tsang was able to demonstrate how in Ultimate Reality the infinitely small contains the infinitely large and the infinitely large the infinitely small, without obstruction. Having done this, he pointed out that this static model was actually very limited and imperfect. It was unable to capture the perpetual, multidimensional motion in the universe and the unimpeded mutual interpenetration of Time and Eternity, as well as past, present, and future.

Metaphors for Creation

People who have envisioned in holotropic states the dynamics of the cosmic creative process and try to describe their insights often lack means of adequate verbal expression. They tend to resort to various symbolic images, metaphors, and parallels from everyday life, hoping that this will help to illustrate some of the experiences and ideas that they are trying to communicate. I will use the same approach in the following description of the creative process, using as illustration images drawn from the circulation of water in nature. References to such natural phenomena are particularly frequent in the accounts from sessions that contain cosmological visions.

Before the onset of creation, Cosmic Consciousness is a boundless undifferentiated field with immense creative potential.

Within it, creation begins as a ripple, as a disturbance of the original unity, that manifests as playful imagining and imaging of various forms. At first, the created entities maintain their contact with the source and the separation is only tentative, relative, and incomplete. Using the water metaphor, the original undivided unity of Absolute Consciousness would have the form of a deep and calm ocean of unimaginable magnitude. The image that can best illustrate the initial stage of the process of creation is the formation of waves on the surface of the ocean.

From one point of view, the waves can be seen and referred to as individual and separate entities. For example, it is possible to talk about a large, fast, and green wave, or one that is good or dangerous for surfers. At the same time, it is quite clear that, in spite of its relative individuality, the wave is also an integral part of the ocean. The differentiation of the waves from the ocean is playful, illusory, and incomplete. A sudden breeze can form waves on the surface of the ocean and when the wind calms down, these waves resume their original full identity with the ocean.

In the stage I have described so far, the creative source generates images different from itself, but these retain the connection with the source and awareness of their essential identity with it. Genuine creation requires that its products become separate and clearly distinguishable from the creative matrix. It begins in a true sense only when the connection with the source is severed and separate identity established. This may at first occur only for a fleeting moment. The corresponding metaphorical image would be that of a wave breaking in the wind or at the shore. As the solid body of water explodes into thousands of little droplets, these assume for an instant separate identity and independent existence, as they are flying through the air. This situation lasts only a very short time, until they all fall back and reunite with the ocean.

In the next phase, the separation is much more definite and the split-off units of consciousness assume their individual identity and independence for a considerable amount of time. This is the beginning of the partitioning, the "cosmic screenwork" or cosmic dissociation and forgetting. The original unity with the source is temporarily lost and the divine identity forgotten. A metaphorical parallel of this situation would be tidal water that got trapped in a pool on a rocky shore when the ocean receded during the low tide. This development involves long-term separation between the maternal waters in the ocean and the water in the pool. Yet during the next high tide the union will be reestablished and the separated mass of water will return to the source.

The continuation of the process of individuation results in a situation in which the separation is complete, convincing, and may appear permanent. A radical metamorphosis occurs and the split-off units of consciousness assume a new identity, quite different from the previous one. The original unity is obscured and concealed, but it is not completely lost. This stage of creation can be illustrated by a body of water that has evaporated from the ocean and has formed a cloud. Before becoming a cloud, the water underwent a profound transformation. The new entity now has a specific and characteristic shape and a life of its own. Yet the little droplets of water that can form in it betray the source and origin of this new phenomenon. They can easily condense, precipitate, and start their way to reunion with the ocean in the form of rain.

In the final phase, the separation is complete and the liaison with the source appears to be all but lost. The transformation is radical and total and the original identity is forgotten. The form of this new unit is distinct, very complex, and solidified. At the same time, the process of multiple divisions has advanced and the consciousness of the created entity appears to represent only an infinitesimal part of the original whole. A good example of this stage is the snowflake that crystallized in the cloud from the water that originally evaporated from the ocean. The snowflake represents only an infinitesimal fragment of the mass of water in the ocean and has a very specific individual shape and structure. The amazing array of forms that the snowflakes assume is a good illustration of the richness of creation characterizing the phenomenal world. The snowflake bears very little similarity to the source and in order to be able to reunite, it has to undergo fundamental changes of its structure and lose its identity.

We could go a step further and think about a block of ice. Here the water is so radically transmuted and so different from its original form that we would not be able to recognize its identity with water if we did not have the intellectual knowledge of the process of freezing and its effects. In sharp contrast to water, ice is dense, solid, hard, and rigid. Like the snowflake, to return to its original aquatic condition, it has to undergo a complete annihilation and lose what appear to be its essential characteristics.

Similar images likening various aspects of creation to water can be found in mystical literature of all ages. Here is how Rūmī describes the Divine and its works: "That is the Ocean of Oneness, wherein is no mate or consort. Its pearls and its fish are none other than its waves. . . . Spirit is truly and always one; but its manifestations on different planes of creation are different. Just as ice, water, and vapor are not three things but only three forms of the same thing, similarly Spirit is one, but its forms are many. In the very highest transcendent realms, it abides as an extremely fine and subtle entity; but as we descend toward less subtle regions, this Spirit also takes less subtle forms."

In the extreme situation, the source is not only lost and forgotten, but its existence is being denied. It would be difficult to find a fitting image for this stage of creation that would be related to the circulation of water in nature. The best example here is the atheist. This is how one of the people with whom I have worked saw the atheist's dilemma in a holotropic state of consciousness:

> An atheist represents the ultimate expression of cosmic humor. It is a split unit of divine consciousness that dedicated its temporary existence to a tragicomic battle for a clearly impossible task. It insists and is determined to prove that the universe and itself represent just accidental assemblies of matter and that the creator does not exist. An atheist has completely forgotten that he or she is of divine origin, does not believe in the existence of God, and can even passionately and violently attack all the believers. Śri Aurobindo described

an atheist as "God who is playing hide and seek with himself."

In addition to the images used above, the entire cycle of circulation of water in nature is often used in its totality to illustrate the character of the cosmic process. Depending on the weather, the ocean shows a beautiful and intricate play of waves that represents an entire world in its own right. The ocean water evaporates and forms clouds, which, in turn, have their own rich inner and external dynamics. The water in the clouds precipitates and returns to the earth in the form of rain, hail, or snow. This is the beginning of the way to reunion. The snow or hail melts, the drops of water merge into trickles and these form creeks, streams, and large rivers. After multiple confluences, this body of water reaches the ocean and reunites with its original source.

The Macrocosm and the Microcosm: As Above, So Below

Another area of everyday life that provides useful images illustrating the creative process is biology, particularly the relationship that exists between cells, tissues, organs, and the organism as a whole, on the one hand, and organisms, species, and ecosystems, on the other. This situation can be used to demonstrate how in the creative process the various units of consciousness are autonomous individuals in their own right, as well as parts of larger wholes and ultimately of the entire cosmic fabric.

The cells are structurally separate entities, but functionally they are integral constituents of tissues and organs. In turn, the tissues and organs are individual forms of increasingly higher orders, but they also have meaningful roles as parts of the entire organism. The fertilized egg in a certain sense contains the entire organism and the embryological development is unfolding of its inner potential. Similarly, the oak can be seen as an unfolded acorn.

We could also pursue this process in the opposite direction, farther into the microworld. The cells contain organelles that are made of molecules and the latter are composed of atoms. The atoms break down into subatomic particles and these, in turn, into quarks, considered currently the smallest constituents of matter. In none of the above examples can the parts be understood as separate entities independent from the system of which they are constituents. They make sense only in the context of larger wholes and ultimately as parts of the totality of creation.

The human body develops from a single undifferentiated source, the fertilized egg, by a complex sequence of divisions resulting in a large number and variety of highly specialized and diversified cells. In its final form, it has a hierarchical arrangement, where each part is also an integrated whole. A complex system of neural and biochemical regulations that transcends the anatomical boundaries on all levels ensures the functional unity of the constituent parts. In addition, each cell harbors a set of chromosomes containing genetic information about the entire organism. Genetic engineering, a science that is in its early stage, has already been able to create from the nucleus of a single cell a clone, an exact replica of the parental organism. The information about the entire body is thus contained in each of its parts in a way that makes the comparison with the cosmic creative process, as we described it earlier, very appropriate.

In the worldview of Tantric science, the relationship between the cosmos and the human organism is not seen as a mere metaphor or a conceptual aid. Ancient Tantric texts suggest that the human body literally is a microcosm that reflects and contains the entire macrocosm. If one could thoroughly explore one's own body and psyche, this would bring the knowledge of all the phenomenal worlds (Mookerjee and Khanna 1977). This is graphically represented in the Purushakāra Yantra, the image of the Cosmic Person. In this figure, the material world in which we live is situated in the area of the belly, the upper part of the body and the head contain the different heavenly realms, and the belly and legs harbor the underworlds.

The Buddha described the relationship between the body and the world in these words: "In truth I say to you that within this fathom-high body lies the world and the rising of the world and the ceasing of the world." In the Cabala, the ten Sefirot, archetypal principles representing various stages of the divine

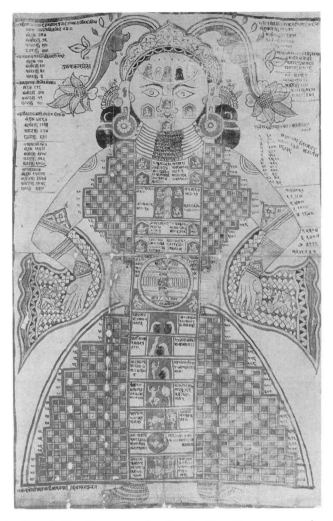

Figure 2. Purushakāra Yantra, or the Cosmic Man Yantra, a grand micro-macro vision of the universe. This eighteenth-century Tantric painting from Rajasthan, India, depicts the human being who has fulfilled his/her immense potentiality and become the entire universe. The seven ascending planes (*lokas*) represent experiences of celestial realms, the central plane those of the earthly plane (*bhurloka*), and the descending ones subnormal states of consciousness.

Source: Philip Rawson, Tantra: The Indian Cult of Ecstasy *(Art and Imagination Series), plate 20, published by Thames and Hudson Ltd. Reprinted with permission of the Ajit Mookerjee Collection. Photograph by Jeff Teasdale.*

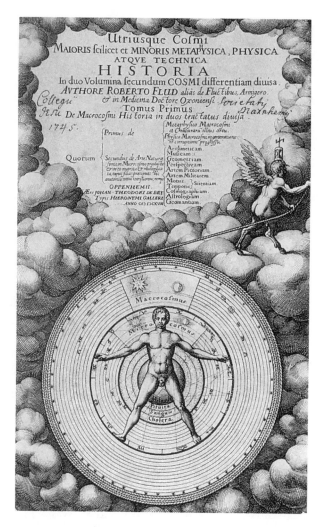

Figure 3. The Hermetic Cosmic Man. Illustration from a seventeenth-century hermetic text by Robert Flud, *Utriusque cosmi historia*, as reproduced in A. Roob's book *Alchemie und Mystik, Köln*, 1996, p. 543, depicting the human being as a microcosm reflecting the macrocosmos. The concentric circles representing the planetary spheres are related to the physical structure of the body. The nine angelic spheres point to the capacity of the individual human to use reason, intellect, and pure mind to achieve the status of the Cosmic Man and even God.

Source: Reprinted with permission of the Old Print Department of the Central Library of the Mannheim University.

Figure 4. **Adam Kadmon**, the Primordial Universal Man of the Cabalists is depicted here as holding the zodiac and supporting the entire solar system. The image of Adam Kadmon, embodying the ten Divine Emanations, the Sephiroth, was seen by the Jewish mystics as the most perfect reflection and representation of Divinity.

Source: Reprinted from Manly Hall's The Secret Teachings of All Ages *copyright and with permission of the Philosophical Research Society in Los Angeles, CA.*

emanation, are seen as the divine body of Adam Kadmon with the head, arms, legs, and sexual organs. The human body is a miniature replica of this primordial form. Similar concepts can also be found in Gnosticism, in the Hermetic tradition, and in other esoteric systems.

This deep connection between the individual human organism and the cosmos suggested by various esoteric traditions has been expressed in the famous statements "As above, so below" or "As without, so within." The observations from modern consciousness research have shed new light on this ancient mystical concept that appears quite absurd from the point of view of materialistic science. Transpersonal psychology has discovered that in holotropic states it is possible to identify experientially with just about any aspect of physical reality, past and present, as well as various aspects of other dimensions of existence. It has confirmed that the entire cosmos is in a mysterious way encoded in the psyche of each of us and becomes accessible in deep systematic self-exploration.

The discussion of the hierarchical arrangements in the universe could also be extended beyond the boundaries of individual organisms, since each life form constitutes a part in larger groups and systems. Animals form colonies, schools, flocks, and herds, and belong to families and species. Individual humans are parts of a family, clan, tribe, culture, nation, gender, race, and so on. Living organisms—plants, animals, and humans—belong to various ecosystems that have developed within the biosphere of our planet. In the complex dynamic structure of the universe, each constituent part is a separate entity, as well as a member of a larger whole. Individuality and participation in a broader context are dialectically combined and integrated.

The Part and the Whole

The new relationship that modern science has discovered between the whole and its parts was explored and systematically described by the British writer and philosopher Arthur Koestler. In his book *Janus,* named after the two-faced Roman god, Koestler coined the term *holon*, reflecting the fact that everything in the universe is simultaneously a whole and a part. The root of this word, *hol-*, suggests wholeness and integrity (from the Greek *holos* = whole) and the suffix *-on*, used customarily in the names of elementary particles, denotes a part or constituent. Holons are Janus-faced entities on the intermediate levels of any hierarchy, which can be described either as wholes or as parts, depending on the way we look at them, whether from "below" or from "above" (Koestler 1978). The concept of holons has been recently further developed in a highly sophisticated and creative way by Ken Wilber (1995).

Holons can accumulate into larger agglomerates. Bacteria, for example, can form a culture or stars can be assembled into a galaxy. These are social holons comprised of elements of the same order. Holons can also create emergent holons of a higher order. Atoms of hydrogen and oxygen can combine into molecules of water, macromolecules can form cells, and cells can get organized into multicellular organisms. These are examples of holons of increasingly higher order. What is important from the point of view of our discussion is that in holotropic states all the different individual, as well as social, holons have corresponding subjective states. These states make it possible for us to experientially identify in a very authentic and convincing way with any aspects of existence that in our ordinary everyday consciousness we experience as objects separate from us.

We are thus able to experience conscious identification with atoms, molecules, or specific cells of the body, either as individuals or as ensembles. Besides experiencing ourselves as other individual human beings, we can also undergo experiential identification with entire human groups, for example, all mothers, soldiers, or Christians of the world. We can envision a single wolf or a pack of wolves and observe them as objects. In addition, we can also identify experientially with a single wolf, as well as experience the consciousness of an entire pack of wolves or even of the entire wolf species.

Some of the people who have experienced holotropic states reported that they experienced consciousness of an ecosystem, of the totality of Life as a cosmic phenomenon, or of our entire planet. In transpersonal states, all aspects of existence as they manifest on different levels and domains of reality, can under certain circumstances become potentially available for conscious experience. This is a very important observation that brings a strong support for understanding the universe and existence as a divine play of Absolute Consciousness.

The following account is an excerpt from the session of Kathleen, who participated in our psychedelic training program of professionals at the Maryland Psychiatric Research Center. It is an example of a transpersonal experience that encompassed all life and reflected its struggle for survival. It resulted in a deep sense of compassion with all living things and a dramatic increase of ecological awareness.

> I seemed to have connected in a very profound way with life on earth. At first, I went through a whole series of identifications with individual animals from various species, but later the experience became more and more encompassing. My identity spread not only horizontally in space to include all living forms, but also vertically in time. I became the Darwinian evolutionary tree in all its ramifications. However incredible this might sound, I experienced myself as the totality of life!
>
> I sensed the cosmic quality of the energies and experiences involved in the world of living forms, the endless curiosity and experimentation characterizing life, and the drive for self-expression and self-preservation operating on many different levels. I realized what we have been doing to life and to the earth since we developed technology. Since technology is also an outgrowth of life, the crucial question I had to deal with was whether life on this planet would survive.
>
> Is life a viable and constructive phenomenon, or a malignant growth on the face of the Earth that contains some fatal flaw in its blueprint condemning it to self-destruction? Is it possible that some basic error occurred when the design for the evolution of organic forms was originally laid down? Can creators of uni-

verses make mistakes as humans do? It seemed at the moment a plausible, but very frightening idea, something I had never considered before.

Kathleen struggled for some time with the question whether it is possible that the creative principle might have made a fundamental error in bringing forth creation and that it might not be fully in control of the process. She concluded that this is probably the case and that the Divine might need assistance from humans to preserve its creation. Having opted for what I have described earlier as the "kaleidoscope" or "chess-game" theory of creation, Kathleen decided to become an active partner of the Divine in the battle for preservation of life. Here is the rest of her session:

> Identifying with life, I experienced and explored an entire spectrum of destructive forces operating in nature and in human beings and saw their dangerous extensions and projections in modern technology threatening to make the earth inhabitable. In this context, I became all the countless victims of the military machinery of modern warfare, prisoners in concentration camps dying in gas chambers, fish poisoned in polluted streams, plants killed by herbicides, and insects sprayed with chemicals.
>
> This alternated with moving experiences of smiling infants, charming children playing in the sand, newly born animals and newly hatched birds in carefully built nests, wise dolphins and whales cruising the crystal-clear waters of the ocean, and images of beautiful pastures and forests. I felt profound empathy with life, strong ecological awareness, and a real determination to join the life-affirming forces on this planet.

Ideas similar to Koestler's concept of the holon were expressed in the seventeenth century in the work of the philosopher and mathematician Gottfried Wilhelm von Leibniz. In his Monadology, Leibniz (1951) described the universe as composed of elementary units called *monads*. These monads have many characteristics of the Jain *jīvas*. As in the Jain worldview, in Leibniz's philosophy all the knowledge about the entire universe can be deduced from the information contained in each single monad.

It is interesting that Leibniz was also the originator of the mathematical technique that was instrumental in the development of optical holography, a new field that provided for the first time a solid scientific basis for the concept of mutual interpenetration. Optical holograms demonstrate very clearly the paradoxical relations that can exist between the parts and the whole, including the possibility of retrieving the information about the whole from each of its parts. It is possible that in creating phenomenal worlds Absolute Consciousness is using the same principles that find their material expression in optical holography. In any case, the holographic model is the best conceptual framework we have to date for the world of transpersonal phenomena.

Creation and the World of Art

In holotropic states, we can realize that existence, human life, and the world around us constitute a fantastic adventure in consciousness, an amazingly complex and intricate cosmic drama. This parallels the concepts found in ancient Indian literature. The Hindu scriptures refer to the divine play of the universe as *līlā* and suggest that the material reality as we perceive it in our everyday life is a product of a fundamental cosmic illusion called *māyā*. Theater, film, and television are artificially created illusory representations of reality. For this reason, these media and various aspects of related artistic activities represent another frequent source of metaphorical images that people who have experienced holotropic states use in describing the process of creation.

The situation of an actor very closely parallels the role each of us plays in the cosmic drama. While on stage and performing a role, good actors can to a great extent lose contact with their real identities and become the characters they represent. For the evening of the performance, they can almost believe they are Othello, Joan of Arc, Ophelia, or Cyrano de Bergerac. Yet the awareness of their real identity remains available and is resumed after the curtain has fallen and the applause of the audience subsides. To a lesser degree, a similar process of identification with the dramatis personae and temporary loss of one's own identity can occur in spectators watching a good movie or a well-performed theater play. The actor or actress have their basic everyday personalities to which they return when the play ends. People who have experienced holotropic states often suggest that something similar happens in the cycles of reincarnation. At the beginning of each lifetime, we assume a different personality and role and, at the time of death, we return to a more basic identity before taking on another incarnation.

Particularly interesting from this point of view is the situation of a playwright, because it can be used to illustrate the complexity of our nature and the problem of determinism versus free will. Since all the boundaries in the universe are ultimately arbitrary, we do not possess a fixed identity; each of us is the creator as well as the creation. The degree of freedom that we have changes dramatically depending on the aspect of creation and the level of the creative process with which we identify. This is similar to the situation of the author of a theater play or a screenplay for a movie. All the characters of a play have their origin in the imagination of the playwright and are thus initially different aspects of a single creative mind. For the purpose of a realistic and effective enactment of the drama the protagonists have to be represented as separate individuals.

This offers the author an opportunity for ambiguous identity in relation to the play and its characters. In the process of writing, he or she has far-reaching freedom to create and shape the characters and determine the course of events. However, the same author can also decide to become one of the players in his or her drama. William Shakespeare, for example, could decide to play the role of Hamlet or Richard Wagner to sing the part of Tannhäuser. In such cases, they would be to a great extent confined and determined by the same scripts that, in another context and on another level, they more or less freely created. In a similar way, each of us appears in the divine play in a dual role of creator and actor. A full and realistic enactment of our role in the cosmic drama requires the suspension of our true identity. We have to forget our authorship and follow the script.

The problem of ambiguity of our identity and of our role in the cosmic drama requires a word of caution. In the last few decades this issue has often been misunderstood and misrepresented in the New Age movement and in popular spirituality. In holotropic states, it is possible to connect with a level of consciousness where it seems very plausible that we have actually chosen our parents and the circumstances of our birth. We can also experience a state of consciousness in which it seems obvious that we are in essence spiritual beings and that as such we have made a free decision to incarnate and engage in the cosmic drama. We can also have a very powerful experience of identification with the creative principle or God. All these experiences can seem very real and convincing.

However, it would be a serious mistake to draw from such insights any conclusions concerning our ordinary identity or our embodied self. In this form we certainly did not make any of the above decisions. If applied to the body-ego, such statements as "You are God and you have created your universe" are confusing and misleading. I remember a workshop at the Esalen Institute in Big Sur, California, in which the leader authoritatively imposed the above statement on the participants. One of the women in the group got seriously upset, since she was the mother of a retarded child. The workshop leader's statement implied that she had chosen this predicament and deliberately created this problem. This would have meant that she, as she experienced herself in her everyday life, was fully responsible for her child's misfortune. Situations of this kind involve a serious confusion of levels and an incorrect use of logic that is technically called "error in logical typing."

The Archetypal Beings and Domains

We can now return to the dynamics of the cosmic creative process as it is revealed in holotropic states of consciousness. I have already described and discussed the frequent insights suggesting that the Universal Mind creates virtual realities through a complex combination of multiple divisions and cosmic dissociation and forgetting. Absolute Consciousness projects itself into countless individual beings that experience themselves as separate from each other and also alienated from their source. In constant dynamic interaction with each other, they generate immensely rich experiential worlds. The material realm which we inhabit and with which we are intimately familiar seems to be just one of these worlds, the farthest outpost of this creative activity.

Of special interest is a domain that lies between our everyday reality and the undifferentiated Absolute Consciousness. It is a mythological realm that has been extensively studied and described by C. G. Jung and his followers. Unlike the material reality, it is not available to ordinary sensory perception; it can be directly experienced only in holotropic states. Jung referred to it as the archetypal realm of the collective unconscious. The beings inhabiting these realms seem to be endowed with extraordinary energy and have an aura of sacredness or numinosity. For this reason, they are usually perceived and described as deities.

The events occurring in this mythic realm unfold in a kind of space and time, but a space and time that are not identical with our experience of these dimensions on the material level. Archetypal sequences lack the geographical and historical integrity that is characteristic for events in material reality. Unlike the happenings in our world, which can be assigned specific spatial and temporal coordinates, the mythical sequences cannot be placed into a coherent fabric of space or time. While it is easy to geographically locate London or assign a specific historical date to the French Revolution, it is impossible to do the same with Shiva's heaven or the battle between the Greek Olympian gods and the Titans. The stories inspired by the mythical realm usually begin: "Once upon a time, in a faraway land," in order to discourage the listener from an attempt to place them geographically or historically into the familiar world of everyday reality.

However, the lack of fixed spatial and temporal coordinates does not make the archetypal world ontologically less real. The encounters with mythological beings and visits to mythic landscapes, as experienced in holotropic states, can be in every respect as real as events in our everyday life, or more so. The archetypal realm is not a figment of human fantasy and imagination; it has an independent existence of its own and a high degree of autonomy. At the same time, its dynamics seem to be intimately connected with material reality and with human life.

The archetypes are clearly supraordinated to the events in the material world and govern, form, and inform what is happening in our everyday reality. The insights from holotropic states of consciousness concerning these connections are similar to the ideas that have been expressed in various books written by the authors inspired by Jungian psychology. These writers showed that our personalities, behaviors, and destinies can be understood in terms of the archetypal divine principles operating in or through our unconscious (Bolen 1984, 1989) and that in our everyday human dramas we act out various mythological themes (Campbell 1972).

The following experience of Helen, a 42-year-old anthropologist, illustrates the way the archetypal world is experienced in holotropic states of consciousness and the insights this can provide.

The sequence that followed was of such grandeur and magnificence that I still feel a deep sense of awe just thinking about it. It was a vision of a world that had some characteristics in common with our everyday reality, yet the amount of energy it was endowed with and the scale on which it existed was beyond anything I could previously have imagined. I saw illustrious anthropomorphic figures, male and female, clad in splendid garments and radiating immense power. It resembled the ancient Greek descriptions of Mount Olympus where the gods feasted on nectar and ambrosia. However, this experience by far surpassed anything I had previously associated with this image.

These suprahuman beings were involved in what resembled social interaction, but their exchange seemed to be of enormous relevance. I felt that what was happening there was intimately connected with our every-day reality and was determining the events in the material world. I remember a particularly impressive detail that can be used as an illustration of this connection and the dimensions involved. At one point, I saw a splendid ring on the finger of one of these divine beings with a stone that seemed to be a cosmic version of a diamond. The reflection from one of its facets struck me as a blinding flash of light and I realized that it projected into our world as explosion of an atomic bomb.

Later I thought in connection with this experience of a movie that I had seen some time ago. I think it was called the Golden Fleece and it featured the adventures of Jason and the Argonauts. The events in this movie unfolded on two levels. One of them portrayed the realm of the Olympian gods, their interactions, affairs, conflicts, clashes, and alliances. Each of these deities had his or her sphere of influence in the cosmos. The protagonists of the story were favorites of some gods and targets of wrath of others. The emotions of the gods manifested on the earthly plane as dynamics of the elements of nature, sudden turns of fortune, or meaningful human encounters.

In view of this experience and the insights associated with it, I feel apologetic about the scientistic hubris with which I used to dismiss the cosmologies of "primitive cultures" as superstition and magical thinking. I realized that this reflected the naiveté of our society in regard to nonordinary states of consciousness. It was very clear to me that once we subject the observations from these states to serious study, our materialistic worldview will have to be drastically revised. We might not use the terms "deities" and "demons" like the "primitive" cultures and might replace them with more respectable terms, such as "archetypal figures." However, once we become familiar with the archetypal dimension, we will not be able to ignore or deny its existence and its importance in the universal scheme of things.

While the above account describes a vision of celestial archetypal regions, other people experienced visits to domains inhabited by various creatures of darkness, as we know them from mythological descriptions of hells or underworlds of different cultures. The following excerpt from a narrative written by Arnold, a forty-year-old teacher, is an example of such an experience.

The next sequence took me into the world of underground tunnels and to what appeared to be sewage systems of all the great metropolis of the world—New York, Paris, London, Tokyo. . . . It seemed that I was getting intimately acquainted with the infrastructure of these cities, with parts and aspects that are indispensable for their existence. I realized to my surprise that there was an entire world there, hidden from the sight of most people and generally unappreciated. I was sinking deeper and deeper into a system of dark mazes until I realized that the domain I was entering did not any more belong to the world of our everyday reality.

Although it certainly felt like the deepest bowels of the earth, it was actually a mythological realm inhabited by strange archetypal creatures. It seemed to me that I was seeing the infrastructure of the cosmos, essential for its existence and proper functioning. Like the underground world of the cities, it was hidden and unappreciated. It was inhabited by gigantic and monstrous chthonic beings of fantastic shapes. They were endowed with titanic energies that made one think of tectonic shifts, earthquakes, and volcanic explosions.

I could not help feeling great appreciation for these homely creatures living their life in darkness and doing patiently the ungrateful labor of running the engine of the universe. They clearly welcomed my visit and responded with great joy to my unspoken compliments. It seemed that they were used to being feared and rejected and showed almost childlike craving for love and acceptance.

As these experiences indicate, there exist various dimensions of reality that are not part of the phenomenal world of our everyday life. They seem to represent different types and levels of experiential realities, different "cosmic channels," to use an analogy with the world of modern electronics. We usually take the material world with all its wonders and complexities for granted and reject the possibility that there might be other domains of reality. However, if we think about it, the sheer mystery of existence—the fact that anything exists at all and that it is possible to experience worlds of any kind—is so stupendous and overwhelming that it makes the question about the specifics of their nature and content a trivial one.

From a larger perspective, the experience of a beautiful sunset over the Pacific Ocean, the vision of the Grand Canyon, or the panorama of downtown Manhattan is not less miraculous than that of Shiva's heaven or the Egyptian underworld. If we accept the existence of a supreme principle that has at its disposal the technology of consciousness and is able to generate experiences, the fact that it can create realities with many different characteristics does not present any serious problems. It would be comparable to the task of a film or TV crew to use the existing technology and produce movies or programs with mythological themes rather than stories from everyday life.

The Mystery Play of the Universe

Since the Hindu philosophers refer to the cosmic process as *līlā*, or divine play, it seems appropriate to illustrate the holotropic insights into the nature of reality by using the analogy with a movie, which is a modern technological version of a magic show. The intention of the moviemakers is to create a reasonable facsimile, a "make-believe" version, of material reality. They use all the available means necessary to achieve this goal. It is usually very easy for the spectators to imagine that the scenes unfolding on the screen represent real events in the material world. In some instances, the impact of a movie on some spectators can be so strong that they respond to it emotionally as if it were real. This happens in spite of the fact that they know intellectually that what they are watching is nothing but a play of electromagnetic waves of different frequencies within a single undivided field of light.

In holotropic states of consciousness we can discover to our surprise that the same applies to our experience of everyday reality. What appears to us as a world of solid objects is a play of vibrations that is essentially empty. Naturally, our experience of the world is fuller and richer than that of a movie, since it includes some dimensions that today's filmmaking technology is incapable of conveying, such as tactile, olfactory, and gustatory qualities. In his famous science fiction novel *The Brave New World,* Aldous Huxley described a future form of entertainment, the "feelies," in which this shortcoming was overcome, since the experiences of the spectators were not limited to the optical and acoustic realms, but included these other sensory qualities. And contemporary researchers in the field of virtual reality are already experimenting with specially designed gloves that would enrich the experience of electronically created visual and acoustic worlds by contributing the tactile dimension.

I described earlier the experience of the "immanent divine," in which the material world is perceived as a dynamic play of cosmic creative energy. This experience also reveals the undivided unity underlying the world of separation. It shows that what we encounter in everyday life are not discrete individuals and solid objects, but integral aspects of a unified energetic field. However absurd this might appear to a naïve realist, this conclusion is in full agreement with the findings of modern physicists. They indicate that what we ordinarily perceive as solid matter is essentially empty. Twentieth-century science has thus provided support for the startling claim of Hindu sages that our perception of the world as made of dense material objects is an illusion (*māyā*).

Let us now develop the analogy between filmmaking and the creation of material reality a step further. By simply watching the movie, we cannot fully understand the process we are involved in, since some important answers about what is happening to us cannot be found on the screen. What we see in the movies does not have independent existence and meaning of its own. The movie is a product of a very complex process and its essential stages are not included in our immediate experience of watching it. To really understand the events we are witnessing, we would have to replace the naïve experience of watching the movie with a systematic in-depth analysis of the process that creates it.

First, we would have to shift our attention away from the screen, turn around, and discover the device responsible for the illusions that we are perceiving. We would detect that its essential component is a powerful source of light that projects the images on the screen. On closer inspection, we would also find the moving celluloid strip that determines the forms and colors we are seeing. This situation is strikingly similar to Plato's famous simile of the cave that he used in his dialogue *The Republic* to describe the illusionary nature of the material world.

In this dialogue Plato (1961b) likens the human condition to a situation in which a group of individuals is confined to the inside of a subterranean grotto. They are firmly fettered to the ground in such a way that they can stare only straight ahead. Behind these prisoners is a bright fire and a low wall above which pupeteers exhibit human and animal effigies and various implements. The prisoners are immersed in watching the shadows on the wall, the only aspect of the whole situation they can actually perceive. Fascinated by the show, they are completely unaware of the true nature of this situation.

In Plato's simile, the objects of our familiar material world are likened to shadows that are cast by a fire on the wall of the cave, while the true nature of reality remains hidden to us. Plato also suggests that the prisoners in the cave believe that the echos of the sounds that originate behind them are actually produced by the shadows. In our movie example, we could similarly identify not only the source of the images, but also discover the origin of the sounds by tracing them to the magnetic tape that generates them.

When we continue our exploration, a closer scrutiny of the projection process will reveal that what we perceive as smooth and continuous movements actually consists of rapid sequences of discontinuous flickering images. This again parallels the insights from nonordinary states of consciousness concerning the nature of reality. I have repeatedly heard reports in this regard from people who had various forms of holotropic experiences. The same insights can be found in traditional spiritual sources. For example, according to Tibetan Buddhism, reality is radically discontinuous. The world is constantly flashing in and out of existence, being dissolved and recreated from one moment to another. Similarly, we ourselves do not have continuous existence from birth to death, but die and are reborn all the time. A modern, scientifically based version of the same concept appears in the philosophy of Alfred North Whitehead (1929).

The next step of our in-depth probing of the movie experience would take us outside of the movie theater altogether. We would discover that the film started as an idea in somebody's mind and that all the processes necessary to make a movie were motivated by the intention to concretize the story in the screenplay and transform it into a convincing vivid experience. The reality portrayed in the movie does not have an independent existence of its own. It cannot be fully understood if we take it out of this larger context. The ultimate reason for the existence of the movie is the intention to provide a specific kind of experience. According to the insights from holotropic states, the same is true about our experience of the material world.

A naïve person, such as a child or a native from a preindustrial culture who has not had exposure to modern technology, could mistake a well-done movie for reality. In the future, holographic movies with holophonic sound, holographic television, and particularly advanced technology of "virtual reality" will make that distinction even more difficult. However, even at present, the idea that our cosmos might be a "virtual reality" produced by superior intelligence does not seem as far-fetched as it would have a hundred or even fifty years ago.

5
The Ways to Reunion
with the Cosmic Source

Now I am moving back. . . . back to the Whole, where I
belong . . . what joy to return. . . . Yes, now I know what I
am, what I have been from the beginning, what I always
will be. . . . a part of the Whole, the restless part that
desires to return, yet lives to seek expression in doing,
creating, building, giving, growing, leaving more than it
takes, and above all desires to bring back gifts of love to
the Whole . . . the paradox of total unity and the continuity of the part. I know the Whole. . . . I am the Whole . . .
even as a part I am the totality.

—Robert Monroe, *The Ultimate Journey*

Whoever has parted from his source
Longs to return to that state of union.

—Rūmī

Involution and Evolution of Consciousness

The process of creation as it was described in the preceding
chapter results in an immensely rich spectrum of entities on
many different levels of reality, ranging from the undifferentiated
Absolute Consciousness through rich pantheons of archetypal
beings to countless individual units constituting the world of
matter. This process of successive divisions combined with increasing separation and alienation represents only one half of the
cosmic cycle. The insights from holotropic states repeatedly reveal
another part of this process consisting of events in consciousness

77

that reflect a movement in the opposite direction—from the worlds of plurality and separation toward increasing dissolution of boundaries and merging into ever larger wholes.

For the sake of brevity, I refer to the descending part of the cosmic process, representing creation (involution of consciousness), as *hylotropic*, or oriented toward the world of matter (from the Greek *hyle* = matter, and *trepein* = moving in the direction of something). In a similar way, I call the ascending aspect of the cosmic process that mediates return to the original undifferentiated unity (evolution of consciousness) *holotropic*, or moving toward wholeness. As I have already mentioned earlier, this latter term is derived from the Greek *holos*, meaning whole, and *trepein*, as above, aiming for something.

These insights parallel the descriptions and discussions of these two cosmic movements described in various spiritual and philosophical systems. In the West, the founder of Neoplatonism, Plotinus (1991), referred to the hylotropic process as Efflux and to the holotropic movement as Reflux. According to the Neoplatonists, the cosmos in all its variety of hierarchical gradations is created by a divine emanation from the supreme One. Humans have a potential access to the highest intellectual and spiritual realms and can rise to the consciousness of the World Soul. Plotinus' ideas became a dominant theme of all Neoplatonic schools, as well as the writings of Christian mystics and German idealistic philosophers. A very comprehensive contemporary synthesis of the ideas concerning Descent and Ascent appears in the work of Ken Wilber (1995).

In the East, similar concepts found its most articulate expression in the writings of the Indian mystic and philosopher Śri Aurobindo (1965). Aurobindo argued that Brahman manifests as the world of matter in a process that he called *involution* and then progressively brings about an unfolding of his latent power in the course of *evolution*. Involution is a process of self-limitation and increasing density, by which the universal Consciousness-Force veils itself by stages and creates planes of existence. In its farthest reaches, it assumes the appearance of the inconscient material world. In each plane all the powers of consciousness belonging to the planes above it are involved, so that the full potential of the original and universal Consciousness-Force is enfolded and hidden even in the Inconscient.

Evolution is the opposite process, by which the Consciousness-Force emerges again from the apparent cosmic Inconscience and manifests its hidden powers. However, it is important to emphasize that for Aurobindo evolution is not an exact reverse of involution. It is not a gradual subtilization and rarefaction plane by plane that would eventually lead to reabsorption of all creation into the One Unmanifest. It is a gradual emergence of higher powers of consciousness in the material universe leading to an ever greater manifestation of the divine Consciousness-Force within its creation.

According to the insights from holotropic states, the universal process offers not only an infinite number of possibilities for becoming a separate individual, but also an equally rich and ingenious range of opportunities for dissolution of boundaries and fusion that mediate experiential return to the source. The unitive experiences make it possible for the individual units of consciousness to overcome their alienation and free themselves from the delusion of their separateness. This transcendence of what earlier appeared to be absolute boundaries and the resulting progressive merging creates larger and larger experiential units. In its farthest reaches, this process dissolves all the boundaries and brings about a reunion with Absolute Consciousness. The sequences of fusions occurring in many forms and on many different levels complete the overall cyclical pattern of the cosmic dance.

Varieties of Unitive Experiences

Although the unitive processes can be observed throughout all domains of existence, they are particularly rich and complex in human beings. Here they can also be studied most directly and systematically in the form of transpersonal experiences. Unfortunately, Western psychiatry does not differentiate between mysticism and psychosis and tends to treat mystical experiences of any kind as manifestations of mental disease. I have met during my professional career many people who received pathological labels, tranquilizing medication, and even shock therapy because they have experienced unity with other other people, nature, cosmos, and God.

Abraham Maslow (1964), the late American psychologist who played an important role in the founding of both humanistic and transpersonal psychology, interviewed hundreds of people who had had spontaneous unitive states, or "peak experiences" as he called them. He was able to show that mystical experiences are not indications of pathology and do not belong into the handbooks of psychiatry. They often occur in people who do not have any serious emotional problems and would otherwise be considered "normal" by standard psychological criteria. Moreover, if these experiences occur in a supportive setting and are well integrated, they can have very beneficial consequences and result in better functioning, higher creativity, and "self-actualization."

The most frequent triggers of unitive experiences are natural and human-made creations of extraordinary aesthetic beauty. For some people, it can be the immensity of the star-filled sky, for others the majesty of giant mountain ranges, or the awesome stillness of the deserts. People visiting such natural wonders as the Grand Canyon, giant waterfalls, or some of the famous stalagmite caverns of the world can feel overwhelmed by their grandeur and experience a mystical rapture. The ocean, with the elemental power manifesting on its surface and the noble silence of its depth, is another frequent source of peak experiences. Similarly, such situations as watching a beautiful sunset, the magic of the aurora borealis, or a total solar eclipse can trigger profound unitive states of consciousness. However, it does not necessarily take events on such a grand scale to inspire mystical awareness. Under the right circumstances, it can be something as "ordinary" as a spider spinning its web or a hummingbird hovering over a flower and sucking nectar.

Exposure to exquisite artistic creations can have a very similar effect. Composers deeply engaged in creative work, performing musicians, as well as people in musical audiences, can occasionally lose their boundaries and literally merge with the music. They can have a sense of actually becoming music, rather than just listening to it. Great dancers, while on stage, often reach states where there is no more difference between the dancer and the dance. European Gothic cathedrals, Moslem mosques, the Taj Mahal, or Hindu and Buddhist temples, by their monumental beauty, have been instrumental in inducing mystical states in many thousands of people. Great sculptures, paintings, and other art objects of all ages and cultures can have a similar effect on sensitive individuals.

Another area of everyday life that is a frequent source of unitive experiences deserves special notice, since most of us probably would not associate it with mystical awareness. Many prominent athletes report that, at the time of their peak performances, they were in states that resembled mystical raptures. We tend to attribute stellar performances in various athletic activities to a combination of special physical endowment, psychological perseverance, unrelenting discipline, and rigorous training. The inside story from some of the world's greatest athletes reveals that the players themselves often see it very differently. They attribute their extraordinary achievments to special states of consciousness that mediate for them capacities that border on the miraculous and supernatural (Murphy and White 1978). An important aspect of these states is typically a sense of losing individual boundaries and merging with various aspects of the environment.

It seems that the mystical raptures triggered by sport activities make it possible to transcend the boundaries of what we usually consider to be humanly possible. I have personally witnessed an astonishing example of such an extraordinary performance associated with a unitive state. It occurred during a monthlong seminar on Buddhism and Western Psychology that we conducted at the Esalen Institute in Big Sur, California. A Korean swordmaster whom we invited as guest faculty offered as part of our program a special demonstration. He asked one of his disciples to lie down on the grass and placed a napkin and a large watermelon on his naked belly. He then retreated about fifteen feet and stood for a few minutes in quiet meditation, his head covered with a tightly fitting bag made of thick black velvet, and holding in his hand a giant, extremely sharp sword.

Suddenly all the dogs in the area started to howl and the swordsman joined in with a wild warrior scream. In a cartwheel fashion, he propelled himself in the direction of his disciple, who was quietly lying on the grass, and with a strong swing of his sword cut the watermelon on his belly in two pieces. There was a slight indention from the sword on the napkin, but the disciple was unscathed. Astounded, the spectators asked how he was able to accomplish such a spectacular feat. Everybody assumed that he was somehow able to remember and visualize the environment as he had seen it before he was blindfolded. He smiled and answered: "No, you meditate and wait until all is one—the swordmaster, the sword, the grass, the melon, the disciple—and then there is no problem!"

Experiences of mystical union have been beautifully captured in the world literature. For example, in Eugene O'Neill's *Long Day's Journey into Night,* Edmund talks about his mystical raptures he experienced in connection with the ocean:

> I lay on the bowsprit, facing astern, with the water foaming into spume under me, the masts with every sail white in the moonlight, towering high above me. I became drunk with the beauty and singing rhythm of it, and for a moment I lost myself—actually lost my life. I was set free! I dissolved in the sea, became white sails and flying spray, became beauty and rhythm, became moonlight and the ship and the high dim-starred sky! I belonged, without past or future, within peace and unity and a wild joy, within something greater than my own life, or the life of Man, to Life itself! To God, if you want to put it that way.
>
> And several other times in my life, when I was swimming far out, or lying alone on a beach, I have had the same experience. Became the sun, the hot sand, green seaweed anchored to a rock, swaying in the tide. Like a saint's vision of beatitude. Like the veil of things as they seem drawn back by an unseen hand. For a second you see—and seeing the secret, are the secret. For a second there is meaning!

Unitive Potential of Death, Sex, and Birth

While unitive experiences happen most likely in emotionally positively charged situations, they can also occur under circumstances that are highly unfavorable, threatening, and critical for the individual. In this case, the ego consciousness is shattered and overwhelmed rather than dissolved and transcended. This happens during severe acute or chronic stress, at the time of intense emotional and physical suffering, or when the integrity or survival of the body are seriously threatened. Deeply depressed people brought by a serious life crisis to the verge of suicide can suddenly experience a profound spiritual opening and transcend their suffering. Many others discover the mystical realms during near-death experiences at the time of accidents, injuries, dangerous diseases, and operations.

Death, an event that ends our individual existence as embodied selves, is a very logical interface with the transpersonal domain. The events leading to death, associated with it, and following it are a frequent source of spiritual opening. Suffering from a terminal illness or being in intimate interaction with people who are dying, particularly close friends or relatives, can activate one's own issues around death and impermanence and be instrumental in a mystical awakening. The training of monks in Tibetan Vajrayana Buddhism requires spending considerable amount of time with dying people. Certain Hindu Tantric traditions involve meditations in cemeteries, in the burning grounds, and in close contact with corpses.

In Middle Ages, Christian monks were asked to imagine in their meditations their own death and to visualize all the stages of decomposition of their bodies until the final disintegration into ashes. "Remember death!", "Dust to dust!", "Death is certain, the hour uncertain!", "Thus passes the glory of the world!" were the mottoes guiding such practice. This was much more than morbid indulgence in death as some modern Westerners would see it. Experiences of deep encounter with death can trigger mystical states. By accepting impermanence and our own mortality on a deep experiential level, we also discover the part of us that is transcendent and immortal.

Various ancient books of the dead offer detailed descriptions of powerful spiritual experiences occurring at the time of biological death (Grof 1994). Modern research in the field of thanatology, a science studying death and dying, has confirmed many important aspects of these accounts (Ring 1982, 1985). It has shown that approximately one-third of the people who come close to death experience powerful visionary states including, among others, a condensed life review, passage through a tunnel, encounter with archetypal beings, contact with transcendental realities, and visions of divine light. In many instances, this can involve "veridical" out-of-body experiences, during which the individual's disembodied consciousness accurately perceives what is happening in various close or remote locations. Survivors of such situations typically undergo a profound spiritual opening, personality transformation, and radical changes in their life values. In a fascinating research project that is currently underway, Kenneth Ring (1995) is studying near-death experiences in congenitally blind people, trying to confirm that in disembodied states they are able to observe their environment.

Talking about triggers of unitive experiences, we should not forget a particularly important category—situations that are associated with human reproductive functions. Many people, both men and women, report that they have experienced profound mystical states during love-making. In some instances, an intense sexual experience can actually be instrumental in what is described in ancient Indian yogic texts as awakening of Kundalinī, or Serpent Power. The yogis see Kundalinī as the creative energy of the universe that is feminine in nature. It lies dormant in the sacral area of the human subtle body until it is activated by a guru, by meditation practice, or by some other influences. The close connection that exists between this spiritual energy and the sexual drive plays an essential role in Kundalini yoga and in Tantric practices.

For women, situations associated with motherhood can become another significant source of unitive experiences. By conceiving, carrying, and delivering a child, women directly participate in the proces of cosmic creation. Under favorable circumstances, the sacred nature of these situations becomes apparent and is consciously experienced. During pregnancy, birth, and nursing, it is not uncommon to sense a mystical connection with the fetus or the infant and even with the world at large. We will return to the relationship between mysticism and the triad birth/sex/death later in this book.

Additional important triggers of unitive states are powerful mind-altering technologies that can facilitate and catalyze their occurrence. Holotropic experiences have played a critical role in the spiritual and ritual life of humanity and much effort has been exerted throughout centuries to develop ways of inducing them. I have briefly reviewed in the introduction to this book the ancient, aboriginal, and modern "technologies of the sacred" and the different contexts in which they have been used, from shamanism through the rites of passage, mysteries of death and rebirth, and various forms of spiritual practice to modern experiential therapies and laboratory consciousness research.

The Immanent and the Transcendent Divine

In holotropic states of consciousness, whether they occur spontaneously or are induced by the ancient and modern mind-altering techniques, it is possible to transcend in various ways the individual boundaries of the embodied self. These experiences offer us the opportunity to become other people, groups of people, animals, plants, or even inorganic elements of nature and of the cosmos. In this process, time does not seem to be an obstacle and past and future events can become as easily available as anything happening at present.

Experiences of this kind convey a very convincing insight that all boundaries in the material world are illusory and that the entire universe as we know it, in both its spatial and temporal aspects, is a unified web of events in consciousness. It becomes very clear that the cosmos is not an ordinary material reality, but a creation of intelligent cosmic energy or the Universal Mind. These experiences thus unveil the "immanent Divine," *deus sive natura*, or God manifested in and as the phenomenal world. They also disclose that each of us is essentially commensurate with the entire web of creation and with all its parts.

While such transpersonal experiences dramatically change our understanding of the nature of everyday material reality, there are others that reveal dimensions of existence that are ordinarily completely hidden to our perception. This category includes discarnate entities, various deities and demons, mythological realms, suprahuman beings, and the divine creative principle itself. In contrast to the "immanent Divine," we can talk here about the "transcendent Divine," since the realms and beings that we encounter under these circumstances are not part of our everyday reality; they belong to a different domain and order of existence.

Experiences of this kind demonstrate that cosmic creation is not limited to our material world, but manifests on many different levels and in many dimensions. Similarly, the possibility of unitive experiences is not confined to the material realm, but extends into other domains. We thus can not only see and encounter the inhabitants of the archetypal regions, we can actually merge with them and become them. And in the farthest reaches of our experiential self-exploration, we can encounter the creative principle itself and recognize our fundamental identity with it.

The experiences of the immanent Divine reveal the sacred nature of everyday reality and the unity underlying the world of matter, which for a naïve observer appears to be made of separate objects. By disclosing that all boundaries within the material world are arbitrary, these experiences make it clear that each of us is essentially identical with the entire field of space-time and ultimately with the cosmic creative energy itself. By comparison, the experiences of the transcendent Divine do not just show us new ways of understanding and perceiving the familiar world of our everyday life. They reveal the existence of dimensions of reality that are ordinarily invisible, or "transphenomenal," particularly those abounding in primordial cosmic forms and patterns that C. G. Jung (1956) called archetypes.

As we have seen earlier, the world of archetypes, although normally imperceptible, is not entirely separate from our everyday material reality. It is intimately interwoven with it and plays a critical role in creating it. In this way, it represents a supraordinated dimension that forms and informs the experience of our everyday life. The archetypal domain thus represents a bridge between the world of matter and the undifferentiated field of Cosmic Consciousness. For this reason, the experience of the transcendent divine is more than just the experience of another "cosmic channel." It also provides insights into the process by which material reality is created; it gives us a "glimpse into the cosmic kitchen," as one of my clients in Prague called it.

The cosmic play offers many opportunities for experiences that make it possible for us to temporarily step out of the role we are playing in the universal script, recognize the illusory nature of everyday reality, and discover the possibility of reunion with the source. Holotropic states provide an understanding of such unitive experiences that is diametrically opposite to the position of mainstream psychiatrists. Rather than being distortions of the correct perception of the material world caused by a pathological process in the brain, these experiences offer profound insights into the true nature of reality. They reveal the existence of phenomena that represent intermediate stages in the process of creation between the undifferentiated consciousness of the Universal Mind and the specifically human experience of the material world. Because they involve transcendence of individual boundaries and expand the sense of one's identity in the holotropic direction, they serve as important landmarks on the journey to spiritual awakening.

The Enigma of Space and Time

Before closing our discussion of the cosmic process as an intricate fabric of hylotropic and holotropic experiences, we have to discuss another important aspect of cosmic creation, namely its relation to space and time. When we describe the creative process as a movement from undifferentiated unity to plurality, our conditioning will very likely lead us to imagine that this process had to begin in a specific location and to unfold in linear time. However, the critical stages of this process occur in regions that lie beyond time and space as we know them. As we have seen, the cosmic creative principle transcends all the distinctions and polarities whatsoever and that includes space and time.

In our everyday life, everything that we encounter has distinct and definite space and time coordinates. Our experience of time as linear and space as three-dimensional is very compelling and convincing. As a result of it, we tend to believe that these characteristics of time and space are mandatory and absolute. In holotropic experiences, we can discover to our surprise that there exist many important alternatives to our usual perception and understanding of these two dimensions. In visionary states, we can experience not only the present, but also the past and, occasionally, even the future. The sequences of events can appear to be circular, they can unfold along spiral trajectories, or actually run backwards. Time can also stop or be altogether transcended. On the levels on which cosmic creation occurs, the past, the present, and the future coexist rather than follow one another and, consequently, all the stages of the process are happening simultaneously.

The concept and experience of space appear to be equally arbitrary when we are in a holotropic state. Any number of different spaces in various hierarchical arrangements can be created in a playful fashion and none of them seems to be more objective, real, and mandatory than others. The transition from the microcosm to the macrocosm does not have to occur in a linear fashion. The small and the large can be freely interchanged in a random and capricious way. Experiential identification with a single cell can effortlessly become one that involves an entire galaxy and vice versa. These two dimensions can also coexist in the experiential space of the same person. Consequently, the baffling paradox of finiteness versus infinity that we experience in our everyday state of consciousness is transcended and ceases to exist.

To illustrate the complexities of experiencing time and space in holotropic states, I will describe one of the most extraordinary adventures in consciousness that I have experienced during the forty years of my inner explorations. It occurred in a high-dose psychedelic session that I had at the Maryland Psychiatric Research Center shortly after my arrival in the United States in 1967. Here is an excerpt from my account of that session:

Somewhere in the second half of my session, I found myself in a very unusual state of mind. It was a feeling of serenity, bliss, and simplicity mixed with awe in regard to the mystery of existence. I sensed that what I was experiencing was similar to what the early Christians must have experienced. It was a world where miracles were possible, acceptable, and even plausible. I was pondering about the problems of time and space and had great difficulty understanding how I could have ever believed that linear time and three-dimensional space are absolute and mandatory dimensions of reality.

It appeared to me rather obvious that there are no limits whatsoever in the realm of spirit and that time and space are arbitrary constructs of the psyche. I suddenly realized that I do not have to be bound by the limitations of time and space and can travel in the time-space continuum quite freely and without any restrictions. This feeling was so convincing and overwhelming that I wanted to test it by an experiment. I decided to try if I could travel to my parents' apartment in Prague, which was many thousand miles away.

After determining the direction and considering the distance, I imagined myself flying through space to the place of my destination. I had the experience of moving through space at an enormous speed but, to my disappointment, I was not getting anywhere. I could not understand why the experiment did not work, since my feeling that such space travel should be possible was very convincing. All of a sudden, I realized that I was still under the influence of my old concepts of time and space. I continued to think in terms of directions and distances and approached the task accordingly. It occurred to me that the proper approach would be to make myself believe that the place of my session was actually identical with the place of my destination. I said to myself: "This is not Baltimore, this is Prague.

Right here and now, I am in my parents' appartment in Prague."

When I approached the task in this way, I experienced peculiar and bizarre sensations. I found myself in a strange, rather congested place full of electric circuits, tubes, wires, resistors, and condensers. After a short period of confusion, I realized that my consciousness was trapped in a TV set located in the corner of the room in my parents' apartment. I was trying, somehow, to use the speakers for hearing and the tube for seeing. After a while, I had to laugh since I realized that this experience was a symbolic spoof ridiculing the fact that I was still imprisoned by my previous beliefs concerning space, time, and matter.

The only way of experiencing distant locations that I could conceive of and accept was one that was mediated by television. Such a transmission, of course, is restricted by the velocity of the electromagnetic waves involved. At the moment when I realized and firmly believed that my consciousness could transcend any limitations whatsoever, including the speed of light, the experience changed rapidly. The television set turned inside out and I found myself walking in the apartment of my parents in Prague.

At this point, I did not feel any drug effect and the experience was as real as any other situation in my life. The door of my parents' bedroom was half open. I looked in, saw their bodies on the bed, and heard them breathing. I walked to the window and looked at the clock on the street corner. It showed a six-hour difference from the time in Baltimore where the experiment took place. In spite of the fact that this number of hours reflected the actual time difference between the two zones, I did not find it to be a convincing evidence. Since I intellectually knew the time difference, my mind could have easily fabricated this experience.

I lay down on the couch in the corner of one of the rooms to reflect on my experience. It was the same couch on which I had spent my last psychedelic session before my departure to the USA. My request for permission to travel to the USA on a fellowship had been initially turned down by the Czech authorities. My last session in Prague happened at a time when I was waiting for the response to my appeal.

Suddenly, I felt a wave of overwhelming anxiety. A strange and uncanny idea emerged in my mind with unusual force and persuasiveness: Maybe I had never left Czechoslovakia and was now coming back from the psychedelic session in Prague. Maybe the positive response to my appeal, the journey to the USA, joining the team in Baltimore, and having a session there was just a visionary journey motivated by strong wishful thinking. I was trapped in an insidious loop, a vicious spatio-temporal circle, unable to determine my real historical and geographic coordinates.

For a long time, I felt suspended between two realities, both of which were equally convincing. I could not tell whether I was experiencing an astral projection to Prague from my session in Baltimore or coming down from a session in Prague in which I had experienced a trip to the United States. I had to think about the Chinese philosopher Chuang-tzu who awoke from a dream in which he was a butterfly and for some time could not decide whether he was not actually a butterfly dreaming of being human.

Meaningful Coincidences and Synchronicities

I would like to discuss in this context another important aspect of holotropic states that has far-reaching implications for our understanding of time and space. Transpersonal experiences are often associated with strange meaningful coincidences that cannot be explained in terms of linear causality. In a universe, as it is described by materialistic science, all events should obey the law of cause and effect. Any coincidences that defy explanation in causal terms are then attributed to the fact that the phenomena involved are too complex and that we lack the knowledge of all the contributing factors. Because of all these unknown "hidden variables," the final outcome can be predicted only statistically, not in specific detail. However, on occasion, the statistical improbability of certain coincidences in our everyday life is so staggering that it makes us question the adequacy of such an interpretation.

A friend of mine recently shared with me a remarkable coincidence that had occurred in his family. His wife and her sister, who lives in another city, were both woken up in the course of the same night by the presence of a bat in their bedrooms. They both responded to this one-time occurrence in their lives in exactly the same way. Although it happened in the middle of the night, they immediately called their father, woke him up and related to him this unusual event. As most of us know, situations violating statistical probabilities are much more frequent than one would expect. I have personally experienced over the years many extraordinary coincidences in my own life. One of them was particularly relevant because of its important consequences and is worth describing.

In 1968 when the Soviet army invaded Czechoslovakia, I was in the United States on a scholarship at the Johns Hopkins University in Baltimore. After the invasion, I was asked by the Czech authorities to return immediately, but decided to disobey and stay in the United States. As a result, I was not able to visit my native country for almost twenty years. During this time, I could not maintain open contact with my friends and colleagues in Czechoslovakia. It would have been politically dangerous for them, because my stay in the United States was considered illegal. After the liberation of Eastern Europe, the board of the International Transpersonal Association (ITA), of which I was president, decided to hold its next meeting in Czechoslovakia and I traveled to Prague to find some potential sites for this meeting.

After my arrival at the Prague airport, I took a taxi to my mother's apartment. After my mother and I had spent some time together and caught up with each other, she went to see a neighbor to make some arrangements and I was in the apartment alone. I sat down in an armchair, had a cup of tea, and reflected about my mission. Because of my long absence, I lost all my contacts, was not familiar with the situation, and did not have an idea where to start. I contemplated the situation for about ten minutes, but was not getting very far. Suddenly my train of thoughts was interrupted by a loud ringing of the doorbell. I answered the door and recognized Thomas, a younger psychiatrist colleague of mine who in the old days used to be my close friend. Before my departure to the United States, we shared some explorations of nonordinary states by sitting for each other in our psychedelic sessions. He had heard from an aquaintance of his about my visit to Prague and came to welcome me.

I found out to my astonishment that just as Thomas was leaving his apartment, his home telephone rang. It was Ivan Havel, a prominent researcher in artificial intelligence and the brother of the Czech president Václav Havel. He and Thomas went to the same school and remained close friends ever since. It turned out that Ivan Havel was also the head of a group of progressive scientists who during the Communist era had secret underground meetings exploring the new paradigm and transpersonal psychology.

This group had heard about my work in the lecture of a friend of mine, a Soviet dissident scientist, Vasily Nalimov. Ivan Havel knew that Thomas and I were friends and called him to mediate contact between me and the group. Because of this peculiar set of coincidences, it took me only ten minutes to get access to the ideal support for the ITA conference—a group of highly competent professionals vitally interested in the subject and the head of the state, who happened to be a deeply spiritually oriented statesman. The conference that was held in 1993 under the aegis of Václav Havel and was very successful.

Probably the most famous case of coincidence is an amusing story about a certain Monsieur Deschamps and a special kind of plum pudding told by the French astronomer Flammarion and quoted by Jung. As a boy, Deschamps was given a piece of this rare pudding by a Monsieur de Fontgibu. For ten years that followed, he had no opportunity to taste this delicacy until he took a trip to Paris. There he saw the same pudding on the menu of a Paris restaurant and asked the waiter for a serving. However, it turned out that the last piece of the pudding was already ordered—by Monsieur de Fontgibu, who just happened to be in the same restaurant at that moment. Many years later, Monsieur Deschamps was invited to a party where this pudding was served as a special rarity. While he was eating it, he remarked that the only thing lacking was Monsieur de Fontgibu. At that moment the door opened and an old man walked in looking very confused. It was Monsieur de Fontgibu, who burst in on the party by mistake because he had been given a wrong address for the place he was supposed to go.

The existence of such extraordinary coincidences is difficult to reconcile with the understanding of the universe developed by materialistic science. It is easier to imagine that these occurrences have some deeper meaning and that they are playful creations of cosmic intelligence. This explanation is particularly plausible when they contain an element of humor, which is often the case. I will use here as an illustration a true story from the life of the American astronaut Neil Armstrong, the first man to land on the moon. The astronomical improbability of something like this happening by chance combined with the exquisite humor of the story makes this certainly one of the most unique "coincidences" of all time.

Descending from the lunar module, just before his foot touched the surface of the moon, Neil Armstrong said his famous words: "One small step for man; one giant step for mankind." It is much less known that, as he was climbing back from the moon surface into the lunar module, he muttered another sentence, "Good luck Mr. Gorski." After his return to earth, curious reporters inquired what this sentence meant, but Armstrong refused to reveal it. Some thought it might have been addressed to a Soviet cosmonaut, but there was no one of that name. After frustrating efforts of the journalists, the entire affair was forgotten.

Last year, at a party in Florida, someone brought it up again. This time, Neil Armstrong felt free to disclose the meaning of the sentence since, in the meantime, Mr. Gorski and his wife had died. When Neil was a boy, the Gorskis were their next-door neighbors. One day, Neil was playing ball in his backyard with his friends. At one point, the ball landed in the Gorskis' garden under the open window of their bedroom and Neil was appointed to retrieve it. The Gorskis were in the middle of a heated argument. As Neil was picking up the ball, he heard Mrs. Gorski screaming: "Oral sex? You want oral sex? You'll get oral sex the day the kid next door walks on the moon!"

Although coincidences of this kind are extremely interesting in and of themselves, the work of C. G. Jung added another fascinating dimension to this challenging phenomenon. The situations discussed above involved highly implausible concatenations of events in the world of matter. Jung observed and described numerous instances of astonishing coincidences in which various events in consensus reality were meaningfully linked to intrapsychic experiences, such as dreams or visions. He coined for this type of coincidence the term *synchronicity*.

In his famous work, *Synchronicity: An Acausal Connecting Principle*, Jung (1960) defined synchronicity as "a simultaneous occurrence of a psychic state with one or more external events which appear as meaningful parallels to the momentary subjective state." Situations of this kind show that our psyche can enter into playful interaction with what appears to be the world of matter. The fact that this can happen blurs the boundaries between subjective and objective reality.

Among the many instances of synchronicity in Jung's own life, one is particularly famous; it occurred during a therapy session with one of his clients. This patient was very resistant to treatment and to the notion of transpersonal realities. Up to the time of this particular event, little or no progress had been made. She had a dream in which she was given a golden scarab. During the analysis of this dream Jung heard a sound of something hitting the window. He went to check what happened and found a shiny rose-chafer beetle on the windowsill trying to get inside. It was a very rare specimen, the nearest analogy to a golden scarab that can be found in that latitude. Nothing like that had ever happened to Jung before. He opened the window, brought the beetle inside, and showed it to the client. This amazing synchronicity had a profound impact on this patient and became an important turning point in her therapy.

Synchronicities and Inner Exploration

Synchronistic events are particularly frequent in the lives of people who experience holotropic states of consciousness in their meditation, psychedelic sessions, experiential psychotherapy, or spontaneous psychospiritual crises. Transpersonal and perinatal experiences are often associated with extraordinary coincidences. For example, when in our inner exploration we are approaching the experience of the ego death, dangerous situations and accidents can suddenly accumulate in our life. I am not talking here only about events in which we ourselves are in some way instrumental, but about those that are caused by other people or by independent external factors. When we face the ego death and experience rebirth in our inner process, such situations tend to clear up as magically as they developed. It seems that we are given the alternative of inner psychological death versus literal physical damage or destruction.

Similarly, when we have a powerful experience of a shamanic type that involves an animal spirit guide, this animal can suddenly keep appearing in in our life in various forms with a frequency that is beyond any reasonable probability. In one of our six-day training modules, a participating psychologist experienced in her holotropic breathwork session a powerful shamanic sequence in which an owl played an important role as her power animal and spirit guide. That same day, she returned from a walk in the forest with remnants of an owl. When she was driving home after the module had ended, she noticed by the side of the road a large wounded bird. She stopped the car and came closer; it was a large owl with a broken wing. The owl allowed her to pick him up and take him to the car without showing any signs of resistance. She took care of the bird until he was able to fly and return to his natural environment.

At the time of inner confrontation with the archetypal images of the Animus, Anima, Wise Old Man, or Terrible Mother, ideal examples of these figures tend to emerge in physical form in our everyday life. It also has been the experience of many people that when they become involved in a project inspired from the transpersonal realms of the psyche, remarkable synchronicities tend to occur and make their work surprisingly easy. My experience with the ITA conference in Prague described earlier would certainly fit into this category.

When we are involved in a systematic inner quest that includes work with holotropic states, we can expect with reasonable certainty that, sooner or later, we will encounter extraordinary meaningful synchronicities. Sometimes, we will notice only occasional individual coincidences, other times, we might be flooded by entire chains of them. According to their content, they can be very uplifting or oppressive and terrifying. In either case, they can lead to serious problems in everyday life if they are convincing and cumulative.

Traditional psychiatry does not distinguish between true synchronicities and psychotic misinterpretation of the world. Since the materialistic worldview is strictly deterministic and does not accept the possibility of "meaningful coincidences," any intimation of extraordinary synchronicities in the client's narrative will be automatically interpreted as delusions of reference, a symptom of serious mental disease. However, there cannot be any doubt about the existence of genuine synchronicities, where any person who has access to the facts has to admit that the coincidences involved are beyond any reasonable statistical probabilities.

Consciousness Research and Modern Physics

Jung was well aware of the fact that the phenomenon of synchronicity was incompatible with traditional thinking in science. Because of the deeply ingrained belief in causality as a central law of nature, he hesitated for many years before he published his observations of events that refused to fit into this mold. He postponed publication of his work on this subject until he and others had collected literally hundreds of convincing examples of synchronicity, making him absolutely sure that he had something valid to report.

Struggling with this phenomenon, Jung became very interested in the developments in quantum-relativistic physics and in the alternative worldview that it was bringing. He had many intellectual exchanges with Wolfgang Pauli, one of the founders of quantum physics, and became familiar with the revolutionary concepts in this field. Jung was aware of the fact that his own observations appeared much more plausible and acceptable in the context of the new emerging image of reality. Additional support for Jung's ideas came from no less than Albert Einstein, who, during a personal visit, encouraged Jung to pursue his idea of synchronicity because it was fully compatible with the new thinking in physics (Jung 1973).

Since the above discussion about the arbitrary and ambiguous nature of time and space might seem implausible or even impossible to somebody who has not had transpersonal experiences, it seems appropriate to mention some astonishing alternatives to our usual understanding of reality that have emerged in the course of this century in modern physics. The fantastic and seemingly absurd insights from holotropic states pale considerably when we compare them with the daring speculations about the microworld and macroworld entertained by many prominent representatives of modern physics. The most outrageous theories concerning the nature of reality that have been formulated by quantum physicists, astrophysicists, and cosmologists are taken seriously when they can be backed by mathematical equations, while similar concepts are met with criticism and even ridicule if their source is consciousness research or transpersonal psychology.

According to a leading cosmogenetic theory, there was a situation about 15 billion years ago when time and space did not exist. They were created together with matter during the Big Bang, when the universe was born in a cataclysmic explosion of unimaginable proportions from a dimensionless point, or singularity. And, conversely, billions of years from now time and space might again cease to exist when the universe collapses into itself. A similar process is already underway in our cosmos in those places where dying giant stars rapidly contract, knock themselves out of existence, and create what the physicists call "black holes." Inside the black holes, beyond a certain boundary that the physicists refer to as the "event horizon," time, space, and physical laws as we know them do not any more exist.

At the beginning of this century, in a conceptual breakthrough of unprecedented proportions, Albert Einstein replaced Newton's three-dimensional space and linear time by a four-dimensional space-time continuum. In Einstein's universe, it is possible to travel in space-time in a way we ordinarily travel in space. Einstein's famous equation suggests that time slows down proportionately to the velocity of a moving system and stops when the velocity reaches the speed of light. In a system moving faster than light, time would actually run backwards. Californian physicist Richard Feynman received a Nobel Prize for his discovery that a particle moving forward in time is identical with its antiparticle moving backward in time.

Theoretical physicists John Wheeler, Hugh Everett, and Neil Graham became known for their "many worlds hypothesis," according to which the universe splits every instant into an infinite number of universes. In his bestselling book, Kip S. Thorne (1994), professor of theoretical physics at the California Institute of Technology, seriously discussed the possibility of using in the future "wormholes" for instant transport to various locations in the universe that lie many light years away and even for travel back in time. According to David Bohm (1980), a longtime co-worker of Albert Einstein, the world as we know it represents only one aspect of reality, its "explicate" or "unfolded order." Its generating matrix is the "implicate order," an ordinarily hidden region in which both space and time are enfolded.

I have included this brief excursion into the world of modern physics because the imaginative and creative thinking in this discipline forms such a striking contrast to the narrow-minded approach of academic psychiatrists and psychologists to the human psyche and consciousness. It is certainly encouraging to see to what extent physicists have been able to overcome many deeply ingrained preconceptions in their search for the understanding of the world of matter. Perhaps the startling speculations of contemporary physics will help us approach with an open mind the extraordinary and challenging findings of modern consciousness research.

The Cosmic Dance

We can now try to summarize the insights from holotropic states describing existence as a fantastic experiential adventure of Absolute Consciousness—an endless cosmic dance, exquisite play, or divine drama. In producing it, the creative principle generates from itself and within itself a countless number of individual images, split units of consciousness, that assume various degrees of relative autonomy and independence. Each of them represents an opportunity for a unique experience, an experiment in consciousness. With the passion of an explorer, scientist, and artist, the creative principle experiments with all the conceivable experiences in their endless variations and combinations.

In this divine play, Absolute Consciousness finds the possibility to express its inner richness, abundance, and immense creativity. Through its creations it experiences myriads of individual roles, encounters, intricate dramas, and adventures on all imaginable levels. This divine play of plays ranges from galaxies, suns, orbiting planets, and moons through plants, animals, and humans to nuclear particles, atoms, and molecules. Additional dramas unfold in the archetypal realms and other dimensions of existence that are not available to our perception in our everyday state of consciousness.

In endless cycles of creation, preservation, and destruction Absolute Consciousness overcomes the feelings of monotony and transcendental boredom. The temporary negation and loss of its pristine state alternates with episodes of its rediscovery and reclaiming. The periods that are full of agony, anguish, and despair are followed by episodes of bliss and ecstatic rapture. When the original undifferentiated consciousness is regained after it was temporarily lost, it is experienced as exciting, surprising, fresh, and new. The existence of agony gives a new dimension to the experience of ecstasy, the knowledge of darkness enhances the appreciation of light, and the extent of enlightenment is directly proportionate to the depth of previous ignorance. In addition, with each excursion into phenomenal worlds followed by return, the Universal Mind is enriched by the experiences of the different roles involved. By having concretized more of its inner potential, it has augmented and deepened its self-knowledge.

For this understanding of the cosmic process it is necessary to assume that the Universal Mind consciously experiences all aspects of creation, both as objects of observation and as subjective states. It can thus explore not only the entire spectrum of specifically human perceptions, emotions, thoughts, and sensations, but also the states of consciousness of all the other life forms of the Darwinian evolutionary tree. On the level of cellular consciousness, it can experience the excitement of the sperm race and the fusion of the sperm with the egg during conception, as well as the activity of the liver cells or neurons in the brain.

Transcending the limits of the animal kingdom and expanding into the botanical world, Absolute Consciousness can become a giant sequoia tree, experience itself as a carnivorous plant catching and digesting a fly, or participate in the photosynthesis in the leaves and germination of seeds. Similarly, the phenomena in the inorganic world, from interatomic bonds through earthquakes and explosions of atomic bombs to quasars and pulsars provide interesting experiential possibilities. And since in its deepest nature our psyche is identical with Absolute Consciousness, these experiential possibilities are, under certain circumstances, open to all of us.

When we view reality from the perspective of the Universal Mind, all the usually experienced polarities are transcended. This applies to such categories as spirit-matter, stability-motion, good-evil, male-female, beauty-ugliness, or agony-ecstasy. In the last analysis, there is no absolute difference between subject and object, observer and the observed, experiencer and the experienced, creator and creation. All the roles in the cosmic drama have ultimately only one protagonist, Absolute Consciousness. This is the single most important truth about existence revealed in the ancient Indian Upanishads. In modern times, it found a beautiful artistic expression in the poem entitled "Please Call Me by My True Names" by the Vietnamese Buddhist teacher Thich Nhat Hahn:

Do not say that I'll depart tomorrow
because even today I still arrive.

Look deeply; I arrive in every second
to be a bud on a spring branch,
to be a tiny bird, with wings still fragile
learning to sing in my new nest,
to be a caterpillar in the heart of a flower,
to be a jewel hiding itself in a stone.

I still arrive, in order to laugh and to cry,
in order to fear and to hope,
the rhythm of my heart is the birth and death
of all that are alive.

I am the mayfly metamorphosing on
the surface of the river,
and I am the bird which, when the springs comes,
arrives in time to eat the mayfly.

I am a frog swimming happily
in the clear water of a pond,
and I am the grass-snake, who, approaching
in silence, feeds itself on the frog.

I am the child in Uganda, all skin and bones,
my legs as thin as bamboo sticks,
and I am the arms merchant,
selling deadly weapons to Uganda.

I am the twelve-year-old girl,
refugee on a small boat,
who throws herself into the ocean
after being raped by a sea pirate,
and I am the pirate,
my heart not yet capable of seeing and loving.

I am a member of the Politburo
with plenty of power in my hands,
And I am the the man
who has to pay his debt of blood
to my people dying slowly in a forced labor camp.

My joy is like spring, so warm it makes
flowers bloom in all walks of life.
My pain is like a river of tears, so full
it fills all four oceans.

Please call me by my true names,
So I can hear all my cries and laughs at once,
So I can see that my pain and my joy are one.

Please call me by my true names
So I can wake up and so the door of my heart
can be left open,
the door of compassion.

6
The Problem of Good and Evil

Consequently: he who wants to have
Right without wrong,
Order without disorder,
Does not understand the principles
Of heaven and earth.
He does not know how
Things hang together.

—Chuang-tzu, *Great and Small*

Ethical Issues in Self-Exploration

One of the most important issues that keeps emerging in holotropic states of consciousness in many different forms and on various levels is the problem of ethics. At the time when our inner experiences focus on biographical issues, the ethical questions usually take the form of a strong need to scrutinize our life from childhood up to the present time and evaluate it from the moral point of view. This tends to be intimately linked with questions concerning self-image and self-esteem. As we review our life history, we might feel an urgent need to examine whether our personality and behavior measure up to moral standards—our own, our family's, or our society's. The criteria here are usually quite relative and idiosyncratic since they necessarily involve a strong personal, familial, and cultural bias. We essentially judge our behavior in terms of the values that have been imposed on us from the outside.

There exists another form of self-judgment in which we evaluate our character and behavior not by the ordinary everyday criteria, but against the background of the universal law and

105

the cosmic order. Experiences of this kind occur in holotropic states of various kinds, but are particularly frequent as part of the life review in near-death situations. Many people who have come close to death talk about their encounters with a Being of Light and describe that in its presence they subjected their lives to merciless reckoning. This strong propensity of the human psyche for moral self-evaluation is reflected in scenes of divine judgment in eschatological mythologies of many different cultures.

As our process of self-exploration deepens, we can discover within ourselves highly problematic emotions and impulses that we were previously completely unaware of—dark and destructive aspects of our unconscious psyche that C. G. Jung referred to as the Shadow. This discovery can be very frightening and disturbing. Some of these dark elements represent our reactions to painful aspects of our history, particularly traumas in infancy and childhood. In addition, powerful destructive potential seems to be associated with the perinatal level of our psyche, the domain of the unconscious that is related to the trauma of birth. The hours of painful and life-threatening experiences associated with the passage through the birth canal naturally provoke a corresponding violent response in the fetus. This results in a repository of aggressive tendencies that we harbor in our unconscious for the rest of our life, unless we make special effort to confront them and transform them in some variety of experiential self-exploration.

In view of these disclosures, it becomes clear that the menacing doubles in such works of art as R. L. Stevenson's *The Strange Case of Dr. Jekyll and Mr. Hyde*, Oscar Wilde's *The Picture of Dorian Gray*, or Edgar Allan Poe's "William Wilson" do not represent fictitious literary characters, but the shadow aspects of an average human personality. Individuals who have been able to look deep into their psyches often describe that they discovered within themselves destructive potential that matches that of evil individuals in the category of Genghis Khan, Hitler, or Stalin. In view of such shattering insights, it is common to experience agonizing misgivings about our own nature and encounter great difficulties in accepting it.

When the experiential self-exploration moves to the transpersonal level, serious ethical questions are typically raised about humanity as a whole, about the entire species of *Homo sapiens*. Transpersonal experiences often portray dramatic historical scenes or even offer a comprehensive panoramic review of history. Such sequences bring powerful evidence that unbridled violence and insatiable greed have always been extremely powerful driving forces in human life. This brings the question about the nature of human beings and the proportion of good and evil in the human species.

Are humans at the core of their being just "naked apes" and is violence wired into the hardware of the human brain? And how do we explain the aspect of human behavior that psychoanalyst Erich Fromm (1973) called "malignant aggression"—viciousness and destructivity that surpasses anything known in the animal kingdom? How do we account for the senseless slaughter in countless wars, for the mass murders of the Inquisition, for the Holocaust, for Stalin's Gulag archipelago, for the massacres in Yugoslavia or Rwanda? It would certainly be difficult to find parallels for these behaviors in any of the animal species!

The present global crisis certainly does not offer a very uplifting and encouraging picture of contemporary humanity. Violence in the form of wars, riots, terrorism, torture, and crime seems to be escalating and the modern weapons have reached apocalyptic efficacy. Billions of dollars are wasted in the insanity of arms race worldwide, while millions of people live in poverty and starvation, or die of diseases for which there are known and inexpensive cures. Several doomsday scenarios, all of them human-made, threaten to destroy our species and with it all life on the planet. To the extent to which *Homo sapiens* is the crown of natural evolution, as we like to believe, is not only humanity, but also the very phenomenon of life, flawed in some fundamental way? In holotropic states, these questions can emerge with agonizing urgency and intensity.

Relativity of the Criteria for Good and Evil

The insights into ethical matters and answers to various moral problems are usually affected considerably as the process of deep self-exploration moves from one level of consciousness to another and we gain access to information that was not available to us before. To some extent, our ethical judgment about everyday matters can change quite drastically even without insights from higher levels of consciousness, simply by acquiring new information. With the benefit of hindsight, seeming blessings can later appear to be major disasters. What at one time was seen as a beneficial action can often take on a very ominous form as we reach deeper and more complete understanding of what is involved.

We can use here as an example the discovery of the insecticide DDT shortly after World War II. Initially, DDT was highly praised as an effective weapon against diseases transmitted by insects. Thousands of tons of this material were dumped into the swamps in various parts of the world in an effort to eradicate yellow fever and malaria, as well as used on a large scale to combat other diseases transmitted by insects. From a limited perspective, this seemed to be a very worthy and commendable project. DDT was considered such a positive contribution to humanity that in 1948 it brought its inventor Paul Müller a Nobel Prize for physiology and medicine. However, what was once considered the epidemiologists' dream turned out to be an ecological nightmare.

It was discovered that DDT was not biodegradable and the entire amount of it that had ever been produced was here to stay. In addition, because of its special affinity to fats, it showed increasing concentration as it moved up the food chain through plankton, small fish, large fish, birds, and mammals. In birds it often reached a concentration that interfered with the capacity to create viable eggshells. Now we know that DDT is responsible for the extinction of pelicans, cormorants, peregrines, eagles, and falcons in some locations. In its geographical spread, it has reached the Arctic and was detected in the fat of the penguins. It even found its way to human mammary glands and into mothers' milk. Although it was taken from the market many years ago, it was recently implicated as a contributing factor in human breast cancer.

The problem of relativity of good and evil was addressed in an artistic way in Jean-Paul Sartre's play *The Devil and the*

Good Lord (Sartre 1960). The chief protagonist, Goetz, is a vicious and merciless military leader who in his unbridled ambition commits many crimes and evil deeds. When he sees the horrors of the pestilence that erupts in the besieged town occupied by his army, he is overwhelmed by fear of death and promises God to change his behavior if He saves his life.

At that moment, a monk miraculously appears and helps him to escape from the town through a secret underground passage. Goetz keeps his promise and begins to lead a life committed to unswerving pursuit of good. However, in its consequences, his new way of life causes more evil than his previous merciless, evil conquests. This play was clearly Sartre's comment on the history of Christianity that is a prime example as to how merciless enforcement of the message of love can result in evil actions and cause suffering of unimaginable proportions.

The issue of ethics is further confounded by the differences in the moral codes from culture to culture. While certain human groups appreciate and cultivate the human body or even see it as sacred, others believe that anything related to flesh and physiological functions is *a priori* corrupt and evil. Some feel casual and natural about nudity, others require that women cover their entire body including parts of their face. In some cultural contexts, adultery was punishable by death, while, according to an old Eskimo custom, the host was expected to offer his wife in the spirit of hospitality to all male visitors of their home. Both polygamy and polyandry have been practiced in human cultural history as acceptable social alternatives. A tribe in New Caledonia used to kill fraternal twins, if one of them was male and the other female, because they committed incest in the womb. By comparison, in ancient Egypt and Peru, the law required that in the royal families the brother married his sister.

In Japan, suicide used to be not only recommended, but practically required in certain situations that were seen as dishonoring. In China and other places, when the ruler died, his wives and servants were killed and buried along with him. According to the Indian custom of *sati*, the widow was expected to follow her dead husband into the flames of the funeral pyre. Together with female infanticide, *sati* was practiced in India long after it had been outlawed by the British in the nineteenth century. Ritual human sacrifice was performed in many human groups and cannibalism was seen as an acceptable practice by some highly cultured groups, such as the Aztecs and the Maori. From a cross-cultural and transpersonal perspective, the rigid observance of customs and rules governing various psychobiological and social practices thus can be seen as a deliberate experiment of cosmic consciousness in which all possible experiential variations have been systematically explored.

Evil as an Intrinsic Part of Creation

One of the most difficult ethical challenges that emerges in holotropic states is to accept the fact that aggression is inextricably woven into the natural order and that it is not possible to be alive without this being at the expense of another life form. Antonie van Leeuwenhoek, a Dutch microbiologist and the inventor of the microscope, summed it up in one sentence: "Life lives on life—it is cruel, but it is God's will." The English poet, Alfred Lord Tennyson called nature "red in tooth and claw." Writing about the Darwinian worldview, biologist George Williams (1966) put it even stronger: "Mother Nature is a wicked old witch." And Marquis de Sade, who gave *sadism* its name, used references to this cruelty of nature as a justification for his own behavior.

Even the most conscientious way of conducting our lives cannot help us to escape this dilemma. Alan Watts (1969) in his article "Murder in the Kitchen" discussed from this point of view the problem of meat-eating versus vegetarianism. The fact that "rabbits scream louder than carrots" did not seem to him a good enough reason to choose the latter. Joseph Campbell expressed the same idea in his tongue-in-cheek definition of a vegetarian as "a person who is not sensitive enough to hear a tomato scream." Since life has to feed on life, whether it is of animal or vegetable nature, Watts recommended as a solution an approach found in many native cultures, both in communities of hunters/gatherers and agricultural societies. These groups use rituals that express gratitude for the eaten one and humble acceptance of their own participation in the food chain in both roles.

Ethical issues and decisions become particularly complex when the relevant insights and information come from levels of consciousness that are not ordinarily easily available, particularly those that include the spiritual dimension. Introducing spiritual criteria into situations of everyday life can become paralyzing if it occurs in an extreme form and is not tempered by practical considerations.

We can mention here as an example an episode from the life of the famous German physician, musician, philanthropist, and philosopher Albert Schweitzer. One day, he was treating in his jungle hospital in Lambarene an African native suffering from a serious septic condition. While he was standing by his body with a syringe filled with an antibiotic, he suddenly had to ask himself what gave him the right to destroy millions of lives of micro-organisms to save one human life. He was questioning by what criteria we assume the right to see human life as superior to that of all the other species.

Joseph Campbell was once asked how we can reconcile our spiritual worldview with the need to make practical decisions in everyday life, including killing to save life. He described as an example the situation of a small child who is in imminent danger of being bitten by a snake. When we intervene under these circumstances, killing the snake does not mean saying "No" to the snake as an integral part of the universal scheme, as a meaningful element of the cosmic order. It is not denying the right of the snake to exist as part of creation and does not necessarily mean that we do not appreciate its existence. This intervention is our reaction to a specific local situation, not a gesture of ultimate cosmic relevance.

Divine Roots of Evil

As we discover the existence of the world of archetypes and realize that its dynamics is instrumental in shaping the events in the material world, the focus of ethical considerations shifts from the personal and cultural levels to the transpersonal domain. The critical issue here is the fundamental dichotomy in the archetypal realm. We become aware of the fact that the pantheon of archetypal beings includes both benefic and malefic principles and forces or, using the terminology of pre-industrial cultures, blissful and wrathful deities. From this perspective, it is they who are responsible for the events in the material world. However, sooner or later it becomes clear that these entities themselves are not autonomous. They are creations or manifestations of a yet higher principle that transcends them and governs them. At this point, the moral inquiry finds a new focus; it is directed to the creative principle itself.

This naturally gives rise to an entirely new series of questions. Is there one creative source that transcends polarities and is responsible for both good and evil? Or is the universe a battlefield where two cosmic forces, one essentially good and the other evil, engage in a universal combat, in the way it has been portrayed in Zoroastrianism, Manichaeanism, and Christianity? If so, which of these two principles is more powerful and will ultimately prevail? If God is good and just, omniscient and omnipotent, as we are told by mainstream Christianity, how do we explain the amount of evil in the world? How is it possible that millions of children are killed in a bestial way or die of starvation, cancer, and infectious diseases long before they could possibly commit any sins? The usual explanation offered by Christian theology, suggesting that God punishes these individuals in advance because He foresees that they would grow up into sinners, certainly is not very convincing.

In many religions, the concept of karma and reincarnation helps to explain how and why something like this can happen. It also accounts for the horrendous inequities among adults and the differences in their destinies. As we will explore later in this book, similar concepts existed also in early Christianity, particularly in its Gnostic form. Gnostic Christianity was condemned as a heresy by the ecclesiastical Church in the second century and, in the fourth century, was severely persecuted with the assistance of Emperor Constantine. Ideas concerning reincarnation of the same soul were banned from Christianity in A.D. 553 at a special congress in Constantinople. This left Christianity with the formidable problem of an omnipotent, just, and benevolent Creator of a world that is full of inequity and evil. The belief in reincarnation can provide answers to some most immediate questions concerning the dark side of existence, but does not address the problem of the origin of the karmic chain of causes and effects.

In holotropic states of consciousness, fundamental ethical questions concerning the nature and origin of evil, the reason for its existence, and its role in the fabric of creation emerge spontaneously and with great urgency. The problem of the morality of the creative principle that is directly responsible for all the suffering and horrors of existence, or that permits and tolerates evil, is truly a formidable one. The ability to accept creation as it is, including its shadow side and one's own role in it, is one of the most challenging tasks we can encounter during an in-depth philosophical and spiritual quest. It is, therefore, interesting to review how these problems appear to those individuals who encounter them on their inner journey.

The experiences of identification with Absolute Consciousness or with the Void involve transcendence of all polarities, including the opposites of good and evil. They contain the entire spectrum of creation from the most beatific to the most diabolical aspects, but in an unmanifested form, as a pure potential. Since ethical considerations are applicable only to the world of manifest phenomena, which involves polarities, the problem of good and evil is intimately connected with the process of cosmic creation. For the purpose of our discussion, it is important to realize that ethical values and norms are themselves parts of creation and thus do not have an absolute independent existence of their own. In the ancient Indian sacred text, the *Katha Upanishad*, we can read:

As the sun, the eye of the whole world,
Is not sullied by the external faults of the eyes,
So the one Inner Soul of all things
Is not sullied by the evil in the world, being
    external to it.

The Role of Evil in the Universal Scheme

Final understanding and philosophical acceptance of evil always seems to involve the recognition that it has an important or even necessary role in the cosmic process. For example, deep experiential insights into ultimate realities that become available in holotropic states might reveal that evil is an essential element in the universal drama. Since cosmic creation is *creatio ex nihilo,* creation out of nothing, it has to be symmetrical. Everything that emerges into existence has to be counterbalanced by its opposite. From this perspective, the existence of polarities of all kinds is an absolutely indispensable prerequisite for the creation of the phenomenal worlds. This fact had its parallel in the speculations of some modern physicists about matter and antimatter, suggesting that in the very first moments of the universe, particles and antiparticles were present in equal numbers.

We have seen earlier that one of the "motives" for creation seems to be the "need" of the creative principle to get to know itself, so that "God can see God" or "Face can behold Face." To the extent to which the divine creates to explore its own inner potential, not expressing the full range of this potential would mean incomplete self-knowledge. And if Absolute Consciousness is also the ultimate Artist, Experimenter, and Explorer, it would compromise the richness of the creation to leave out some significant options. Artists do not limit their topics to those that are beautiful, ethical, and uplifting. They portray any aspects of life that can render interesting images or promise intriguing stories.

The existence of the shadow side of creation enhances its light aspects by providing contrast and gives extraordinary richness and depth to the universal drama. The conflict between good and evil in all the domains and on all the levels of existence is an inexhaustible source of inspiration for fascinating stories. A disciple once asked Sri Ramakrishna, the great Indian visionary, saint, and spiritual teacher: "Swamiji, why is evil in the world?" After a short deliberation, Ramakrishna replied succinctly: "To thicken the plot." This answer might appear cynical in view of the nature and scope of suffering in the world, seen in a concrete form of millions of children dying of starvation or various diseases, the insanity of wars throughout history, countless sacrificed and tortured victims, and the desolation of natural disasters. However, a mental experiment can help us to get a different perspective.

Let us for a moment imagine that we can eliminate from the universal scheme anything that is generally considered bad or evil, all the elements that we feel should not be part of life. Initially, it might seem that this would create an ideal world, a true paradise on earth. However, as we proceed, we see that the situation is much more complex. Suppose we start with the elimination of diseases, something that certainly belongs to the dark side of existence, and imagine that they have never existed. We soon discover that this is not an isolated intervention that selectively eradicates an evil aspect of the world. This interference has a profound effect on many positive aspects of life and creation that we hold in great esteem.

Together with the diseases we eliminate the entire history of medicine—medical research and the knowledge it imparts, the discovery of the causes of dangerous illnesses, as well as miraculous cures for them, such as vitamins, antibiotics, and hormones. There are no more miracles of modern medicine—life-saving operations, organ transplants, and genetic engineering. We lose all the great pioneers of science, like Virchow, Semmelweiss, and Pasteur, the heroes who dedicated their entire lives to a passionate search for answers to medical problems. There is also no need for the love and compassion of all those who take care of ailing people, from physicians and nurses to a variety of good Samaritans. We lose Mother Teresa together with the reason to award her a Nobel Prize. Here go the shamans and indigenous healers with their colorful rituals and knowledge of medicinal herbs, the miracles in Lourdes, and the Filipino psychic surgeons!

Another obviously dark and evil aspect of creation is the existence of oppressive regimes, totalitarian systems, genocide, and wars. When we focus our cosmic sanitation efforts on this area, we eliminate a significant part of human history. In this process, we lose all the heroic acts of freedom fighters of all times who sacrificed their lives for just causes and for the liberty of their countries and compatriots. There are no more triumphs of victory over evil empires and the intoxication of newly achieved freedom. We have to remove from the world the fortified castles of all historical periods and countries, as well as museums documenting the ingenuity of weapon-making, the mastery of defense, and the richness of military attires. Naturally, the elimination of violence from the cosmic drama will have profound reverberations in the world of art. The libraries, art museums, music collections, and movie archives would shrink considerably when we remove from them all the pieces of art inspired by violence and the fight against it.

The absence of metaphysical evil would drastically reduce the need for religion, since God without a powerful adversary would become a guaranteed commodity that would be taken for granted. Everything related to ritual and the spiritual life of humanity would now be missing from the universal scheme and none of the historical events inspired by religion have ever happened. Needless to say, we would also lose some of the best works of art—literature, music, paintings, sculptures, and movies—inspired by the conflict between the divine and the demonic. The world would be without its glorious Gothic cathedrals, Moslem mosques, synagogues, and Hindu and Buddhist temples, as well as other architectural gems inspired by religion.

If we continued further with this process of purging the universal shadow, creation would lose its immense depth and richness and we would eventually end up with a very colorless and uninteresting world. If this kind of reality were portrayed in a Hollywood movie, we probably would not find it worth seeing and the movie theaters would be empty. A widely used manual for successful screenplay writing stresses the importance of tension, conflict, and drama as necessary prerequisites for a successful movie. It actually specifically warns that portraying "life in a happy village" would guarantee a certain flop and box office disaster.

The filmmakers, who have a free choice to select any themes for their movies, do not usually choose sweet uneventful stories with a happy ending. They typically include suspense, danger, difficulties, serious emotional conflicts, sex, violence, and evil. And, of course, the creators of movies themselves are significantly influenced by the taste and demands of the audiences. To the extent to which God created humans according to his/her image, as we are told, it should not be surprising that cosmic creation follows the same principles that govern creative activity and entertainment in our world.

In the process of deep experiential self-exploration, we discover that creation is dichotomized on all the levels where we encounter forms and separate phenomena. Absolute Consciousness and the Void exist beyond the world of phenomena and thus transcend all polarities. Good and Evil as separate entities come into existence and manifest in the initial stages of creation when the dark and the light aspect of the Divine emerge from the undifferentiated matrix of the Void and Absolute Consciousness. While these two aspects of existence represent polar opposites and are antagonistic toward each other, they are both necessary elements in creation. In a complex and intricate interplay, they generate the countless characters and events on many different levels and in many dimensions of reality that constitute the cosmic drama.

Two Faces of God

In holotropic states, we can directly experience not only the unified creative principle, as I described earlier, but also separately either its benevolent or its malevolent form as two discrete entities. When we encounter the benevolent form of God, we selectively tune into the positive aspects of creation. At this point, we are not aware of the shadow side of existence and we see the cosmic play in its entirety as being essentially radiant and ecstatic. Evil appears to be ephemeral or entirely absent from the universal scheme of things.

The best approximation to the understanding of the nature of this experience is to describe it in terms of the ancient Indian concept of *Sacchidānanda*. This composite Sanskrit word consists of three separate roots: *sat* meaning existence or being; *chit*, which translates as awareness; and *ānanda*, which signifies bliss. All we can say about this experience is that we are identified with a radiant, boundless, and dimensionless principle, or state of being, that seems to be endowed with infinite existence, has infinite awareness or wisdom, and experiences infinite bliss. It also possesses an infinite capacity to create forms and experiential worlds out of itself.

This experience of Sacchidānanda, or Existence-Awareness-Bliss, has its counterpart—a cosmic principle that epitomizes all the negative potential of the Divine. It represents a negative mirror image or an exact polar opposite of the basic attributes of Sacchidānanda. We can think here of the introductory scene from Goethe's *Faust*, in which Mephistopheles introduces himself to Faust: "I am the spirit that negates" ("Ich bin der Geist der stets verneint"). When we look at the phenomena that we consider bad or evil, we will see that they fall into three distinct categories, each of which represents the negation of one of the basic characteristics or attributes of Sacchidānanda.

The first of the three basic qualities of the positive Divine is *sat*, or infinite existence. The corresponding category of evil is related to the concepts and experiences related to limited existence, termination of existence, and nonexistence. Here belongs the impermanence that rules the phenomenal world and the inevitable prospect of final annihilation of everything. This includes our own demise, the death of all living organisms, and the ultimate destruction of the earth, the solar system, and the universe. We can think here of the dismay of Gautama Buddha, when during his rides outside of his father's palace he discovered the facts of disease, old age, and death. In our own tradition, medieval Christian clergy coined many laconic phrases reminding the population of this aspect of existence: "Dust to dust, and to dust thou will return," "Remember death," "This is how passeth the glory of the world," or "Death is certain, its hour uncertain."

The second important aspect of Sacchidānanda is *chit*, or infinite awareness, wisdom, and intelligence. The corresponding category of evil is related to various forms and levels of limited awareness and ignorance. It covers a wide range of phenomena from harmful consequences of lack of knowledge, inadequate information, and misunderstanding in matters of everyday life to self-deception and basic ignorance about the nature of existence on a high metaphysical level (*avidyā*). This type of ignorance was described by the Buddha and some other spiritual teachers as one of the important roots of suffering. The form of knowledge that can penetrate the veil of this ignorance and lead to liberation from suffering is called in the East *prajñāpāramitā*, or transcendental wisdom.

The third category of phenomena experienced as bad or evil includes elements that represent negation of another major characteristic of Sacchidānanda, the element of unlimited bliss, or *ānanda*. The experiences belonging here and their causes reflect the dark side in the most direct, obvious, and explicit way, because they interfere with an ecstatic experience of existence. They involve an entire range of difficult emotions and unpleasant physical sensations that are direct opposites of divine pleasure, such as physical pain, anxiety, shame, sense of inadequacy, depression, and guilt.

The evil demiurgic principle, the negative mirror image of Sacchidānanda mentioned earlier, can be experienced in a purely abstract form or as a more or less concrete manifestation. Some people describe it as Cosmic Shadow, an immense field of ominous energy, endowed with consciousness, intelligence, destructive potential, and monstrous determination to cause chaos, suffering, and disaster. Others experience it as an anthropomorphic figure of immense proportions representing the all-pervading universal evil, or the Dark God. The encounter with the shadow side of existence can also take a more culture-bound form of specific deities, as exemplified by Satan, Lucifer, Ahriman, Hades, Lilith, Moloch, Kālī, or Coatlicue.

I will use here as an illustration an excerpt from the report of Jane, a thirty-five-year-old psychologist, who experienced in her training session a shattering confrontation with the dark side of existence that culminated in an encounter with a horrifying personification of universal evil.

> It seemed to me that I had lived my life up to this point with rosy glasses on my eyes that prevented me from seeing the monstrosity of existence. I saw

countless images of various forms of life in nature
being attacked and devoured by others. The entire
chain of life, from the lowest organisms to the most
highly developed ones, suddenly appeared as a brutal
drama in which the small and weak get eaten by the
large and strong. This dimension of nature was so
striking and overbearing that I could hardly see any
other aspects, such as the beauty of animals or ingenuity and creative intelligence of the life force. It was
a shattering illustration of the fact that the very basis
of life is violence; life cannot survive without feeding
on itself. A herbivore is just a more hidden and mitigated example of predatory existence in this biological
holocaust. The sentence "nature is criminal" that the
Marquis de Sade used to justify his own behavior
suddenly made new sense.

Other images took me on a tour of human history
and provided clear evidence that it has been dominated by violence and greed. I saw the vicious com-
bats of the cavemen using primitive clubs, as well as
the mass slaughter caused by increasingly sophisticated
weapons. Visions of the Mongolian hordes of Genghis
Khan, sweeping through Asia senselessly killing and
burning villages, were followed by the horrors of Nazi
Germany, Stalin's Russia, and the African Apartheid.
And yet other images portrayed the insatiable acquisi-
tiveness and insanity of our technological society that
threatens to destroy all life on this planet!

The ultimate irony and cruel joke in this dismal
portrait of humanity appeared to be the role of the
world's great religions. It was clear that these institutions promising to mediate contact with the divine
have often actually been a channel for evil. From the
history of Islam spread by sword and spear through
the Christian crusades and atrocities of the Inquisition
to more recent religiously motivated cruelties, religion
has been part of the problem rather than its solution.

Up to this point in the session, Jane had to witness a selective display of the shadow aspects of life, both in nature and in human society, without getting any insights concerning the causes of greed and violence. In a later phase, the experience took her directly to what seemed to be the metaphysical source of all evil in the world.

> Suddenly the experience changed and I came face to face with the entity responsible for all I had seen. It was the image embodying the quintessence of timeless Evil, an incredibly ominous towering figure, radiating unimaginable power. Although I had no concrete measure, it seemed immense, possibly the size of entire galaxies. Although it was generally anthropomorphic and I could roughly recognize specific part of its body, it had no concrete form.
>
> It was composed of rapidly changing dynamic images that flowed in holographic interpenetration. They portrayed various forms of evil and appeared in appropriate parts of the anatomy of this God of Evil. Thus the belly contained hundreds of images of greed, gluttony, and disgust, the genital area scenes of erotic perversion, rape, and sexual murder, the arms and hands violence committed by swords, daggers, and firearms. I felt awe and indescribable terror. The names Satan, Lucifer, and Ahriman emerged in my mind. But these were ridiculously meek labels for what I was experiencing.

The Separating Power of Evil

Some of the people who had experienced personal encounter with the Cosmic Evil had some interesting insights about its nature and function in the universal scheme of things. They saw that this principle is intricately woven into the fabric of existence and that it permeates in increasingly concrete forms all the levels of creation. Its various manifestations are expressions of the energy that makes the split-off units of consciousness feel separate from each other. It also alienates them from their cosmic source, the undifferentiated Absolute Consciousness. It thus prevents them from the realization of their essential identity with this source and also of their basic unity with each other.

From this point of view, evil is intimately linked with the dynamism to which I referred earlier as "partitioning," "screen-work," or "forgetting." Since the divine play, the cosmic drama, is unimaginable without individual protagonists, without dictinct separate entities, the existence of evil is absolutely essential for the creation of the world as we know it. This understanding is in basic agreement with the notion found in some Christian mystical scriptures according to which the fallen angel Lucifer (literally, "Light-Bearer"), as a representative of polarities, is seen as a demiurgic figure. He takes humanity on a fantastic journey into the world of matter. Approaching this problem from another perspective we can say that, in the last analysis, evil and suffering are based on a false perception of reality, particularly the belief of sentient beings in their separate individual self. This insight forms an essential part of the Buddhist doctrine of *anatta* or *Anātman* (no-self).

The insight that evil is a separating force in the universe also helps to understand certain typical experiential patterns and sequences in holotropic states. Thus, ecstatic experiences of unification and consciousness expansion are often preceded by shattering encounters with the forces of darkness, in the form of evil archetypal figures, or passing through demonic screens. This is regularly associated with extreme emotional and physical suffering. The most salient example illustrating this connection is the process of psychospiritual death and rebirth, in which experiences of agony, terror, and annihilation by wrathful deities are followed by a sense of reunion with the spiritual source. This connection seems to have found a concrete expression in the Japanese Buddhist temples, such as the splendid Todaiji in Nara, where one has to pass by terrifying figures of wrathful guardians before entering the inside of the temple and facing the radiant image of the Buddha.

One in Many, Many in One

Any attempt to apply ethical values to the process of cosmic creation has to take into consideration an important fact. According to the insights presented in this book, all boundaries that we ordinarily perceive in the universe are arbitrary and ultimately illusory. The entire cosmos is in its deepest nature a single entity of unimaginable dimensions, Absolute Consciousness. As we saw earlier, in the beautiful poem by Thich Nhat Hahn, all the roles in the cosmic drama have, in the last analysis, only one protagonist. In all the situations that involve the element of evil, such as hatred, cruelty, violence, misery, and suffering, the creative principle is playing a complicated game with itself. The aggressor is identical with the attacked, the dictator with the oppressed, the rapist with the raped, and the murderer with his victim. The infected patient is not different from the bacterial agents that invaded her and caused the disease, or from the doctor who applies the antibiotic to stop the infection.

The following excerpt from a session of Christopher Bache, the professor of philosophy and religion whose description of the experience of the Void I cited earlier, is a very vivid illustration of the shattering realization of our essential identity with the creative principle:

> At the center came forward the theme of sex. At first sex emerged in its pleasant form as mutual delight and erotic satisfaction, but soon it changed into in its violent form, as attack, assault, injury, and hurt. The forces of sexual assault were building in the crisscrossing fields of humanity as well. I was facing these brutal forces, and behind my back was a child. I was trying to protect this child from them, to hold them back and prevent them from reaching it. The horror intensified as the child became my precious three year old daughter. It was she and it was all children of the world simultaneously.

> I kept trying to protect her, to hold back the attack that was pushing through me, and yet I knew that

eventually I would fail. The longer I held the forces in check, the more powerful they became. The "I" here was not just a personal "I" but thousands and thousands of people. The horror was beyond anything I can describe. Glancing over my shoulder I could feel the field of frightened innocence, but now there was another element added to it—a strain of mystical embrace. Superimposed upon the child was the Primal Female, the Mother Goddess herself. She beckoned me to embrace her, and I knew instinctively that there could be no greater sweetness than the one found in her arms.

In holding myself back from violent sexual assault, I was also holding myself back from the mystical embrace of the Goddess, yet I could not bring myself to rape and kill my child no matter how sweet the promise of redemption. The frenzy continued to build until eventually I began to turn. Still holding back the terrible onslaught of killing, I was now facing my victim and being torn apart by the forces of passion on one side and protection on the other. My victim was at once my helpless, innocent, fragile daughter and the Primal Woman inviting me to a sexual embrace of cosmic proportions.

After a long period of agonizing battle against the horifying onslaught of violent impulses, Chris was gradually able to surrender to them and let them play themselves out. The resolution of this excruciating situation came when he was able to discover that behind the separate protagonists of these violent scenes was only one entity—himself as the creative principle.

No matter how hard I fought what was happening, I was being drawn to unleash the fury. In horror and blind thirst I was turning to attack, to rape, to kill, and yet I continued to fight what was happening with every ounce of my strength. The struggle drove me to deeper and deeper levels of intensity until suddenly something broke open, and I came to the shattering realization that I was turning to kill and rape myself. This breakthrough was very multidimensional and confusing. The intensity of my struggle drove me beyond a breaking point where I suddenly confronted the reality that I was both the raping killer and the victim. Experientially I knew that we were the same. In looking into my victim's eyes, I discovered that I was looking into my own face. I sobbed and sobbed. "I'm doing it to myself."

This was not a karmic inversion, a flip into a former life where victim and victimizer changed places. Rather, it was a quantum jump to an experiential level that dissolved all dualities into a single, encompassing flow. The "I" I now became was not in any way personal, but an underlying oneness that subsumed all persons. It was collective in the sense of including all human experience, but utterly simple and undivided. I was one. I was aggressor and victim. I was rapist and raped. I was killer and killed. I was doing it to myself. Through all of history, I have been doing it to myself.

The pain of human history was my pain. There were no victims. Nothing was outside of me doing this to me. I was responsible for everything that I was experiencing, for everything that had ever happened. I was looking into the face of my creation. I did this. I am doing this. I chose for all this to happen. I chose to create all these horrible, horrible worlds.

The Forms of Emptiness and the Emptiness of Forms

In any metaphysical discussion concerning the existence of evil, we have to take into consideration another important factor. Careful analysis of the nature of reality, whether experiential, scientific, or philosophical, will reveal that the material world and all the events in it are essentially void. The texts of various Buddhist schools offer meditational practices through which we can discover the emptiness of all material objects and the absence of a separate self in our own being. By following the instructions for spiritual practice, we can reach experiential confirmation of the basic tenet of Buddhism—that form is emptiness and emptiness is form.

This statement, which appears paradoxical or even absurd to our everyday state of consciousness, reveals a profound truth about reality that has been confirmed by modern science. In the first decades of this century, physicists conducted systematic research exploring the composition of matter all the way to a subatomic level. They discovered in this process that what they had earlier considered to be solid matter turned out to be increasingly empty. Eventually, anything even remotely resembling solid "stuff" completely disappeared from the picture and was replaced by abstract probabilistic equations.

What the Buddhists discovered experientially and modern physicists experimentally is in essential agreement with the metaphysical speculations of Alfred North Whitehead (1967), one of the greatest philosophers of this century. Whitehead calls the belief in enduring existence of separate material objects the "fallacy of misplaced concreteness." According to him, the universe is composed of countless discontinuous bursts of experiential activity. The basic element of which the universe is made is not enduring substance, but moment of experience, called in his terminology *actual occasion.* This term applies to phenomena on all the levels of reality, from subatomic particles to human souls.

As the above discussion suggests, none of the events from our everyday life, and, for that matter, none of the situations that involve suffering and evil, are ultimately real in the sense we usually think about them and experience them. To illustrate this, I will return to the movie analogy that I used earlier. When we are watching a movie or a television show, what we see as separate protagonists are actually various aspects of one and the same undivided field of light. We have the choice to interpret our perceptions as a complex real-life drama or realize that we are witnessing a dance of electromagnetic and acoustic waves of various frequencies that are carefully orchestrated and synchronized for a specific effect. While an unsophisticated person or a child might mistake the movie for reality, a typical moviegoer is well aware of the fact that he or she is participating in a virtual, make-believe reality.

The reason we decide to interpret the play of light and sound as a real story and the progonists as separate entities is that we are interested in the experience that results from such a strategy. We actually make a voluntary choice to go to the movie theater and agree to pay the entrance fee, because we actively seek the experiences involved. And while we decide to react to the situation as if it were real, we are, on another level, aware that the characters in the movie are fictional and that the protagonists are actors who volunteered to participate. Particularly important from the point of view of our discussion is the knowledge of the moviegoers that the persons killed in the movie did not really die.

According to the insights decribed in this book, the human predicament closely parallels that of the moviegoer. We made, on another level of reality, the decision to incarnate, because we were attracted by the experiences that material existence provides. The separate identity of the protagonists in the cosmic drama, including our own, is an illusion and the matter of which the universe seems to be made is essentially empty. The world in which we live does not really exist in the form in which we perceive it. The spiritual scriptures of the East compare our everyday experience of the world to a dream from which we can awaken. Frithjof Schuon (1969) put it very succinctly: "The universe is a dream woven of dreams: the self alone is awake."

In the cosmic drama, as in a movie or a theater play, nobody is killed or dies, since a larger and deeper identity is assumed or resumed after a particular role ends. In a certain sense, the protagonists and the drama do not exist at all, or they exist and do not exist at the same time. From this point of view, to blame the Universal Mind for the existence of evil in the world would be equally absurd as to sentence a movie director for the crimes or murders committed on the screen. Naturally, there is one important difference between sentient beings and the protagonists in the movies. Even if the beings in the material world are not what they appear to be, the experiences of physical pain and emotional suffering associated with their role are real. This, of course, is not the case as far as the movie actors are concerned.

This way of looking at creation can be very disturbing, in spite of the fact that it is based on very convincing personal experiences in holotropic states and is also generally compatible with scientific findings about the nature of reality. The problems become obvious as we start thinking about the practical consequences that such a perspective has for our life and our everyday conduct. At first sight, seeing the material world as "virtual reality" and comparing human existence to a movie seems to trivialize life and make light of the depth of human misery. It might appear that such a perspective denies the seriousness of human suffering and fosters an attitude of cynical indifference, where nothing really matters. Similarly, accepting evil as an integral part of creation and seeing its relativity could easily be seen as a justification for suspending any ethical constraints and for unlimited pursuit of egotistical goals. It might also seem to sabotage any effort to actively combat evil in the world.

However, the situation in this regard is much more complex than it might appear at a superficial glance. First of all, practical experience shows that the awareness of the emptiness behind all forms is not at all incompatible with genuine appreciation and love for all creation. Transcendental experiences leading to profound metaphysical insights into the nature of reality actually engender reverence toward all sentient beings and responsible engagement in the process of life. Our compassion does not require objects that have material substance. It can just as easily be addressed to sentient beings who are units of consciousness.

The awareness of the emptiness underlying the world of forms can help us significantly in coping with difficult life situations. At the same time, it does not in any way make existence less meaningful or interfere with our ability to enjoy the beautiful and pleasant aspects of life. Deep compassion and admiration for creation is in no way incompatible with the realization that the material world does not exist in the form in which we experience it. After all, we can have an intense emotional reaction to powerful works of art and profoundly empathize with their characters! And, unlike in the works of art, in life all the experiences of the protagonists are real!

Impact of the Holotropic Process on
Ethical Values and Behavior

Before we can fully appreciate the ethical implications that deep transcendental insights can have for our behavior, we have to take into consideration some additional factors. Experiential exploration that makes such profound insights available typically reveals important biographical, perinatal, and transpersonal sources of violence and greed in our unconscious. Psychological work on this material leads to a significant reduction of aggression and to an increase of tolerance. We also encounter a large spectrum of transpersonal experiences in which we identify with various aspects of creation. This results in deep reverence for life and empathy with all sentient beings. The same process through which we are discovering the emptiness of forms and the relativity of ethical values thus also significantly reduces our proclivity to immoral and antisocial behavior and teaches us love and compassion.

We develop a new system of values that is not based on conventional norms, precepts, commandments, and fear of punishment, but on our knowledge and understanding of the universal order. We realize that we are an integral part of creation and that by hurting others we would be hurting ourselves. In addition, deep self-exploration leads to the experiential discovery of reincarnation and of the law of karma. This brings us awareness of the possibility of serious experiential repercussions of harmful behaviors, even those that escape societal retributions.

Plato was clearly aware of the profound moral implications of our beliefs concerning the possibility of life continuing beyond the biological demise. In *Laws* (Plato 1961a) he has Socrates say that disconcern for the *postmortem* consequences of our deeds would be "a boon to the wicked." In advanced stages of spiritual development, a combination of the decrease of aggression, decline of egocentric orientation, sense of oneness with sentient beings, and the awareness of karma become important factors governing our everyday conduct.

It is interesting to mention in this context C. G. Jung and the crisis he experienced when he became aware of the relativity of all ethical norms and values. At that point, he seriously questioned whether, from a higher perspective, it really matters at all what behavior we choose and whether we follow ethical precepts. After some deliberation, he finally found a satisfying personal answer to this problem. He concluded that, since there are no absolute criteria for morality, every ethical decision is a creative act that reflects our present stage of consciousness development and the information that is available to us. When these factors change, we may retrospectively see the situation differently. However, that does not mean that our original decision was wrong. What is important is that we did the best we could do under the circumstances.

Although in advanced transpersonal experiences we can transcend evil, its existence appears to be very real in our everyday life and in various other experiential realms, particularly in the archetypal domain. In the world of religion, we often encounter tendencies to portray evil as something that is separate from the Divine and alien to it. Holotropic experiences lead to an understanding that one of my clients called "transcendental realism." It is an attitude that accepts the fact that evil is an intrinsic part of creation and that all realms that contain separate individuals will always have both a light and a shadow side. Since evil is inextricably woven into the cosmic fabric and indispensable for the existence of experiential worlds, it cannot be defeated and eradicated. However, while we cannot eliminate evil from the universal scheme of things, we can certainly transform ourselves and develop radically different ways of coping with the dark side of existence.

In deep experiential work we realize that we have to experience in our life a certain amount of physical and emotional pain and discomfort that is intrinsic to incarnate existence in general. The First Noble Truth of the Buddha reminds us that life means suffering *(duḥkha)* and it specifically refers to situations and circumstances that are responsible for our misery—birth, old age, disease, dying, association with what we do not like, separation from what is dear to us, and not getting that which we wish for. In addition, each of us experiences suffering that is specific for us and reflects our destiny and karmic past.

While we cannot avoid suffering, we can have a certain influence on its timing and the form it takes. My observations from the work with holotropic states indicate that when we confront the dark side of existence in a focused and condensed form in deliberately planned sessions, we can significantly reduce its various manifestations in our everyday life. There are some other ways in which systematic self-exploration can help us to cope with suffering and with the experience of the difficult aspects of existence. After we have learned to endure the extreme intensity of the experiences in holotropic states, our baseline and threshold for suffering undergo profound changes and the trials and tribulations of everyday life are much easier to bear.

We also discover that we are not body egos or what the Hindus call name and form (*nāmarūpa*). In the course of our self-exploration, we experience radical shifts in our sense of identity. In holotropic states, we can identify with anything from an insignificant speck of protoplasm in a vast material universe to the totality of existence and Absolute Consciousness itself. Whether we see ourselves as helpless victims of overwhelming cosmic forces or the co-authors of our life scripts will naturally have a far-reaching impact on the degree of suffering we experience in life or, conversely, on the amount of delight and freedom we enjoy.

Evil Archetypes and the Future of Humanity

Before closing this chapter, I would like to mention some interesting insights from holotropic states concerning the relationship between evil, the future of humanity, and survival of life on our planet. We are all painfully aware of the severe and dangerous global crisis that we are facing as we are about to enter into the next millennium. We clearly cannot continue acting as we have in the past throughout most of human history and hope to survive. It has become imperative to find ways to curb human violence, to dismantle weapons of mass destruction, and to secure peace in the world. Equally important is to stop industrial pollution of the air, water, and soil and to reorient our economy to renewable sources of energy. Another important task is to eliminate poverty and hunger in the world and to provide treatment for all the people suffering from curable diseases.

Many of us are deeply concerned about this situation and have a sincere desire to avert it and to create a better world. It is obvious that the situation in the world is critical and it is hard to imagine any easy remedial actions that would correct it. The difficulty in finding solutions is usually attributed to the fact that the current global crisis is extremely complex and involves an intricate web of problems that have economic, political, ethnic, military, psychological, and other dimensions. The solutions, if they were possible, are seen as corrections of the deviant trends in these different areas.

In holotropic states, we discover that this problem has also a disturbing metaphysical dimension. We become aware of the fact that what is happening in our world is not determined solely by material causes. In the last analysis, it is a direct reflection of the dynamics in the archetypal domain. The forces and entities operating in this domain are strongly polarized; the pantheon of archetypal figures includes both benevolent and malefic deities. The archetypal principles—good, neutral, and evil—represent an integral part of creation and indispensable elements in the cosmic game. For this reason, it is not possible to eliminate evil from the universal scheme of things. Half of the archetypal pantheon cannot be simply "put out of business."

In view of these insights, it becomes obvious that if we want to improve the situation in the world and reduce the influence of evil elements on our everyday affairs, we have to find less destructive and less dangerous forms of expression for the archetypal forces responsible for them. It is imperative to create appropriate contexts that would make it possible to honor these archetypal forces and to offer them alternative outlets that would enhance instead of destroy life. Occasionally, holotropic states bring interesting ideas suggesting what these activities and institutions would look like.

The primary strategy for reducing the impact of the potentially destructive archetypal forces in our world would be to find for them safe channels of expression in holotropic states of consciousness. This could include programs of systematic spiritual practice of different orientations, various experiential forms of psychotherapy mediating access to perinatal and transpersonal experiences, and centers offering supervised psychedelic sessions. Of great importance would also be a return to socially sanctioned ritual activities comparable to those that existed in all ancient and aboriginal cultures. Modern versions of rites of passage would make it possible to consciously experience and integrate various difficult destructive and self-destructive energies that would otherwise have a disturbing effect on society. Additional interesting alternatives would be dynamic new art forms and entertainment modalities using the technology of virtual reality.

These transformative technologies could be complemented by various outward-oriented activities serving the same purpose. Thus the powerful and potentially destructive explosive energies that are currently expressed in internecine wars could be partially channeled through a large scale globally integrated space program or other similar technical projects. Another possibility would be competitive events of various kinds, from sports tournaments to racing events involving modern technology. Some of the energy could also be channeled through sophisticated amusement parks, elaborate carnivals, and pageants similar to the festivities of the ancient and medieval royalty, aristocracy, gentry, and general population. If there is any validity in the above insights, the task of developing these new forms certainly represents an interesting challenge.

7
Birth, Sex, and Death:
The Cosmic Connection

Death borders upon our birth, and our cradle stands in the grave.

—Joseph Hall

Man puts himself at once on the level of the beast if he seeks to gratify lust alone, but he elevates his superior position when, by curbing the animal desire, he combines with the sexual functions ideas of mortality, of the sublime, and of the beautiful.

—Baron Richard von Krafft-Ebing

Intimate Links between Birth, Sex, and Death

In the chapter exploring the ways to reunion with the cosmic source, I briefly mentioned three aspects of human life that have a particularly close connection with the transpersonal domain: birth, sex, and death. As we saw, all three of them represent important gateways to transcendence and unique opportunities for cosmic reunion. This is true whether our encounter with one of these areas occurs in a symbolic way in the process of deep experiential self-exploration or in situations of our everyday life.

Delivering women and people participating in the delivery as assistants or observers can experience a powerful spiritual opening. This is particularly true if birth does not occur in the dehumanized context of a hospital, but under circumstances where it is possible to experience its full psychological and spiritual impact. Similarly, having a close personal brush with death or spending intimate time with dying people can be a powerful catalyst for mystical experiences. And love-making with a highly compatible partner can be a profoundly spiritual event and, on occasion, even initiate an ongoing process of consciousness evolution. The close connection between sexuality and spirituality is the basis of Eastern Tantric practices.

Besides their intimate link with spirituality, birth, sex, and death also show a significant experiential overlap with each other. For many women, an uncomplicated delivery under favorable conditions can be the strongest sexual experience of their life. Conversely, a powerful sexual orgasm in women, as well as men, can occasionally take the form of psychospiritual rebirth. The orgasm can also be so overpowering that it can be subjectively experienced as dying. The connection between sexual orgasm and death is reflected in the French language that refers to it as "small death" ("la petite mort"). And dying, particularly if it is associated with choking, can have a strong sexual component.

Equally close is the relationship between birth and death. In advanced stages of pregnancy, many women have dreams that contain the motifs of death and destruction. Childbirth is a potentially life-threatening event for the mother, as well as the child. And delivery can be associated with strong fears of dying, even if it is not particularly difficult and does not endanger life. The reverse is also true; the near-death experiences share certain elements with birth, particularly the frequent sense of passing through a tunnel or funnel and emerging into light.

In the work with holotropic states, we can get deep insights into the nature of these experiential connections between birth, sex, and death. In the unconscious psyche, these three crucial areas of our life are so intimately linked and interwoven that it is impossible to experience one of them without touching upon the other two. This comes as a surprise, because in our everyday life we usually think about these three areas as separate and discuss them in different contexts. Birth is something that marks the beginning of our life and involves an infant. Death, unless it is a result of a serious disease or accident, is associated with old age and thus with the final stage of our life. Sexuality, in the full sense of the word, belongs to an intermediate period of our life characterized by physical maturity.

Birth, Sex, and Death in the Perinatal Process

This conventional view of the relationship between birth, sex, and death undergoes profound changes when our process of deep experiential self-exploration moves beyond the level of memories from childhood and infancy and reaches back to birth, to the perinatal domain of the psyche. We start encountering emotions and physical sensations of extreme intensity, often surpassing anything we previously considered humanly possible. At this point, the experiences become a strange mixture of the themes of birth and death. They involve a sense of a severe, life-threatening confinement and a desperate and determined struggle to free ourselves and survive. This intimate relationship between birth and death on the perinatal level reflects the fact that birth is a potentially life-threatening event. The child and the mother can actually lose their lives during this process and children might be born severely blue from asphyxiation, or even dead and in need of resuscitation.

The reliving of various aspects of biological birth can be very authentic and convincing and often replays this process in photographic detail. This can occur even in people who have no intellectual knowledge about their birth and lack elementary obstetric information. We can, for example, discover through direct experience that we had a breech birth, that a forceps was used during our delivery, or that we were born with the umbilical cord twisted around the neck. We can feel the anxiety, biological fury, physical pain, and suffocation associated with this terrifying event and even accurately recognize the type of anesthesia used when we were born. This is often accompanied by various postures and movements of the head and body that accurately recreate the mechanics of a particular type of delivery. All these details can be confirmed if good birth records or reliable personal witnesses are available.

The strong representation of birth and death in our psyche and the close association between them might surprise traditional psychologists and psychiatrists, but is actually logical and easily understandable. The delivery brutally terminates the intrauterine existence of the fetus. He or she "dies" as an aquatic organism and is born as an air-breathing, physiologically and even anatomically different, form of life. And the passage through the birth canal is itself a difficult and potentially life-threatening situation.

It is not so easy to understand, why the perinatal dynamics also regularly includes a sexual component. And yet, when we are reliving the final stages of birth in the role of the fetus, this is typically associated with an unusually strong sexual arousal. The same is true for delivering women, who can experience a mixture of fear of death and intense sexual excitement. This connection seems strange and puzzling, particularly as far as the fetus is concerned, and certainly deserves a few words of explanation.

There seems to be a mechanism in the human organism that transforms extreme suffering, especially when it is associated with suffocation, into a particular form of sexual arousal. This experiential connection can be observed in a variety of situations other than birth. People who had tried to hang themselves and were rescued in the last moment typically describe that, at the height of suffocation, they felt an almost unbearable sexual arousal. It is known that males executed by hanging typically have an erection and even ejaculate. The literature on torture and brain-washing describes that inhuman physical suffering often triggers states of sexual ecstasy. In a less extreme form, this mechanism operates in various sadomasochistic practices that include stran-gulation and choking. In the sects of flagellants, who regularly engage in self-inflicted torture, and in religious martyrs, subjected to unimaginable torments, extreme physical pain at a certain point changes into sexual arousal and eventually results in ec-static rapture and transcendental experiences.

Dynamics and Symbolism of the Basic Perinatal Matrices (BPMs)

So far, we have focused primarily on the emotional and physical aspects of the birth experiences. However, the experiential spec-trum of the perinatal domain of the unconscious is not limited to elements that can be derived from the biological processes involved in childbirth. It also involves rich symbolic imagery that is drawn from the transpersonal realms. The perinatal domain is an important interface between the biographical and the transpersonal levels of the psyche. It represents a gateway to the historical and archetypal aspects of the collective unconscious in the Jungian sense. Since the specific symbolism of these experiences has its origin in the collective unconscious, and not in the individual memory banks, it can come from any geographical and historical context, as well as any spiritual tradition of the world, quite independently from our racial, cultural, educational, or religious background.

Identification with the infant facing the ordeal of the passage through the birth canal seems to provide access to experiences of people from other times and cultures, of various animals, and even mythological figures. It is as if by connecting with the experience of the fetus struggling to be born, one reaches an intimate, almost mystical, connection with the consciousness of the human species and with other sentient beings who are or have been in a similar difficult predicament.

Experiential confrontation with birth and death seems to result automatically in a spiritual opening and discovery of the mystical dimensions of the psyche and of existence. As I mentioned before, it does not seem to make a difference whether this encounter with birth and death occurs in actual life situations, such as in delivering women and in the context of near-death experiences, or is purely symbolic. Powerful perinatal sequences in psychedelic and holotropic sessions or in the course of spontaneous psychospiritual crises (spiritual emergencies) seem to have the same effect.

Biological birth has three distinct stages. In the first one, the fetus is periodically constricted by uterine contractions without having any chance of escaping this situation, since the cervix is firmly closed. Continued contractions pull the cervix over the fetus' head until it is sufficiently dilated to allow the passage through the birth canal. Full dilation of the cervix marks the transition from the first to the second stage of delivery, which is characterized by the descent of the head into the pelvis and its gradual, difficult propulsion through the birth pathways. And finally, in the third stage, the newborn emerges from the birth canal and, after the umbilical cord is cut, he or she becomes an anatomically independent organism.

At each of these stages, the baby experiences a specific and typical set of intense emotions and physical sensations. These experiences leave deep unconscious imprints in the psyche that later in life play an important role in the life of the individual. Reinforced by emotionally important experiences from infancy and childhood, the birth memories can shape the perception of the world, profoundly influence everyday behavior, and contribute to the development of various emotional and psychosomatic disorders. In holotropic states, this unconscious material can surface and be fully experienced. When our process of deep self-exploration takes us back to birth, we discover that reliving each stage of delivery is associated with a distinct experiential pattern, characterized by a specific combination of emotions, physical feelings, and symbolic images. I refer to these patterns of experience as basic perinatal matrices (BPMs).

First Basic Perinatal Matrix (BPM I)

The first perinatal matrix (BPM I) is related to the intrauterine experience immediately preceding birth and the remaining three matrices (BPM II–BPM IV) to the three clinical stages of delivery described above. Besides containing elements that represent a replay of the original situation of the fetus at a particular stage of birth, the basic perinatal matrices also include various natural, historical, and mythological scenes with similar experiential qualities drawn from the transpersonal realms. In what follows, I will briefly outline the specific connections between the perinatal dynamics and the transpersonal domain.

I would like to emphasize that the connections between the experiences of the consecutive stages of biological birth and various symbolic images associated with them are very specific and consistent. The reason they emerge together is not understandable in terms of conventional logic. However, that does not mean that these associations are arbitrary and random. They have their own deep order that can best be described as "experiential logic." What this means is that the connection between the experiences characteristic for various stages of birth and the concomitant symbolic themes are not based on some formal external similarity, but on the fact that they share the same emotional feelings and physical sensations.

While experiencing the episodes of undisturbed embryonal existence (BPM I), we often encounter images of vast regions with no boundaries or limits. Sometimes we identify with galaxies, interstellar space, or the entire cosmos other times we have the experience of floating in the ocean or of becoming various aquatic animals, such as fish, dolphins, or whales. The undisturbed intrauterine experience can also open into visions of nature—safe, beautiful, and unconditionally nourishing, like a good womb (Mother Nature). We can see luscious orchards, fields of ripe corn, agricultural terraces in the Andes, or unspoiled Polynesian islands. The experience of the good womb can also provide selective access to the archetypal domain of the collective unconscious and open into images of paradises or heavens as they are described in the mythologies of different cultures.

When we are reliving episodes of intrauterine disturbances, or "bad womb" experiences, we have a sense of dark and ominous threat and we often feel that we are being poisoned. We might see images that portray polluted waters and toxic dumps. This reflects the fact that many prenatal disturbances are caused by toxic changes in the body of the pregnant mother. The experience of the toxic womb can be associated with visions of frightening demonic figures from the archetypal realms of the collective unconscious. Reliving of more violent interferences during prenatal existence, such as an imminent miscarriage or attempted abortion, is usually connected with a sense of universal threat or with bloody apocalyptic visions of the end of the world.

Second Basic Perinatal Matrix (BPM II)

When the experiential regression reaches the onset of biological birth, we typically feel that we are being sucked into a gigantic whirlpool or swallowed by some mythical beast. We might also experience that the entire world or even cosmos is being engulfed. This can be associated with images of devouring or entangling archetypal monsters, such as leviathans, dragons, giant snakes, tarantulas, and octopuses. The sense of overwhelming vital threat can lead to intense anxiety and general mistrust bordering on paranoia. We can also experience a descent into the depths of the underworld, the realm of death, or hell. As mythologist Joseph Campbell so eloquently described, this is a universal motif in the mythologies of the hero's journey (Campbell 1968).

Reliving the fully developed first stage of biological birth when the uterus is contracting, but the cervix is not yet open (BPM II), is one of the worst experiences a human being can have. We feel caught in a monstrous claustrophobic nightmare, are suffering agonizing emotional and physical pain, and have a sense of utter helplessness and hopelessness. Our feelings of loneliness, guilt, absurdity of life, and existential despair can reach metaphysical proportions. We lose connection with linear time and become convinced that this situation will never end and that there is absolutely no way out. There is no doubt in our mind that what is happening to us is what the religions refer to as Hell—unbearable emotional and physical torment without any hope for redemption. This can actually be accompanied by archetypal images of devils and infernal landscapes from different cultures.

When we are facing the dismal situation of no exit in the clutches of uterine contractions, we can experientially connect with sequences from the collective unconscious that involve people, animals, and even mythological beings who are in a similar painful and hopeless predicament. We identify with prisoners in dungeons, inmates of concentration camps or insane asylums, and with animals caught in traps. We might experience the intolerable tortures of sinners in hell or of Sisyphus rolling his boulder up the mountain in the deepest pit of Hades. Our pain can become the agony of Christ asking God why He has abandoned him. It seems to us that we are facing the prospect of eternal damnation. This state of darkness and abysmal despair is known from the spiritual literature as the Dark Night of the Soul. From a broader perspective, in spite of the feelings of utter hopelessness that it entails, this state is an important stage of spiritual opening. If it is experienced to its full depth, it can have an immensely purging and liberating effect on those who experience it.

Third Basic Perinatal Matrix (BPM III)

The experience of the second stage of birth, the propulsion through the birth canal after the cervix opens and the head descends (BPM III), is unusually rich and dynamic. Facing the clashing energies and hydraulic pressures involved in the delivery, we are flooded with images from the collective unconscious portraying sequences of titanic battles and scenes of bloody violence and torture. It is also during this phase that we are confronted with sexual impulses and energies of a problematic nature and unusual intensity.

I have already described earlier that sexual arousal is an important part of the experience of birth. This places our first encounter with sexuality into a very precarious context, into a situation where our life is threatened, where we are suffering pain as well as inflicting pain, and where we are unable to breathe. At the same time, we are experiencing a mixture of vital anxiety and primitive biological fury, the latter being an understandable reaction of the fetus to this painful and life-threatening experience. In the final stages of birth, we can also encounter various forms of biological material—blood, mucus, urine, and even feces.

Because of these problematic connections, the experiences and images that we encounter in this phase typically present sex in a grossly distorted form. The strange mixture of sexual arousal with physical pain, aggression, vital anxiety, and biological material leads to sequences that are pornographic, aberrant, sadomasochistic, scatological, or even satanic. We can be overwhelmed by dramatic scenes of sexual abuse, perversions, rapes, and erotically-motivated murders.

On occasion, these experiences can take the form of participation in rituals featuring witches and satanists. This seems to be related to the fact that reliving this stage of birth involves the same strange combination of emotions, sensations, and elements that characterizes the archetypal scenes of the Black Mass and of the Witches' Sabbath (Walpurgi's Night). It is a mixture of sexual arousal, panic anxiety, aggression, vital threat, pain, sacrifice, and encounter with ordinarily repulsive biological materials. This peculiar experiential amalgam is associated with a sense of sacredness or numinosity that reflects the fact that all this is unfolding in close proximity to a spiritual opening.

This stage of the birth process can also be associated with countless images from the collective unconscious portraying scenes of murderous aggression, such as vicious battles, bloody revolutions, gory massacres, and genocide. In all the violent and sexual scenes that we encounter at this stage, we alternate between the role of the perpetrator and that of the victim. This is the time of a major encounter with the dark side of our personality, Jung's Shadow, which we discussed in the chapter on good and evil. As this perinatal phase is culminating and approaching resolution, many people envision Jesus, the Way of the Cross, and crucifixion, or even actually experience full identification with Jesus' suffering. The archetypal domain of the collective unconscious contributes to this phase heroic mythological figures and deities representing death and rebirth, such as the Egyptian god Osiris, the Greek deities Dionysus and Persephone, or the Sumerian goddess Inanna.

Fourth Perinatal Matrix (BPM IV)

The reliving of the third stage of the birth process, of the actual emergence into the world (BPM IV), is typically initiated by the motif of fire. We can have the feeling that our body is consumed by searing heat, have visions of burning cities and forests, or identify with victims of immolation. The archetypal versions of this fire can take the form of the cleansing flames of Purgatory or of the legendary bird Phoenix, dying in the heat of his burning nest and emerging from the ashes reborn and rejuvenated. The purifying fire seems to destroy in us whatever is corrupted and prepare us for spiritual rebirth. When we are reliving the actual moment of birth, we experience it as complete annihilation and subsequent rebirth and resurrection.

To understand why we experience the reliving of biological birth as death and rebirth, one has to realize that what happens to us is much more than just a replay of the original event of childbirth. During the delivery, we are completely confined in the birth canal and have no way of expressing the extreme emotions and sensations involved. Our memory of this event thus remains psychologically undigested and unassimilated. Much of our later self-definition and our attitudes toward the world are heavily contaminated by this constant deep reminder of the vulnerability, inadequacy, and weakness that we experienced at birth. In a sense, we were born anatomically but have not really caught up emotionally with the fact that the emergency and danger are over. The "dying" and the agony during the struggle for rebirth reflect the actual pain and vital threat of the biological birth process. However, the ego death that immediately precedes rebirth is the death of our old concepts of who we are and what the world is like, which were forged by the traumatic imprint of birth.

As we are purging these old programs from our psyche and body by letting them emerge into consciousness, we are reducing their energetic charge and curtailing their destructive influence on our life. From a larger perspective, this process is actually very healing and transforming. And yet, as we are nearing its final resolution, we might paradoxically feel that, as the old imprints are leaving our system, we are dying with them. Sometimes, we not only experience the sense of personal annihilation, but also the destruction of the world as we know it.

While only a small step separates us from the experience of radical liberation, we have a sense of all-pervading anxiety and impending catastrophy of enormous proportions. The impression of imminent doom can be very convincing and overwhelming. The predominant feeling is that we are losing all that we know and that we are. At the same time, we have no idea what is on the other side, or even if there is anything there at all. This fear is the reason that at this stage many people desperately resist the process if they can. As a result, they can remain psychologically stuck in this problematic territory for an indefinite period of time.

The encounter with the ego death is a stage of the spiritual journey when we might need much encouragement and psychological support. When we succeed in overcoming the metaphysical fear associated with this important juncture and decide to let things happen, we experience total annihilation on all imaginable levels. It involves physical destruction, emotional disaster, intellectual and philosophical defeat, ultimate moral failure, and even spiritual damnation. During this experience, all reference points, everything that is important and meaningful in our life, seems to be mercilessly destroyed.

Immediately following the experience of total annihilation—"hitting cosmic bottom"—we are overwhelmed by visions of light that has a supernatural radiance and beauty and is usually perceived as sacred. This divine epiphany can be associated with displays of beautiful rainbows, diaphanous peacock designs, and visions of celestial realms with angelic beings or deities appearing in light. This is also the time when we can experience a profound encounter with the archetypal figure of the Great Mother Goddess or one of her many culture-bound forms.

The experience of psychospiritual death and rebirth is a major step in the direction of the weakening of our identification with the "skin-encapsulated ego" and reconnecting with the transcendental domain. We feel redeemed, liberated, and blessed and have a new awareness of our divine nature and cosmic status. We also typically experience a strong surge of positive emotions toward ourselves, other people, nature, God, and existence in general. We are filled with optimism and have a sense of emotional and physical well-being.

It is important to emphasize that this kind of healing and life-changing experience occurs when the final stages of biological birth had a more or less natural course. If the delivery was very debilitating or confounded by heavy anesthesia, the experience of rebirth does not have the quality of triumphant emergence into light. It is more like awakening and recovering from a hangover with dizziness, nausea, and clouded consciousness. Much additional psychological work might be needed to work through these additional issues and the positive results are much less striking.

Perinatal Process and the Collective Unconscious

From what I have described, we can see that the perinatal domain of the psyche represents an experiential crossroad of critical importance. It is not only the meeting point of three absolutely crucial aspects of human biological existence—birth, sex, and death—but also the dividing line between life and death, the individual and the species, and the psyche and the spirit. Full conscious experience of the contents of this domain of the psyche with good subsequent integration can have far-reaching consequences and lead to spiritual opening and deep personal transformation.

People usually begin the process of intensive experiential self-exploration for very personal reasons—either for therapeutic purposes or for their own emotional and spiritual growth. However, certain aspects of perinatal experiences strongly suggest that what is happening here is an event that in its significance transcends by far the narrow interests of the individual. The intensity of the emotions and physical sensations involved and the frequent identification with countless other people throughout history give these experiences a distinctly transpersonal quality.

The following excerpt from an account of a powerful session involving a holotropic state of consciousness, beautifully captures the nature of perinatal experiences, their intensity, and the degree to which they engage the collective unconscious of humanity. (Bache 1997)

I was surprised and caught off guard by how terribly painful this session was. It was not personal and had little to do with my biological birth. The pain I was suffering was clearly related to the birthing of the species first, and my birthing second. My experiential bound-

aries stretched to include the entire human race and all
of human history, and this "I" was caught up in a
horror that I am incapable of describing with any
accuracy. It was a raging insanity, a surging kaleido-
scopic field of chaos, pain, and destruction. It was as
if the entire human race had gathered from all corners
of the globe and gone absolutely stark raving mad.

People were attacking each other with a rabid sav-
agery augmented by science fiction technology. There
were many currents crossing and crisscrossing in front
of me, each composed of thousands of people—some
killing in multiple ways, some being killed, some fleeing
in panic, others being rounded up, others witnessing
and screaming in terror, others witnessing and having
their hearts broken by a species gone mad—and "I"
was all their experiences. The magnitude of the deaths
and the insanity is impossible to describe. The problem
is finding a frame of reference. The only categories I
have available to me are simplistic approximations that
can give only a vague sense of it.

This kind of suffering comprises all of human history. It is at once species-specific and archetypal. It
comprises the wildest science fiction worlds of horror
beyond our imagination. It involves not only human
beings but billions and billions of pieces of matter in
agonizing galactic explosions. Horror beyond any scope.
It is a convulsing of the human species, a convulsing
of the universe. Floating through it were scenes of
tragic suffering caused by nature and human indifference. Thousands of starving children from around the
globe, their bodies bloated in death, their eyes staring
out blankly at a humanity that was killing them through
systemic ecological abuse and human neglect. Lots of
violence between men and women—rape, beating, in-
timidation, retaliation—cycles and cycles of destruction.

The extraordinary nature of perinatal experiences raises some
interesting and important questions. Why is it that in the process

of deep self-exploration we reach a phase when we transcend our individual boundaries and connect with the collective unconscious and the history of our species? Why does this involve such intimate connection with death and with the reliving of birth? How and why is this process so closely associated with sexuality? What role does the frequent participation of the archetypal elements play in these experiences? And finally, what is the function and meaning of this process and how is it related to spirituality and consciousness evolution?

I would like to refer here to the work of Christopher Bache (1996), who has made an interesting attempt to clarify the problem of the presence of collective suffering at the perinatal level and the role of the individual in the spiritual awakening of the species. Bache pointed out that the key to the understanding of the perinatal process is the fact that its function is to liberate us from the confines of separate unenlightened existence and awaken in us the realization of our true nature, our essential identity with the creative principle. Like the Roman god Janus, the perinatal domain has a dual nature. It will show us a very different face, depending on the direction from which we look at it, whether from the point of view of the body-ego or our transpersonal Self.

Seen from the personal perspective, the perinatal domain appears to be the basement of our individual unconscious, a repository of undigested fragments of those experiences that most seriously challenged our survival and body integrity. From this angle, we perceive the perinatal process, and the violence that it entails, above all as a threat to our individual existence. From the transpersonal perspective, the identification with the body-ego appears to be the product of fundamental ignorance, a dangerous illusion that is responsible for the fact that we live our lives in an unfulfilling, destructive, and self-destructive way. Once we understand this fundamental truth of existence, we see the perinatal experiences, in spite of their violent and painful nature, as radical and drastic, but loving, attempts to liberate us spiritually by demolishing the prison of our false identity. We are not being annihilated, but birthed to a higher reality where we reconnect with our true nature.

Individual Transformation and Healing of
Species Consciousness

We know from the practice of experiential therapy that it is possible to purge from our unconscious undigested memories of emotional and physical pain from our infancy, childhood, and later life by fully experiencing them. This, together with ensuing positive experiences that become available in this process, frees us from the distorting influence of past traumas that make our daily life inauthentic and unsatisfactory. Christopher Bache suggests that, in a similar way, perinatal experiences might play an important role in the healing of the traumatic past of the human species.

Is it not possible, he asks, that the memory of the violence and insatiable greed that is woven into the fabric of human history, causes disturbances in the collective unconscious that contaminate humanity's present? Why could not the healing impact reach beyond the individual person, as our consciousness expands beyond the body-ego? Is it not conceivable that by experiencing the pain that countless generations of people inflicted on each other in the course of human history, we are actually clearing the collective unconscious and contributing to a better planetary future?

Spiritual literature offers great examples of individual suffering that has redeeming influence on the world. In the Christian tradition, it is Jesus Christ, who died on the cross for the sins of humanity. This is vividly reflected in the mythological theme of the Harrowing of Hell depicting Jesus, at the time between death on the Cross and his resurrection, descending into Hell and liberating sinners from its jaws by the power of his suffering and sacrifice. The Hindu tradition accepts the possibility that very advanced yogis can significantly positively influence the situation in the world and the collective problems of humanity by confronting them internally in deep meditation, without actually physically leaving their caves.

Mahāyāna Buddhism has the beautiful archetypal image of the Bodhisattva who reaches enlightenment, but refuses to enter nirvāṇa and makes a sacred commitment to continue reincarnating until all sentient beings are liberated. The Bodhisattva's determination to take on the suffering of incarnate existence in order to help others is expressed in his powerful vow:

> Sentient beings are numberless;
> I vow to save them all.
> Delusions are inexhaustible;
> I vow to end them all.
> The gates of Dharma are manifold;
> I vow to enter them all.
> The Buddha way is supreme.
> I vow to complete it.

Dying Before Dying

Many people who have experienced holotropic states describe the perinatal level of the psyche as a gate between the transcendental realm and material reality, a passageway that functions in both directions. At the time of our biological birth, when we emerge into the material world, we "die" to the transcendental dimension and, conversely, our physical demise can be seen as birth into the world of spirit.

However, the spiritual birth does not have to be associated with the death of the body. It can occur at any time in the course of deep self-exploration or even during a spontaneous psychospiritual crisis (spiritual emergency). It is then a purely symbolic event, an "ego death," or "dying before dying," which does not involve any biological damage. Abraham à Sancta Clara, a seventeenth-century German Augustinian monk, summed it up in one sentence when he wrote: "The man who dies before he dies, does not die when he dies."

This "dying before dying" has played an important role in all shamanic traditions. By undergoing death and rebirth in their initiatory crises, shamans lose the fear of death and become familiar and comfortable with its experiential territory. As a result, they can later visit this realm on their own terms and mediate similar experiences for others. In the mysteries of death and rebirth, which were widespread in the Mediterranean area and other parts of the ancient world, initiates experienced a profound symbolic confrontation with death. In this process, they lost the fear of death and developed an entirely new set of values and strategy of life.

The experience of psychospiritual death and rebirth ("second birth," "birth from water and spirit," becoming a *dvija*) has played an important role in many religious traditions. All pre-industrial cultures attributed great significance to these experiences from a personal as well as collective perspective and developed safe and effective ways to induce them in various ritual contexts. Modern psychiatry sees the same experiences as pathological phenomena and indiscriminately suppresses them when they occur spontaneously in contemporary individuals. This unfortunate strategy has been a significant contributing factor in Western civilization's loss of spirituality.

Sexuality: Way to Liberation or Pitfall on the Spiritual Path?

Sex shows a similar inherent ambiguity as birth and death. Depending on circumstances, it can mediate deep unitive states or deepen separation and alienation. Which of these two modes will manifest in a particular case will depend on the circumstances and on the attitude of the individuals involved. If the partners who are interacting sexually do not feel love and respect for each other and are driven only by instinctual impulses or by the need for power and domination, having intercourse will very likely intensify their feelings of separation and alienation. If the sexual union occurs between two partners who are personally mature and have not only good biological compatibility, but also deep emotional resonance and mutual understanding, love-making can result in a profound spiritual experience. Under these circumstances, they can transcend their individual boundaries and experience feelings of oneness with each other and, at the same time, have a sense of reunion with the cosmic source.

This spiritual potential of sex is the basis of the ancient Indian Tantric practices. Pañchamakāra is a complex Tantric ceremony that involves ingestion of powerful Ayurvedic herbal mixtures combining aphrodisiac and psychedelic properties. An intricate, highly stylized ritual procedure helps the partners identify with the archetypal principles of the feminine and masculine. It culminates in a ritualized sexual union maintained for a long period of time (*maithuna*).

With special training, participants are able to suppress the biological orgasm and the extended sexual arousal then triggers a mystical experience. In the course of this ritual event, the partners transcend their everyday identities. In full identification with archetypal beings, Shiva and Shakti, they experience a sacred marriage, a divine union with each other and with the cosmic source. In Tantric symbolism, various aspects of sexuality and reproductive functions, such as genital union, menstrual flux, pregnancy, and delivery, not only have literal biological meaning, but also refer to various higher levels of the cosmic creative process.

Practical Implications of the Insights from Consciousness Research Concerning Birth, Sex, and Death

The observations described in this chapter have important practical implications. They strongly indicate that changes of our attitudes to the triad birth/sex/death and of our practices related to them could have a profound influence not only on the quality of our personal life, but also on the future of the human species and our planet. We have seen that the memories of prenatal existence, birth, and early postnatal events leave deep imprints in our unconscious and exert a profound influence on our life. It is, therefore, imperative that in the future we do whatever is possible to improve the conditions under which children are conceived, develop as embryos, are born, and are treated after delivery.

This should begin with education of the young generation providing the necessary sexual information without irrational moral and religious distortions and unrealistic injunctions, prohibitions, and expectations. However, it would not be sufficient to offer unbiased technical data about reproductive functions. It is essential that we raise the image of sex, which is currently seen as a purely biological affair and often portrayed in its worst manifestations, to that of a spiritually based activity. Another important task is to bring awareness to the fact that the fetus is a conscious being. This would increase the responsibility in regard to conceiving a child and bring attention to the importance of the emotional and physical condition of the pregnant mother. It would also make a big difference, if the education in postadolescence could include elements increasing psychospiritual maturity for future parenthood.

The delivery typically activates the mother's own perinatal unconscious, which can interfere with the birth process, both emotionally and physiologically. It would, therefore, be ideal if women could do their own deep experiential work before becoming pregnant to eliminate these potentially disturbing elements from their unconscious. Special attention should then be given to the delivery itself. This would include good psychological and technical preparation for delivery, natural conditions for childbirth, and loving postnatal care with adequate physical contact between the infant and the mother. There are good reasons to believe that the circumstances of birth play an important role in creating a disposition for future violence and self-destructive tendencies or, conversely, for loving behavior and healthy interpersonal relationships.

The French obstetrician Michel Odent (1995) has shown how this perinatal imprinting, which has the potential to sway our emotional life in the direction of love or hatred, can be understood from the history of our species. The birth process has two different aspects and each of them involves specific hormones. The stressful activity of the mother during the delivery itself is primarily associated with the adrenaline system. The adrenaline mechanisms also played an important role in the evolution of the species as mediators of the aggressive and protective instincts of the mother at times when birth was typically occurring in open natural environments. They made it possible for females to rapidly shift from delivering to fight or flight when an attack by a predator made it necessary.

The other task associated with birth, which is equally important from the evolutionary point of view, is the creation of the bond between the mother and the newborn. This process involves the hormone oxytocine, which induces maternal behavior in animals and humans, and endorphins that foster dependency and attachment. Prolactine, the hormone that is instrumental in nursing, has similar effects. The busy, noisy, and chaotic milieu of many hospitals induces anxiety and unnecessarily engages the adrenaline mechanisms. It conveys and imprints the picture of a world that is potentially dangerous. Like the jungle setting in the primordial times, such a situation calls for aggressive responses. Conversely, a quiet, safe, and private environment creates an atmosphere of safety that engenders affectionate patterns of relating. Radical improvement of birth practices could have a far-reaching positive influence on the emotional and physical well-being of the human species and assuage the insanity of its behavior that is currently threatening to destroy the very basis of life on this planet.

The prenatal and perinatal history also has important implications for our spiritual life. As we have seen earlier, incarnation and birth represent separation and alienation from our true nature, which is Absolute Consciousness. Positive experiences in the womb and after birth are the closest contacts with the Divine that we can experience during our embryonal life or in infancy. The "good womb" and "good breast" thus represent experiential bridges to the transcendental level. Conversely, negative and painful experiences that we encounter in the intrauterine period, during birth, and in the early postnatal period send us deeper into the state of alienation from the divine source.

When our prenatal and early postnatal experiences are predominantly positive, we tend to maintain throughout our life a natural connection with the cosmic source. We can sense the divine dimension in nature and in the cosmos and are able to enjoy to a great degree the incarnate existence. Conversely, when our early development was just a series of continuing traumas, the loss of connection with the spiritual source can be so complete that our existence in the material world is a painful ordeal full of emotional torment.

I should also mention that sometimes an extremely severe trauma can result in a situation where consciousness splits from the body and is catapulted into the transpersonal realm. This can establish an escape route that is regularly used as a defense mechanism in later difficult life situations. This form of spiritual connection can help to protect us from excessive pain, but it does not enhance the quality of life, since this mechanism is not well integrated with the rest of the personality.

Substantial changes are also necessary in our attitude toward death. We have seen that death has a powerful and important representation in our unconscious. Its deepest manifestations are transpersonal in nature and have the form of wrathful archetypal figures and karmic records of life-threatening situations from other incarnations. The memories of vital threats in the womb, during delivery, and after birth represent additional important sources of fear of death. For many of us, this is complemented by memories of serious traumas that we experienced later in life. The menacing specter of death that we harbor in our unconscious interferes with our everyday existence and makes our life in many ways inauthentic. In technological societies, the predominant reactions to this situation are massive denial and avoidance that are in their consequences destructive and self-destructive on an individual as well as a collective level.

It is essential for the future of humanity that we break through this denial and come to terms with the problem of impermanence and of our mortality. There exist ancient and modern methods of deep self-exploration that can help us to confront the fear of death, bring it fully into consciousness, and overcome it. We have already seen how "dying before dying" can open for us the channels to the transcendental dimension of existence and initiate a journey that can eventually lead to the discovery of our true identity. In this process, we can experience emotional and psychosomatic healing and our life becomes more satisfying and authentic. This profound psychospiritual transformation can raise our consciousness to an entirely different level and make our life less taxing and more rewarding.

It is important to be aware of the existence and nature of this process and to provide guidance and support for people who experience it unintentionally in near-death situations or spontaneous psychospiritual crises (spiritual emergencies). Another important step is to make available, on a large scale, various ancient and modern methods of deep self-exploration that make it possible to undergo this process deliberately. Pre-industrial and ancient societies had certain procedures in the form of rites of passage and mysteries of death and rebirth that were designed specifically for this purpose. Thanks to the ancient knowledge that, in the last several decades, has been re-discovered by consciousness research, transpersonal psychology, and thanatology, we have now the possibility of substantially improving the emotional quality of our life, as well as our death.

People, who have during their lifetime experientially confronted birth and death and connected with the transpersonal dimension, have good reasons to believe that their physical demise will not mean the end of their existence. They have personally experienced in a very convincing way that their consciousness transcends the boundaries of their physical body and is capable of functioning independently of it. As a result, they tend to see death as a transition into a different state of existence and an awe-inspiring adventure in consciousness rather than final defeat and annihilation. Naturally, this attitude can in itself substantially change the approach to death and the experience of dying. In addition, people who are involved in deep self-exploration have the opportunity to gradually come to terms with many difficult aspects of their unconscious that we otherwise have to deal with in the final period of our life.

The insights from the work with holotropic states also have important implications for the way we practically approach the final stages of life, our own as well as those of other people. When we believe that the critical dimension of our existence is consciousness and not matter, we will be concerned about the nature and quality of our experience of dying and death rather than a mechanical prolongation of life at all costs. In the work with other people who are dying, we will put emphasis on the quality of communication and will offer meaningful psychospiritual support. We will complement, and in some instances replace, the technological wizardry of modern medicine with genuine human care. If the information conveyed by the *Bardo Thödol, The Tibetan Book of the Dead*, is correct, the way we approach death and experience it is of critical importance. If we are adequately prepared, this time is a unique opportunity to achieve instant spiritual liberation. According to the Tibetan teachings, even if we do not succeed, the quality of our preparation for death or the lack thereof will determine the nature of our next incarnation.

8
The Mystery of Karma and Reincarnation

For I have already at times been a boy and a girl, and a
bush and a bird and a mute fish in the salty waves.

—Empedocles

Were an Asiatic to ask me for a definition of Europe, I
should be forced to answer him: It is that part of the
world which is haunted by the incredible delusion that
man was created out of nothing, and that his present
birth is his first entrance into life.

—Arthur Schopenhauer, *Parerga and Paralipomena*

Crosscultural Perspective on Reincarnation

According to Western materialistic science, our lifespan is limited
to the period between our conception and our biological death.
This assumption is a logical consequence of the conviction that
we are essentially our bodies. Since the body perishes and de-
composes at the time of biological death, it seems obvious that
at this point we cease to exist. This perspective is in conflict with
the beliefs of all the great religions and spiritual systems of the
ancient and pre-industrial cultures who have seen death as an
important transition, rather than the final end of any form of
existence. Most Western scientists dismiss or even ridicule the
belief that our existence can continue beyond death. They attribute this idea to lack of education, to superstition, or to primitive wishful thinking of people who are unable to face and
accept the grim reality of impermanence and death.

In pre-industrial societies, the belief in life after death is not
limited to a vague notion that there might be a Beyond.

159

Mythologies of many cultures offer very specific descriptions of what happens after we die. They provide intricate maps of the posthumous journey of the soul and depict various abodes—heavens, paradises, and hells—that harbor discarnate beings. Of particular interest is the belief in reincarnation, according to which the individual units of consciousness keep returning to earth and experience entire chains of embodied existences. Some spiritual systems combine the belief in reincarnation with the law of karma, suggesting that the merits and debits from previous lifetimes determine the quality of subsequent incarnations. Various forms of the belief in reincarnation show a wide distribution over geographical space and historical time. They have developed, often independently, in cultures separated by many thousands of miles and by many centuries.

The concept of reincarnation and karma is the cornerstone of many Asian religions—Hinduism, Buddhism, Jainism, Sikhism, Zoroastrianism, the Tibetan Vajrayāna, Japanese Shintoism, and Chinese Taoism. Similar ideas can be found in such historically, geographically, and culturally diverse groups as various African tribes, American Indians, Pre-Columbian cultures, Polynesian kahunas, practitioners of the Brazilian *umbanda*, the Gauls, and the Druids. In ancient Greece, several important schools of thought subscribed to this doctrine, among them the Pythagoreans, the Orphics, and the Platonists. The concept of reincarnation was adopted by the Essenes, the Pharisees, the Karaites, and other Jewish and semi-Jewish groups. It also formed an important part of the cabalistic theology of medieval Jewry. This list would not be complete without mentioning the Neoplatonists and Gnostics and in modern times the Theosophists, Anthroposophists, and certain spiritualists.

Although the belief in reincarnation is not a part of modern Christianity, similar concepts existed also among the early Christians. According to St. Jerome (A.D. 340–420), reincarnation was given an esoteric interpretation that was communicated to a select elite. It appears that the belief in reincarnation was an integral part of Gnostic Christianity, best known from the scrolls discovered in 1945 at Nag Hammadi. In the Gnostic text called *Faith Wisdom* or *Pistis Sophia* (1921) Jesus teaches his disciples how failures in one life are transferred to another. Thus, for example, people who use curses against others will in their new life be "continually troubled in their hearts," while arrogant and immoderate persons might be reborn in a deformed body and be looked down upon by others.

The most famous Christian thinker speculating about the pre-existence of souls and world cycles was Origen (A.D. 186–253), one of the greatest Church Fathers of all times. In his writings, particularly in the book *De Principiis*, or *On First Principles* (Origenes Adamantius 1973), he expressed his opinion that certain scriptural passages could only be explained in the light of reincarnation. His teachings were condemned by the Second Council of Constantinople convened by Emperor Justinian in A.D. 553 and became a heretical doctrine. The verdict read: "If anyone assert the fabulous pre-existence of souls and shall submit to the monstrous doctrine that follows from it, let him be anathema!" However, some scholars believe that they can detect traces of the teachings in the writings of St. Augustine, St. Gregory, and even St. Francis of Assisi.

How can we explain that so many cultural groups in the course of history have held this extraordinary belief and that they formulated complex and intricate theoretical systems describing it? How is it possible that they were all in agreement about an issue that is alien to the Western industrial civilization and that is considered utterly absurd by Western materialistic science? The usual explanation is that these differences reflect our superiority in the scientific understanding of the universe and of human nature. However, closer examination reveals that the real reason for this difference is the tendency of Western scientists to adhere to their belief system and to ignore, censor, or distort all observations that are in conflict with it. More specifically, this attitude reflects the reluctance of Western psychologists and psychiatrists to pay attention to the experiences and observations from holotropic states of consciousness.

Empirical Evidence for Reincarnation

The concept of reincarnation and karma is not a "belief" in the usual sense of the word, meaning an ungrounded and arbitrary theoretical and emotional position that is not supported by facts.

For the Hindus, Buddhists, Taoists, and other groups for whom it constitutes an important part of their religion, reincarnation is not a matter of belief. It is an eminently empirical issue, based on very specific experiences and observations. This is also true for open-minded and knowledgeable Western consciousness researchers. They are not naïve, ignorant, and unfamiliar with the philosophical position and worldview of materialistic science, as their critics like to portray them.

Many of these researchers have good academic training and impressive credentials. The reason for their position is that they have made some important observations concerning reincarnation for which their academic training failed to provide adequate explanations. In many instances, they also had extraordinary personal experiences that they could not easily dismiss. According to Christopher Bache, a researcher who has thoroughly reviewed the literature on reincarnation and encountered past life experiences in his own inner search, the evidence in this area is so rich and remarkable that scientists who do not think the problem of reincarnation deserves serious study are either uninformed or "boneheaded" (Bache 1990).

Let us take a brief look at the existing evidence that one should be familiar with before making any judgments concerning reincarnation. The nature of this evidence is described in a mythological language in a passage written by Sholem Ash (1967), a twentieth-century Hassidic scholar: "Not the power to remember, but its very opposite, the power to forget, is a necessary condition of our existence. If the lore of the transmigration of souls is a true one, then these souls, between their exchange of bodies, must pass through the sea of forgetfulness. According to the Jewish view, we make the transition under the overlordship of the Angel of Forgetfulness. But it sometimes happens that the Angel of Forgetfulness himself forgets to remove from our memories the records of the former world; and then our senses are haunted by fragmentary recollections of another life. They drift like torn clouds above the hills and valleys of the mind, and weave themselves into the incidents of our current existence."

Modern researchers have amassed a large amount of observations suggesting partial lifting of the veil of forgetfulness that

Sholem Ash talks about. Many of them studied and described vivid past life experiences that occur spontaneously in everyday life or in the course of various therapeutic sessions involving holotropic states of consciousness. Others collected additional information about reincarnation by guiding people to specific areas of their psyche with the use of hypnosis or some other approaches. There have also been interesting attempts at experimental verification of the authenticity of such guided past life experiences (Wambach 1979). And finally, there are certain intriguing data from the Tibetan spiritual tradition that provide valuable insights into this area from yet another angle.

Children Remember Past Lives

Among the most interesting phenomena related to the problem of reincarnation are spontaneous past life experiences in children. Reports from many different countries of the world indicate that, occasionally, small children remember and describe their previous life in another body, another time and place, and with other people. These memories can present many problems in the lives of these children and their parents. They are often associated with various "carry-over pathologies," such as phobias, unusual idiosyncrasies, and strange reactions to certain people, places, and situations. There exist reports of child psychiatrists who treated and described cases of this kind. Access to these memories usually appears around the age of three and gradually disappears between the ages of five and eight.

Ian Stevenson, professor of psychology at the University of Virginia in Charlottesville, has conducted meticulous studies of over three thousand of such cases and reported about them in his books (Stevenson 1966, 1984, 1987). Stevenson's cases were not only from "primitive," "exotic" cultures with an *a priori* belief in reincarnation, but also from Western countries, including Great Britain and the United States. Being a cautious and conservative researcher, Stevenson reported only several hundred of them, because many have not met the high standards he had set for his research. Only the cases with the best scientific evidence were included. Stevenson eliminated many of the observations, because the family benefited from the behavior of their children financially, in terms of social prestige, or public attention. Additional reasons for not including certain cases were inconsistent testimony, false memory (cryptomnesia), witnesses of questionable character, or indication of fraud.

The findings of Stevenson's research are remarkable. Although he had eliminated in all the reported cases the possibility that these children could have obtained the information through the conventional channels, he was able to confirm their stories, often with incredible details. In some cases, he actually took the children into the village or town that they had remembered from their previous life. Although they had never been there in their current lifetime, they were familiar with the topography of the village and were able to find the home they had allegedly lived in. They even recognized the members of their "family" and the villagers and knew their names. Possibly the strongest evidence in support of the reincarnation hypothesis was the incidence of striking birthmarks that specifically reflected injuries and other events from the remembered life; this could be confirmed by independent research (Stevenson, 1997).

Past Life Memories in Adults

Spontaneous, vivid reliving of past life memories in adults occurs most frequently during episodes of psychospiritual crises (spiritual emergencies). However, various degrees of remembering can also happen in more or less ordinary states of consciousness in the circumstances of everyday life. Mainstream psychiatrists are aware of the existence of past life experiences, but they treat them routinely as indications of serious psychopathology, usually by suppressive pharmacological medication. The leading theories of personality in contemporary psychology are firmly anchored in the materialistic paradigm and thus naturally subscribe to the "one-timer view."

Past life experiences can be facilitated by a wide variety of techniques that mediate access to deep levels of the psyche, such as meditation, hypnosis, use of psychedelic substances, and stays in a sensory isolation tank. They can emerge during body work and in sessions of experiential psychotherapy, for example, in the course of rebirthing, holotropic breathwork, or primal therapy. I have heard of many instances where past life episodes appeared unsolicited in sessions with therapists who had a very conventional theoretical framework and did not believe in reincarnation, or even those who were violently opposed to the concept. The emergence of karmic material is also completely independent of the experiencer's previous philosophical and religious belief system.

In a fully developed past life experience, we find ourselves involved in an emotionally highly charged situation that is happening in another historical period and in another location. Our sense of personal identity is preserved, but it is experienced in relation to another person and another time and place. These experiences often involve other people with whom we have an intense relationship in this lifetime. The emotional quality of these episodes is usually very negative. Sometimes, they are associated with physical pain, panic anxiety, deep sadness, or guilt feelings. Other times, it is consuming hatred, murderous anger, or insane jealousy. However, in some instances, these sequences can reflect great emotional fulfillment and happiness. They portray passionate love affairs, devoted friendships, or spiritual partnerships.

The most characteristic aspect of past life experiences is a convinced feeling that the situation we are facing is not new. We clearly remember that it happened to us before, that we once actually were this other person in one of our previous lives. This sense of reliving something that one has seen before (déjà vu) or experienced before (déjà vécu) in a previous incarnation is very basic and cannot be analyzed any further. It is comparable to the ability to distinguish in everyday life our memories of events that actually happened from our dreams, daydreams, and fantasies. It would be difficult to convince a person, who is relating to us a memory of something that happened last week, that the event did not really occur and that he or she is just imagining it. Past incarnation memories have a similar subjective quality of authenticity and reality.

Unique Features of Past Life Phenomena

Past life experiences have some extraordinary characteristics for which they deserve serious attention of researchers studying consciousness and the human psyche. Considered in their totality, these features leave no doubt that karmic sequences represent unique phenomena *sui generis* and not simply fantasies or figments of pathological imagination. Past life experiences occur on the same continuum with accurate memories from adolescence, childhood, infancy, birth, and intrauterine existence, phenomena that can often be reliably verified. Sometimes they appear simultaneously or alternate with biographical material from our current life (Grof 1988, 1992).

Another interesting feature of past life experiences is that they are often intimately connected with important issues and circumstances in our present life. When karmic sequences emerge fully into consciousness, either spontaneously or in the context of deep experiential psychotherapy, they can provide illuminating insights into various previously incomprehensible and puzzling aspects of our everyday existence. This includes a wide variety of emotional, psychosomatic, and interpersonal problems for which conventional forms of psychotherapy failed to provide explanation.

Experiences of past life memories typically provide more than just new understanding of these problems. This process can also often result in alleviation or complete disappearance of various difficult symptoms, such as various phobias, psychosomatic pains, or asthma. It can also be instrumental in healing of troublesome relationships with other people. Past life experiences can thus contribute significantly to the understanding of psychopathology and play an essential role in successful therapy. Therapists who refuse to work with these experiences because they reject the concept of reincarnation are depriving their patients of a very effective therapeutic mechanism.

The persons who experience karmic phenomena often gain accurate insights into the time and culture involved, concerning social structure, beliefs, rituals, customs, architecture, costumes, weapons, and other aspects of life. In many instances the nature and quality of this information makes it unlikely that these people could have acquired it through the conventional channels. Occasionally, past life experiences render information about specific historical events.

Verification of Past Life Memories

The criteria for verification of past life memories are the same as those that we use when we relive events from infancy and childhood of the present lifetime. We try to get as many details of the retrieved memory as possible and then search for independent evidence corroborating or disproving its content. Unfortunately, in many past life experiences, this information is not specific enough to allow independent verification. Other times, the quality of the information is adequate, but it is impossible to find sufficiently specific and detailed historical sources that would make the verification procedure possible.

Most past life memories in adults do not permit the same degree of verification as Stevenson's spontaneous memories in children, which are typically more recent. To appreciate the challenge associated with such an endeavor, it is important to consider that even our memories from this lifetime do not always lend themselves easily to objective verification. Psychotherapists are well aware of the problems associated with the attempts to evaluate the veracity of memories from childhood and infancy retrieved in verbal or regressive therapy. Naturally, the task to verify past life experiences is incomparably more difficult than similar efforts concerning material from the present lifetime. Even if such experiences contain very specific details, which is not always the case, objective evidence is incomparably harder to come by, since the material is much older and often involves other countries and cultures.

In spite of all these difficulties, there are some rare instances in which all the necessary criteria are met. The result of such independent research can be truly extraordinary. Over the years, I have been able to make in my work several observations, in which the content of past life experiences could be corroborated in remarkable detail. In all these cases, I have not been able to find a natural explanation for the phenomena involved. There is no doubt in my mind that the information conveyed by these experiences came through extrasensory channels. I have also heard similar stories from other researchers.

In my previous publications (Grof 1975, 1988), I have described two such case histories. The first one involved a neurotic patient undergoing psychedelic therapy. She experienced in four consecutive sessions many episodes from a life of a seventeenth-century Czech nobleman. This man had been publicly executed in the Old Town Square in Prague together with twenty-six other prominent aristocrats. This public execution was an effort of the Hapsburgs to break the moral of the Czechs after they had defeated the Czech king in the battle of the White Mountain. In this case, the patient's father conducted, unbeknownst to her, independent genealogical research of the family's pedigree, which confirmed that they were descendents of one of these unfortunate men.

The second example was a man who relived in his primal work and later in his holotropic breathwork sessions during our monthlong seminar at the Esalen Institute a number of episodes from the war between England and Spain in the sixteenth century. They revolved around the mass slaughter of Spanish soldiers by the British in the besieged fortress of Dunanoir on the western coast of Ireland. During these sessions, he experienced himself as a priest who accompanied these soldiers and was killed with them. At one point, he saw on his hand a seal ring with engraved initials and drew a picture of it.

In his later historical research, he was able to confirm the veracity of this entire episode that he previously had not known anything about. One of the documents he found in historical archives gave the name of the priest who had accompanied the Spanish soldiers on their military expedition. To his and our surprise, the initials of this name were identical with those that were carved on the seal ring he had seen in his session and captured in a detailed drawing.

A striking aspect of past life experiences is their frequent association with remarkable synchronicities involving other people and situations. The protagonists in our past life memories often are important persons from our present life, such as parents, children, spouses, boyfriends, girlfriends, or superiors. It seems to make sense that an intense past life experience could result in dramatic changes in our own feelings and behavior toward the person who was an important part of our karmic scenario. However, these experiences also often show unexplainable mysterious synchronistic links with specific changes in the lives of other persons whom we identified as protagonists in our past life memory. These persons could be hundreds or thousands of miles away from the place where our experience happens and have absolutely no knowledge that it takes place. Yet they can independently undergo, at exactly the same time, a dramatic complementary change in their feelings and attitude toward us.

The Karmic Triangle

I will use here an example from my own life to illustrate this remarkable phenomenon. Over the years, I have observed many similar occurrences involving other people. The episode I am about to describe happened shortly after my arrival in the United States. My emigration to the United States in 1967 brought about radical changes in my personal, professional, political, and cultural environment. I arrived in Baltimore with some fifty pounds of luggage. Over half of the total content of my luggage was the documentation of my psychedelic research in Prague and the rest were my personal belongings. This was all that was left of my old life in Europe. It was a new beginning for me on all imaginable levels. While I thoroughly enjoyed the inspiring team of my professional colleagues at Spring Grove, the undreamed of freedom of expression, and all the novel things I was discovering in the world around me, I did not have much success in creating a satisfactory personal life.

All the women in my social sphere who were of appropriate age for me and shared my interests seemed to be married or otherwise committed. It was a frustrating situation since I was at a stage of life when I felt a deep need for partnership. My friends

and colleagues at Spring Grove seemed to be even more concerned about this situation than I was myself and exerted great
effort to remedy it. They searched for potential partners for me
and kept inviting them for various social occasions. This resulted
in a few frustrating and somewhat awkward situations, but did
not bear any fruit. And then this situation suddenly changed in
the most unexpected and very radical way.

A difficult relationship of a fellow therapist, Seymour, had
abruptly ended and my friends invited his ex-girlfriend Monica
for dinner. When Monica and I first met, I immediately felt a
strong attraction to her and had a sense of instant deep connection. It was not difficult for me to fall in love with her. She was
of European origin like myself, single, beautiful, and bright. Her
unusual charm, wit, and facility with words quickly made her the
center of attention of every party she attended. I felt rapidly
drawn into the relationship and was unable to be objective and
realistic about it.

I did not see any problem in the fact that Monica was
considerably younger than myself. I also chose to ignore her
stories about her extremely traumatic childhood and tumultuous
interpersonal history that I would have normally seen as serious
warning signs. I was able to reassure myself that all these were
details, nothing that we would not be able to work out. Had I
been able to be analytic under the circumstances, I would have
recognized that I had met what C. G. Jung called an *anima
figure*. Monica and I started dating and had a passionate and
unusually stormy relationship.

Monica's moods and behavior seemed to change from one
day to another, or even from hour to hour. Waves of intense
affection toward me alternated with episodes of aloofness, eva-
siveness, and withdrawal. The situation seemed to be further
complicated by two unusual circumstances. Since my arrival in
Baltimore, I lived in a studio that had been at one time rented
by Monica's ex-boyfriend Seymour and she used to visit him
there. She was now coming to the same apartment to see a
different man. In addition, Monica's brother Wolfgang hated me
since the very first time we had met. He and Monica had an
unusually strong relationship that seemed to have distinct inces-

tuous features. Wolfgang was violently opposed to my relationship with Monica and treated me like a rival.

I was very committed to make the relationship work, but
nothing I was able to do had any influence on the crazy
rollercoster ride we seemed to be taking together. I felt like I
was alternately exposed to hot and cold showers. I found it very
frustrating but, at the same time, my attraction to Monica had a
strange magnetic quality and I was unable to terminate this
confusing and unfulfilling relationship.

I desperately needed some insight into the baffling dynamic
I was caught in. Our institute had a program offering mental
health professionals the opportunity to have up to three psychedelic sessions. The members of our therapeutic team were eli-
gible for this program. In an effort to reach some clarity in my
relationship with Monica, I applied for an LSD session just as our
difficulties were reaching their peak. The following is an excerpt
from that session, describing my first introduction to the world
of past life experiences and to the law of karma:

> In the middle of this session I suddenly had a vision
> of a dark rock of irregular shape that looked like a
> giant meteorite and seemed extremely ancient. The sky
> opened up and a lightning bolt of immense intensity
> hit its surface and started to burn into it some myste-
> rious arcane symbols. Once these strange hieroglyphs
> were carved into the surface of the rock, they contin-
> ued to burn and emit blinding incandescent light. Al-
> though I was unable to decipher the hieroglyphs and
> read them, I sensed they were sacred and I could
> somehow understand the message they were convey-
> ing. They revealed to me that I had had a long series
> of lives preceding this one and that, according to the
> law of karma, I was responsible for my actions in these
> lives, although I could not remember them.
>
> I tried to refuse responsibility for things of which
> I did not have any memory, but was not able to resist
> the enormous psychological pressure forcing me to
> surrender. Finally, I had to accept what clearly was an

ancient universal law against which there was no re-
course. Once I yielded, I found myself holding in my
arms Monica, just as I remembered holding her on the
previous weekend. We were floating in air in an archetypal pit of immense size, slowly descending in an
extended spiral. I felt instinctively that this was the
Abyss of Ages and that we were traveling back in time.

The descent took forever; it seemed it would never
end. Finally we reached the bottom of the pit. Monica
disappeared from my arms and I found myself walking
in a hall of an ancient Egyptian palace, dressed in
ornate clothes. All around me on the walls were beautiful reliefs accompanied by carved hieroglyphs. I could
understand their meaning in the same way I would
understand the message of the posters pasted on a
Baltimore billboard. On the other side of the large hall,
I saw a figure that was slowly approaching me. I knew
that I was the son of an aristocratic Egyptian family
and that the man approaching me was my brother in
that lifetime.

As the figure came closer, I recognized it was
Wolfgang. He stopped about ten feet from me and
looked at me with immense hatred. I realized that in
this incarnation Wolfgang, Monica, and I were siblings.
I was the first born and as such I had married Monica
and received many other privileges that came with that
status. Wolfgang felt deprived and experienced agonizing jealousy and strong hatred toward me. I saw clearly
that this was the basis of a destructive karmic pattern
that then repeated itself in many variations throughout
ages.

I stood in the hall facing Wolgang and feeling his
deep hatred toward me. In an attempt to resolve this
painful situation, I tried to send him a telepathic message: "I do not know which form I am in and how I
got here. I am a time traveler from the twentieth century, where I took a powerful mind-altering drug. I am
very unhappy about the tension that exists between us

and want to do anything to resolve it." I stretched my arms into a very open position and sent him the following message: "Here I am, this is all I have! Please, do anything you need to do to liberate us from this bondage, to set both of us free!"

Wolfgang seemed very excited about my offer and accepted it. His hatred seemed to take the form of two intense rays of energy resembling powerful laser beams that burned my body and caused me extreme pain. After what seemed an extremely long time of excruciating torture, the beams gradually lost their power and eventually completely faded. Wolfgang and the hall disappeared and I found myself holding Monica again in my arms.

This time we ascended through the same Abyss of Ages, moving forward in time. The walls of this archetypal pit were opening into scenes from different historical periods showing Monica, Wolfgang, and myself in many previous lifetimes. All of them depicted difficult and destructive triangular situations, in which we seriously hurt each other. It seemed that a strong wind, a "karmic hurricane," was blowing through centuries, dissipating the pain of these situations and releasing the three of us from a fatal painful bondage.

When this sequence ended and I returned fully into the present, I was in a state of indescribable bliss and ecstatic rapture. I felt that even if I would not achieve anything else during the rest of my days, my life had been productive and successful. Resolution and release from one powerful karmic pattern seemed a sufficient accomplishment for one lifetime!

Monica's presence in my experience was so intense that I was convinced she had to feel the impact of what was happening with me. When we saw each other the next week, I decided to find out what was her experience in the afternoon when I had the session. At first, I deliberately did not tell her anything about my session, trying to avoid any possibility of suggestion. I simply asked her what she did between 4 and 4.30 p.m. when I was experiencing the Egyptian karmic sequence in my session. "Strange that you should ask me," she answered, "it was probably the worst time of my entire life!"

She then proceeded to describe a dramatic showdown she had had with her superior that ended by her storming out of the office. She was sure she had lost her job, felt desperate, and ended up in a nearby bar drinking heavily. At one point, the door of the bar opened up and a man walked in. Monica recognized Robert, a man with whom she had had a sexual relationship at the time she met me. Robert was very rich and gave her many expensive gifts, including a new car and a horse.

Unbeknownst to me, Monica continued the relationship with him after we started dating, not being able to make a choice between the two of us. When she now saw Robert entering the bar, she walked to him and wanted to give him a hug and a kiss. Robert made an evasive maneuver and shook her hand instead. Monica noticed that he was accompanied by an elegant woman. Clearly perplexed, Robert introduced her to Monica; it happened to be his wife. For Monica this was a shock, since during their entire relationship Robert had pretended that he was single.

At this point, Monica felt that the ground disappeared from under her feet. She left the bar and ran to her car, the one that Robert had given her. Severely drunk and in heavy rain, she raced down the beltway reaching the speed of over 90 miles per hour, determined to end it all. Too much had happened that day and she did not care any more! It turned out that exactly at the time when I reached the resolution of the karmic pattern in my session, my image emerged in Monica's mind. She started thinking about me and about our relationship. Realizing that she still had somebody in her life she could rely on, she calmed down. She slowed down the car, drove it off the beltway, and parked it at the curbside. When she sobered up to the point that she could drive safely, she returned home and went to bed.

The day after this discussion with Monica, I received a phone call from Wolfgang, who asked for an appointment with me. This was an absolutely unexpected and surprising development, since Wolfgang had never called me before, let alone asked for a meeting. When he arrived, he told me that he came to see me about a very intimate and embarassing matter. It was a problem that is called in psychoanalysis the prostitute-Madonna complex. He had had a number of casual and superficial sexual relationships in his life, including many one-night stands, and never had had any problems developing and maintaining erection. Now he felt that he had found the woman of his dreams and, for the first time in his life, was deeply in love. However, he was unable to have sex with her and experienced repeated painful failures.

Wolfgang was desperate and afraid that he would lose this relationship unless he did something about his impotence. He told me that he was too embarassed to talk about his problem with a stranger. He thought about discussing the issue with me, but rejected the idea, because he had strong negative feelings toward me. At one point, his attitude toward me suddenly changed radically. His hatred dissolved as if by magic and he decided to call me and seek help. When I asked him when this had happened, I found out that it exactly coincided with the time when I had completed the reliving of the Egyptian sequence.

A few weeks later, I retrieved the missing piece of the Egyptian story. I did a hypnotic session with Pauline McCririck, a psychoanalyst from London. The following is an excerpt from my account of this experience.

> I lay in the sand of a hot sun-scorched desert. I felt agonizing pain in my belly and my entire body was in spasms. I knew I had been poisoned and was going to die. I realized from the context that the only people who could have poisoned me had to be Monica and her lover. By the Egyptian law, she had to marry me as her oldest brother, but her affection belonged to another man. I had found out about their affair and had attempted to interfere with their relationship. The realization that I had been betrayed and poisoned filled me with blind anger. I died alone in the desert with my entire being filled with hatred.

The reliving of this situation brought another interesting insight. I seemed to remember that in this Egyptian lifetime, I was actively involved in the mysteries of Isis and Osiris and knew their secrets. I felt that the poison and the hatred intoxicated my mind and obscured everything else, including this knowledge. This made it impossible for me to take advantage of the secret teachings at the time of my death. For the same reason, my connection with this arcane knowledge was brutally severed.

I suddenly saw that much of my present life had been dedicated to an unrelenting search for these lost teachings. I remembered how excited I had been every time I had come across some information that was directly or indirectly related to this area. In the light of this insight, my work with psychedelics revolving around psychospiritual death and rebirth seemed to be a rediscovery and modern reformulation of the processes involved in the ancient mysteries.

In a subsequent meditation, I was unexpectedly flooded with a fugue of images representing highlights of my experiences with Monica and Wolfgang, some of them from real life, others from my sessions. The intensity and speed of this review rapidly increased until it reached an explosive climax. In an instant, I felt a deep sense of resolution and peace. I knew that the karmic pattern was now fully resolved. Monica and I remained friends for the rest of my stay in Baltimore. The tension and chaos disappeared from our interactions and neither of us felt any compulsion to continue an intimate relationship. We both understood that we were not meant to be partners in our present lifetime.

Reincarnation and Karma in Tibetan Buddhism

There exists another interesting piece of the puzzle of reincarnation. It is the information we have about certain Tibetan teachings and practices concerning the degree to which it is possible to actually influence the process of death and reincarnation. Tibetan literature describes that certain highly developed spiritual masters are able to choose the time of their death and predict or select the time and place of their next incarnation. Others have developed the capacity to maintain continuity of consciousness during their passage through the bardos, intermediate states between death and the next incarnation.

Conversely, according to these reports, accomplished Tibetan monks can use certain specific clues, received in dreams and meditations, as well as various external omens, to locate and identify the child who is the reincarnation of a *tulku* or a Dalai Lama. Eventually, the child is found, brought to the monastery, and exposed to a series of tests during which it has to correctly identify from several sets of similar objects those that belonged to the deceased. Some aspects of this practice could, at least theoretically, be subjected to a rather rigorous testing following Western standards.

Reincarnation: Fact or Fiction?

We can now summarize the objective evidence that forms the basis of the widespread "belief" in reincarnation and karma. The term *belief* is actually inappropriate when applied to this area. Properly understood, it is a theoretical system of thought, a conceptual framework that is trying to provide explanation for a large number of unusual experiences and observations. In holotropic states, spontaneous or induced, it is not only possible but very common to experience episodes from the lives of people in various historical periods and different countries of the world. When we experience these sequences, we feel completely identified with these individuals. In addition, we have a convinced feeling that we actually once were these persons and lived their lives. These experiences are typically very vivid and can engage all our senses.

In terms of their content, past life experiences transcend racial and cultural boundaries and can take place in any country of the world and at any time of human history or prehistory. They often provide detailed information about the countries, cultures, and times involved. In many instances, this information by far surpasses our previous knowledge of these matters and our general educational background. On occasion, the sequences from past lives can feature animal protagonists. For example, we can experience a situation in which we were killed by a tiger or trampled to death by an elephant. Over the years, I have also witnessed some past life experiences with only one protagonist, such as episodes where the experiencer died in an avalanche or was crushed by a falling tree. The therapeutic potential of past life experiences and the synchronicities associated with them are additional remarkable features of these phenomena. These are the facts that we have to know before we attempt to pass a judgment concerning the "belief" in reincarnation and karma.

These extraordinary characteristics of past life experiences have been repeatedly confirmed by independent observers. However, all these impressive facts do not necessarily constitute a definitive "proof" that we survive death and reincarnate as the same separate unit of consciousness, or the same individual soul. This conclusion is just one possible interpretation of the existing evidence. This is essentially the same situation that we encounter in science, where we have certain facts of observation and look for a theory that would explain them and put them into a coherent conceptual framework.

One of the basic rules in modern philosophy of science is that a theory should never be confused with the reality that it describes. The history of science clearly shows that there always exists more than one way to interpret the available data. In the study of past life phenomena, as in any other area of exploration, we have to separate facts of observation from the theories that try to make sense of them. For example, the falling of objects is a fact of observation, whereas the theories trying to explain why it happens have changed several times in the course of history and undoubtedly will change again.

The existence of past life experiences with all their remarkable characteristics is an unquestionable fact that can be verified by any serious researcher who is sufficiently open-minded and interested to check the evidence. It is also clear that there is no plausible explanation for these phenomena within the conceptual framework of mainstream psychiatry and psychology. On the other hand, the interpretation of the existing data is a much more complex and difficult matter. The popular understanding of reincarnation as a repeated cycle of life, death, and rebirth of the same individual is a reasonable conclusion from the available evidence. It certainly is far superior to the attitude of traditional psychologists and psychiatrists, who ignore all the available evidence and rigidly adhere to the established ways of thinking. However, it is not difficult to imagine some alternative interpretations of the same data. Naturally, none of these explanations is congruent with the materialistic paradigm.

At least two such alternatives can already be found in the spiritual literature. In the Hindu tradition, the belief in reincarnation of separate individuals is seen as a popular and unsophisticated understanding of reincarnation. In the last analysis, there is only one being that has true existence and that is Brahman, or the creative principle itself. All separate individuals in all the dimensions of existence are just products of infinite metamorphoses of this one immense entity. Since all the divisions and boundaries in the universe are illusory and arbitrary, only Brahman really incarnates. All the protagonists in the divine play of existence are different aspects of this One. When we attain this ultimate knowledge, we are able to see that our past incarnation experiences represent just another level of illusion or *māyā*. To see these lives as "our lives" requires perception of the karmic players as separate individuals and reflects ignorance concerning the fundamental unity of everything.

In his book *Lifecycles*, Christopher Bache (1990) discusses another interesting concept of reincarnation found in the books by Jane Roberts (1973) and in the works of other authors. Here the emphasis is neither on the individual unit of consciousness nor on God, but on the Oversoul, an entity that lies in between the two. If the term soul refers to the consciousness that collects and integrates the experiences of an individual incarnation, the Oversoul or Soul is the name given to the larger consciousness that collects and integrates the experiences of many incarnations.

According to this view, it is the Oversoul that incarnates, not the individual unit of consciousness.

Bache points out that if we are extensions of our former lives, we clearly are not the summation of all the experiences that they have contained. The purpose that the Oversoul has for incarnating is to collect specific experiences. A full involvement in a particular life requires severing the connection with the Oversoul and assuming discrete personal identity. At the time of death, the separate individual dissolves in the Oversoul, leaving only a mosaic of unassimilated difficult experiences. These then become assigned to the life of other incarnated beings in a process that can be compared to dealing a hand of cards in a card game.

In this model, there is no true continuity between the lives of the individuals that incarnate at diffferent times. By experiencing undigested parts of other lives, we are not dealing with our personal karma, but actually clearing the field of the Oversoul. The image that Bache uses to illustrate the relationship between the individual soul and the Oversoul is that of a nautilus shell. Here each chamber represents a separate unit and reflects a certain period in the life of the mollusk, but it is also integrated into a larger whole.

We have so far discussed three different ways of interpreting the observations related to past life phenomena. The incarnating units were, respectively, the individual unit of consciousness, Absolute Consciousness, and the Oversoul. However, we have not exhausted all the possibilities of alternative explanations that could account for the observed facts. Because of the arbitrary nature of all boundaries in the universe, we could just as easily define as the incarnating principle a unit larger than the Oversoul, for example, the field of consciousness of the entire human species or that of all life forms.

We could also take our analysis a step further and explore the factors that determine the specific choice of the karmic experiences that are assigned to the incarnating unit of consciousness. For example, some people with whom I have worked had convincing insights that an important factor in the selection process might be the relationship between karmic patterns and the time and place of a particular incarnation with its specific astro-logical correlates. This notion is in general agreement with the observations from psychedelic sessions, holotropic breathwork, and spontaneous episodes of psychospiritual crises. They show that in all these situations the content and timing of nonordinary states are closely correlated with planetary transits (Tarnas, in press).

Holotropic Experiences and Their Influence on Our Belief System

To get a more comprehensive perspective on the subject of reincarnation, let us explore the changes in our beliefs that occur during systematic inner work involving holotropic states. Our belief or disbelief in reincarnation, as well as our understanding of what might survive death, reflect the nature and level of the experiences we have had. A typical member of the Western industrial civilization believes that he or she is a physical body. This clearly limits individual existence to a lifespan that reaches from conception to the moment of death. As we saw, this "one-timer" approach is in conflict with the perspective of many other human groups throughout history. In our culture, it is strongly endorsed by an unlikely alliance of materialistic science and the Christian Church. The problem of reincarnation is one of the rare areas where both of these institutions reach complete agreement.

Personal experiences of past life memories that we encoun-ter in meditation, experiential psychotherapy, psychedelic ses-sions, or "spiritual emergency" can be extremely authentic and convincing. They can bring about a drastic change in our worldview and open us up to the concept of reincarnation, not as a belief, but as an experiential reality. Consequently, the emphasis in our self-exploration tends to change considerably. Previously, we might have felt that it was all-important to work through our traumas from childhood, infancy, and birth, because we realized that they were a source of difficulties in our present life. After the discovery of the karmic realm, we become more concerned about attaining release from traumatic karmic patterns, because they have the potential to contaminate not one lifetime, but many consecutive ones.

At this stage, we often continue having additional past life experiences that can be very rich in accurate detail and be associated with remarkable synchronicities. We thus keep obtaining convincing evidence about the reality and authenticity of this way of understanding existence. We do not think about ourselves any more as Alan Watts' "skin-encapsulated egos." Instead of identifying with one specific individual who lives from conception to death, we now have a much larger concept of who we are.

Our new identity is that of a being whose existence spans many lifetimes; some of them have already passed, others still await us in the future. To see ourselves in this way, we have to transcend our previous belief that our lifespan is temporally limited to the period between conception and death. At the same time, we have to continue believing in the absolute nature of spatial boundaries that separate us from other people and from the rest of the world. We think about ourselves as open-ended chains of lifetimes and see our karmic partners in the same way.

If we continue our inner journey, additional holotropic experiences can show us that even spatial boundaries are ultimately illusory and can be dissolved. This creates an entirely new perspective on the problem of reincarnation. We have now transcended the concept of karma, as it is usually understood, because we have reached a level where there are no more separate individuals. And the existence of discrete characters is a necessary prerequisite for any karmic interaction. At this point, we identify with the unified field of cosmic creative energy and with Absolute Consciousness. From this perspective, the past life dramas represent just another level of illusion, the play of *māyā*. It becomes clear that all lives have ultimately only one protagonist and that, in the last analysis, they are all empty of substance.

We now do not believe in karma any more, certainly not in the same sense as we did before. This form of disbelief is of an entirely different kind and order than the attitude of a materialistic skeptic and atheist. We still remember the time when we lived in a completely constricted state of consciousness and rejected the idea of reincarnation as utterly ridiculous and absurd. We are also aware of the fact that powerful and compelling experiences can move us to a level of consciousness where reincarnation is not a concept, but lived reality. And we know that even this stage can be transcended when our process of inner self-exploration confronts us with experiences that make us understand the relativity of all boundaries and the fundamental emptiness of all forms.

Neither a categorical denial of the possibility of reincarnation, nor the belief in its objective existence are true in an absolute sense. All the three approaches to this problem mentioned above are experientially very real and each of them reflects a certain level of insight into the universal scheme of things. In the last analysis, only the existence of the creative principle itself is real. Both the world in which reincarnation seems impossible and the one where it seems to be an undeniable fact are virtual realities created by orchestration of experiences. For this reason, the cosmic game can include scripts that from our limited everyday perspective might appear to be incompatible and in conflict with each other. In the Universal Mind and its divine play they can coexist without any problem.

9
The Taboo against Knowing Who You Are

We are not human beings having a spiritual experience.
We are spiritual beings having a human experience.

—Teilhard de Chardin: *The Phenomenon of Man*

Our birth is but a sleep and a forgetting:
The Soul that rises with us, our life's Star,
Hath had elsewhere its setting,
And cometh from afar:
Not in entire forgetfulness,
And not in utter nakedness,
But trailing clouds of glory do we come
From God who is our home:
Heaven lies about us in our infancy!
Shades of the prison house begin to close
Upon the growing boy.

—William Wordsworth, "Ode: Intimations of Immortality"

The Perfect Illusion

In holotropic states, we can transcend the boundaries of the
embodied ego with which we usually identify and have convincing experiences of becoming other people, animals, plants, and
even inorganic parts of nature or various mythological beings.
We discover that the separation and discontinuity that we usually
perceive within creation are arbitrary and illusory. And when all
the boundaries dissolve and we transcend them, we can experience identification with the creative source itself, either in the

form of Absolute Consciousness or the Cosmic Void. We thus discover that our real identity is not the individual self, but the Universal Self.

If it is true that our deepest nature is divine and that we are identical with the creative principle of the universe, how do we account for the intensity of our belief that we are physical bodies existing in a material world? What is the nature of this fundamental ignorance concerning our true identity, this mysterious veil of forgetting that Alan Watts called "the taboo against knowing who you are"? (Watts 1966). How is it possible that an infinite and timeless spiritual entity creates from itself and within itself a virtual facsimile of a tangible reality populated by sentient beings who experience themselves as separate from their source and from each other? How can the actors in the world drama be deluded into believing in the objective existence of their illusory reality?

The best explanation I have heard from the people with whom I have worked is that the cosmic creative principle traps itself by its own perfection. The creative intention behind the divine play is to call into being experiential realities that would offer the best opportunities for adventures in consciousness. To meet this requirement, they have to be convincing and believable in all details. We can use here as an example works of art such as theater plays or movies. These can occasionally be enacted and performed with such perfection that they make us forget that the events we are witnessing are illusory and react to them as if they were real. Also, a good actor and actress can sometimes lose their true identity and temporarily merge with the characters they are impersonating.

The world in which we live has many characteristics that Absolute Consciousness in its pure form is missing, such as plurality, polarity, density, physicality, change, and impermanence. The project of creating a facsimile of a material reality endowed with these properties is executed with such artistic and scientific perfection that the split-off units of the Universal Mind find it entirely convincing and mistake it for reality. In the extreme expression of its artistry, represented by the atheist, the Divine actually succeeds in bringing forth arguments not only against its involvement in creation, but against its very existence.

One of the important ploys that help to create the illu-sion of an ordinary material reality is the existence of the trivial and ugly. If we all were radiant ethereal beings, draw-ing our life energy directly from the sun and living in a world where all the landscapes would look like the Himalayas, the Grand Canyon, and unspoiled Pacific islands, it would be too obvious to us that we are part of a divine reality. Similarly, if all the buildings in our world looked like Alhambra, the Taj Mahal, Xanadu, or the cathedral in Chartres, and we were surrounded by Michelangelo's sculptures and listen to Beethoven's or Bach's music, the divine nature of our world would be easily discernible.

The fact that we have physical bodies with all their secre-tions, excretions, odors, imperfections, and pathologies, as well as a gastrointestinal system with its repulsive contents, certainly effectively obscures and confuses the issue of our divinity. Vari-ous physiological functions like vomiting, burping, passing gas, defecating, and urinating, together with the final decomposition of the human body further complicate the picture. Similarly, the existence of unattractive natural scenes, junkyards, polluted in-dustrial areas, foul-smelling toilets with obscene graffiti, urban ghettoes, and millions of funky houses make it very difficult to realize that our life is a divine play. The existence of evil and the fact that the very nature of life is predatory makes this task almost impossible for an average person. For educated Western-ers, the worldview created by materialistic science is an addi-tional serious hurdle.

It is certainly easier to associate divinity with beauty than with ugliness. However, in a larger context, including ugliness into the universal scheme makes the spectrum of existence fuller and richer and helps to disguise the divine nature of creation. The image of the hideous can be executed with great perfection and to be able to do it constitutes an interesting challenge. When we realize that the complex nature of Cosmic Consciousness includes, among others, certain characteristics that we find on our level reflected in artists and scientists, the tendency to ex-plore the entire spectrum of possibilities, including the ugly and disgusting, suddenly does not seem very surprising.

The world of art, including painting, literature, and movies, can hardly be accused of onesidedly favoring the beautiful and uplifting. Similarly, scientists certainly do not shy away from exploring any aspect of existence and many of them do not hesitate to pursue their passionate quest even if their discoveries have dismal and ugly consequences for our world. Once we realize the origin and purpose of the cosmic drama, the usual criteria for perfection and beauty have to be drastically revised. One of the important tasks on the spiritual journey is to be able to see the divine not only in the extraordinary and ordinary, but also in the lowly and ugly.

According to our usual criteria, Albert Einstein is a genius who certainly towers high above his fellow humans, let alone above a primate like a chimpanzee. However, from a cosmic perspective, there is no hierarchical difference between Einstein and an ape, since they are both perfect specimens of what they were intended to be. Within a Shakespeare play, a king is certainly superior to his court jester. However, the status of Lawrence Olivier as an actor does not oscillate depending on which of them he plays, as long as he delivers a perfect performance. Similarly, Einstein is God impeccably impersonating Albert Einstein and a chimpanzee is God playing perfectly the role of a chimpanzee.

Ordinarily, possessing a reasonable esthetic sense, we would admire the work of Michelangelo or Vincent van Gogh and not feel much appreciation for kitsch. This would make perfect sense if we were comparing ordinary human efforts that have such drastically different results. However, the true originators of these works were not the embodied selves of the authors but the Absolute Consciousness and the cosmic creative energy working through them with a specific purpose. If the creative intention was not to produce a great piece of art, but quite specifically to add the phenomenon of kitsch to the cosmic game, this project was perfect in its own way.

The same can be said about an ugly toad, a creature that was included in the universal scheme for a specific purpose by the same source that was capable of creating swallowtail butterflies, peacocks, and gazelles. It is the absolute perfection of creation, understood in this sense, that seems to be responsible for the "taboo against knowing who we are." The virtual reality simulating a material universe is worked out with such an acute sense for miniscule detail that the result is absolutely convincing and believable. The units of consciousness cast as the protagonists in the countless roles of this play of plays get entangled and caught in the complex and intricate web of its illusionary magic.

Creative Play of the Demiurges

The insights into the nature and dynamics of the cosmic game do not have to emerge on the level of the supreme creative principle. Gail, a minister who participated in our training program for professionals at the Maryland Psychiatric Research Center, had in her psychedelic session an interesting sequence that portrayed cosmogony as a competitive creative game of four demiurgic suprahuman entities. Although her experience is very unusual, since it involves several demiurgic beings rather than one creative principle, I will include it here. It illustrates with exceptional clarity many of the issues related to the problem of incarnation of spiritual beings and the "taboo against knowing who you are." Here is the corresponding excerpt from her session:

> I found myself in a dimension that seemed to lie beyond space and time as we know it. What comes to my mind when I think about it now is the concept of hyperspace used by modern physicists. However, such a technical term would not describe the profound feeling of sacredness, the awesome sense of numinosity associated with my experience. I realized that I was a suprahuman being of immense proportions, possibly one that transcended all limitations, or one that existed before any limitations were known. I did not have any form, being just pure consciousness with superb intelligence suspended in Absolute Space. Although there was no source of light there, I cannot say I was in complete darkness.

I shared this space with three other beings. Although they were purely abstract and amorphous like myself, I could clearly feel their separate presence and communicate with them in a complex telepathic fashion. We amused each other by various brilliant intellectual games; fireworks of extraordinary ideas were being thrown back and forth. The complexity, intricacy, and level of imagination involved in these games by far surpassed anything known among humans. It was all pure entertainment, *l'art pour l'art*, since in the form we were, none of it had any practical implications.

I have to think in this context about whales who float in the ocean with their enormous brains and are endowed with intelligence that matches or surpasses ours. Since nature does not create and maintain organs and functions that are not being used, the mental activity of the cetaceans has to be comparable to that of humans. Yet. because of their anatomy, they have only minimal capacity to give any tangible physical expression to what is going on in their minds. I once read a speculation of a researcher who suggested that the whales may be spending most of their time entertaining each other using their amazing voices that carry in the ocean over distances of hundreds of miles. Do they tell each other stories and communicate artistic creations? Do they have philosophical dialogues or play sophisticated games? Or are they like Indian or Tibetan yogis who in their deep meditations, in the solitude of their caves and cells, experience connection with the entire history of the cosmos and other realities?

After this introduction, describing the general ambience and context of her experience and reflecting on the disembodied existence as a purely spiritual being, Gail focused on the part of her session that has immediate relevance for our discussion about the "taboo against knowing who we are."

One of the beings came up with an intriguing idea. It suggested that it would be possible to create a game involving a reality with many different creatures of various sizes and forms. They would appear to be dense and solid and exist in a world filled with objects of different shapes, textures, and consistencies. The beings would come into existence, evolve, have complex interactions and adventures with each other, and then cease to exist. There would be groups of creatures of various orders, each existing in two forms—male and female—that would complement each other and participate in reproduction.

This reality would be bound by distinct space and time coordinates. Time would show a mandatory flow from the past through the present to the future and later events would appear to be caused by the preceding ones. There would be vast historical periods, each different from the others. One would have to travel to get from one place to another and there would be many different ways to do it. A variety of rigid limitations, rules, and laws would govern all the events in this world, as it is with all the games. Entering this reality and assuming different roles in it would provide exquisite entertainment of a very unique type.

The three spiritual beings were intrigued, but incredulous, and expressed serious doubts about the suggested project. As exciting as it sounded, it seemed unlikely that it could be implemented. How could an unlimited spiritual being existing in the world of all possibilities be made to believe that it is confined to a solid body of a strange shape, with a head, trunk, and extremities, and that it critically depends on the ingestion of other dead creatures and the presence of a gas called oxygen? How could it be convinced that it has a limited intellectual capacity and that its ability to perceive is constrained by the range of something like the sensory organs. It seemed too fantastic to be seriously considered! In what follows, Gail describes how the demiurgic beings resolved the problem.

A heated intellectual exchange ensued. The originator of this plan responded to all our objections, insisting that the project was perfectly feasible. He/she was convinced that sufficient complexity and intriguing nature of the script, consistent association of specific situations with compelling experiences, and careful covering of all the loopholes was all that was necessary. It would trap the participant into an intricate net of illusions and trick him/her into believing in the reality of the game. We were getting increasingly fascinated by all the possibilities and finally became convinced that this unusual project was viable. We agreed to enter the game of incarnation excited by the promise of extraordinary adventures in consciousness.

This experience has somehow resolved whatever concerns I have ever had regarding the matter of karma. It left me with a firm conviction that I am in essence a spiritual being and that the only way I could have possibly gotten involved in the cosmic drama was through a free decision. The choice to incarnate involves voluntary acceptance of a large number of limitations, rules, and laws, as it always does when we decide to play a game. From this perspective, it does not make sense to blame anybody for anything that happens in our life. The fact that, on a higher level, we have a free choice whether or not we enter the cosmic game creates a metaframework that redefines everything that occurs within it.

Vicissitudes and Pitfalls of the Return Journey

There exists another important reason why it is so difficult to free ourselves from the illusion that we are separate individuals living in a material world. The ways to reunion with the divine source are fraught with many hardships, risks, and challenges. The divine play is not a completely closed system; it offers the protagonists the possibility to discover the true nature of creation, including their own cosmic status. However, the ways leading out of self-deception to enlightenment and to reunion with the source present serious problems and most of the potential loopholes in creation are carefully hidden. This is absolutely necessary for the maintenance of stability and balance in the cosmic scheme. These vicissitudes and pitfalls of the spiritual path represent an important part of the "taboo against knowing who we are."

All the situations that provide opportunities for spiritual opening are typically associated with a variety of strong opposing forces. Some of the obstacles that make the way to liberation and enlightenment extremely difficult and dangerous are intrapsychic in nature. Here belong terrifying experiences that can deter less courageous and determined seekers, such as encounters with dark archetypal forces, fear of death, and the specter of insanity. Even more problematic are various interferences and interventions that come from the external world. In the Middle Ages, many people who had spontaneous mystical experiences were risking torture, trial, and execution by the Holy Inquisition. In our time, stigmatizing psychiatric labels and drastic therapeutic measures replaced accusations of witchcraft, tortures, and autos-da-fé. Materialistic scientism of the twentieth century has ridiculed and pathologized any spiritual effort, no matter how well founded and sophisticated.

The authority that science enjoys in modern society makes it difficult to take spirituality seriously and pursue the path of spiritual discovery. In addition, the dogmas and activities of mainstream religions tend to obscure the fact that the only place where true spirituality can be found is inside the psyche of each of us. At its worst, organized religion can actually function as a grave impediment for any serious spiritual search, rather than an institution that can help us connect with the Divine.

The technologies of the sacred developed by various aboriginal cultures have in the West been dismissed as products of magical thinking and primitive superstitions of the savages. The spiritual potential of sexuality that finds its expression in Tantra is by far outweighed by the pitfalls of sex as a powerful animal instinct. The advent of psychedelics that have the capacity to open wide the gates to the transcendental dimension was soon followed by irresponsible secular misuse of these compounds and the threats of insanity, chromosomal damage, and legal sanctions.

Failed Experiment in Astral Projection

We are so deeply imbedded in our belief in an objectively existing and predictable material world that a sudden collapse of our familiar reality and violation of the "taboo against knowing who we are" can be associated with indescribable metaphysical terror. I will illustrate this point by completing the story about my "astral projection" from Baltimore to Prague that I introduced earlier (p. 89–91). I interrupted my account at the point where I felt trapped in a space-time loop, not knowing in which of these two cities I actually was. Here is the rest of this extraordinary adventure in consciousness:

> I felt that I needed a much more convincing proof of whether or not what I was experiencing was "objectively real" in the usual sense. I finally decided to perform a test—to take a picture from the wall and later check in the correspondence with my parents if something unusual had happened at that time in their apartment. I reached for the picture, but before I was able to touch the frame, I was overcome by an increasingly alarming feeling that it was an extremely risky and dangerous undertaking. I suddenly felt under the attack of evil forces and perilous black magic. It seemed to me that what I was about to do was a hazardous gamble, in which the price was my soul.
>
> I paused and made a desperate effort to understand what was happening. Images from the world's famous casinos were flashing in front of my eyes—Monte Carlo, Lido in Venice, Las Vegas, Reno—I saw roulette balls spiraling at intoxicating speeds, the levers of the slot machines moving up and down, and dice rolling on the green surface of the tables during a game of craps. There were circles of players passing around cards, groups

of gamblers involved in baccarat, and crowds watching the flickering lights of the keno panels. This was followed by scenes of secret meetings of statesmen, politicians, army officials, and topnotch scientists.

I finally got the message and realized that I had not yet overcome my egocentrism and was not able to resist the temptation of power. The possibility of transcending the limitations of time and space appeared to me to be intoxicating and dangerously seductive. If I could exert control over time and space, an unlimited supply of money appeared to be guaranteed, together with everything that money can buy. All I would have to do under those circumstances was to go to the nearest casino, stock market, or lottery office. No secrets would exist for me if I could have mastery over time and space. I would be able to eavesdrop on summit meetings of political leaders and have access to top-secret discoveries. This would open undreamed-of possibilities for directing the course of events in the world.

I understood the dangers involved in my experiment. I remembered passages from different spiritual books warning against toying with supernatural powers before we overcome the limitations of our egos and reach spiritual maturity. There was something that appeared even more relevant. I found out that I was extremely ambivalent in regard to the outcome of my test. On the one hand, it seemed extremely enticing to be able to liberate myself from the slavery of time and space. On the other hand, it was obvious that a positive outcome of this test would have far-reaching and serious consequences. It clearly could not be seen as an isolated experiment revealing the arbitrary nature of space and time.

If I could get confirmation that it was possible to manipulate the physical environment at a distance of several thousand miles, my whole universe would collapse as a result of this one experiment, and I would find myself in a state of utter metaphysical confusion. The world as I had known it would not exist any more. I would lose all the maps I relied on and felt comfortable with. I would not know who, where, and when I was and would be lost in a totally new, frightening universe, the laws of which would be alien and unfamiliar to me. If I had these powers, there would likely be many others who would have them too. I would have no privacy anywhere and doors and walls would not protect me anymore. My new world would be full of potential dangers of unforeseeable kind and unimaginable proportions.

I could not bring myself to carry out the experiment and decided to leave the problem of the objectivity and reality of the experience unresolved. This made it possible for me to toy with the idea that I had been able to transcend time and space. At the same time, it left open the possibility to see the entire episode as a peculiar deception caused by a powerful psychedelic substance. The idea that the destruction of reality as I knew it was objectively verified beyond any reasonable doubt was simply too frightening.

The moment I gave up the experiment, I found myself back in the room in Baltimore where I took the substance and within a couple of hours my experience stabilized and congealed into the familiar "objective reality." I never forgave myself for having wasted such a unique and fantastic experiment. However, the memory of the metaphysical terror involved in this test makes me doubt that I would be more courageous if I were given a similar chance in the future.

The Secrets of False Identity

We can now sum up the insights from holotropic states concerning the "taboo against knowing who we are." On all the levels of creation, with the exception of the Absolute, the participation in the cosmic game requires that the units of consciousness forget their true identity, assume a separate individuality, and perceive and treat other protagonists as fundamentally different from themselves. The creative process generates many domains with different characteristics and each of them offers unique opportunities for exquisite adventures in consciousness. The experience of the world of gross matter and the identification with a biological organism existing in this world is just an extreme form of this universal process.

The mastery with which the creative principle is able to portray the different realms of existence seems to make the experiences of the roles involved so believable and convincing that it is extremely difficult to detect their illusory nature. In addition, the possibilities of overcoming the illusion of separation and experiencing reunion are associated with extreme difficulties and complex ambiguities. In essence, we do not have a fixed identity and can experience ourselves as anything on the continuum between the embodied self and Absolute Consciousness. The extent and degree of free choice, that we have as protagonists on the different levels of the cosmic game, decreases as consciousness descends from the Absolute to the plane of material existence and increases in the course of the spiritual return journey. Since by our true nature we are unlimited spiritual beings, we enter the cosmic game on the basis of a free decision and get trapped by the perfection with which it is executed.

10

Playing the Cosmic Game

Two birds beautiful of wing, friends and comrades, cling
to a common tree, and one eats the sweet fruit, the
other regards him and eats not.

—*Rig Veda*

How little do we know that which we are!
How less what we may be!

—George Gordon Lord Byron

The Three Poisons of Tibetan Buddhism

We have now explored in some detail the large and encompassing vision of creation and the exalted image of human nature
that have emerged from the work with holotropic states. As we
are nearing the end of our story, it seems appropriate to examine
the practical implications of this information for our everyday
life. How does systematic self-exploration using holotropic states
influence our emotional and physical well-being, our personality,
worldview, and system of values? Can the new discoveries give
us any specific guidelines that would help us to derive maximum
benefit from what we have learned? Can we use the new knowledge in a way that would make our life more fulfilling and
rewarding?

Spiritual teachers of all ages seem to agree that pursuit of
material goals, in and of itself, cannot bring us fulfillment, happiness, and inner peace. The rapidly escalating global crisis,
moral deterioration, and growing discontent accompanying the
increase of material affluence in the industrial societies bear

witness to this ancient truth. There seems to be general agreement in the mystical literature that the remedy for the existential malaise that besets humanity is to turn inside, look for the answers in our own psyche, and undergo a deep psychospiritual transformation.

It is not difficult to understand that an important prerequisite for successful existence is general intelligence—the ability to learn and recall, think and reason, and adequately respond to our material environment. More recent research emphasized the importance of "emotional intelligence"—the capacity to adequately respond to our human environment and adequately handle our interpersonal relationships (Goleman 1996).

Observations from the study of holotropic states confirm the basic tenet of perennial philosophy that the quality of our life ultimately depends on what can be called "spiritual intelligence." It is the capacity to conduct our life in such a way that it reflects deep philosophical and metaphysical understanding of reality and of ourselves. This, of course, raises questions about the nature of the psychospiritual transformation that is necessary to achieve this form of intelligence, the direction of the changes that we have to undergo, and the means that can facilitate such development.

A very clear and specific answer to this question can be found in different schools of Mahāyāna Buddhism. We can use here as the basis for our discussion the famous Tibetan screen-painting (*thangka*) portraying the cycle of life, death, and reincarnation. It depicts the Wheel of Life held in the grip of the horrifying Lord of Death. The wheel is divided into six segments representing the different *lokas*, or realms into which we can be born. The celestial domain of gods is shown as being challenged from the adjacent segment by the jealous warrior gods, or *asuras*. The region of hungry ghosts is inhabited by *pretas*, pitiful creatures representing insatiable greed. They have giant bellies, enormous appetites, and the mouths the size of a pinhole. The remaining sections of the wheel depict the world of human beings, the realm of wild beasts, and hell. Inside the wheel are two concentric circles. The outer one shows the ascending and descending paths along which souls travel. The innermost circle contains three animals—a pig, a snake, and a rooster.

Figure 5. The Tibetan Wheel of Life, held in the grip of the Lord of Death. In the middle are three animals symbolizing the forces perpetuating the cycles of death and rebirth: cock (lust), snake (aggression), and pig (ignorance). On their right side is the dark path with descending victims of bad karma and on the left side the light ascending path of the good karma. The six large segments of the wheel represent the realms of existence into which one can be born: realm of the gods, realm of the warrior deities, realm of the hungry ghosts, hell, the animal realm, and the realm of the human beings. The pictures on the rim of the wheel represent the chain of causation leading to rebirth.

The animals in the center of the wheel represent the "three poisons" or forces that, according to Buddhist teachings, perpetuate the cycles of birth and death and are responsible for all the suffering in our life. The pig symbolizes the ignorance concerning the nature of reality and our own nature, the snake stands for anger and aggression, and the rooster depicts desire and lust leading to attachment. The quality of our life and our ability to cope with the challenges of existence depend critically on the degree to which we are able to eliminate or transform these forces that run the world of sentient beings. Let us now look from this perspective at the process of systematic self-exploration involving holotropic states of consciousness.

Practical Knowledge and Transcendental Wisdom

The most obvious benefit that we can obtain from deep experiential work is access to extraordinary knowledge about ourselves, other people, nature, and the cosmos. In holotropic states, we can reach deep understanding of the unconscious dynamics of our psyche. We can discover how our perception of ourselves and of the world is influenced by forgotten or repressed memories from childhood, infancy, birth, and prenatal existence. In addition, in transpersonal experiences we can identify with other people, various animals, plants, and elements of the inorganic world. Experiences of this kind represent an extremely rich source of unique insights about the world we live in.

In this process, we can gain considerable amount of knowledge that can be useful in our everyday life. However, the ignorance symbolized in the Tibetan *thangkas* by the pig is not the absence or lack of knowledge in the ordinary sense. It does not mean simply inadequate information about various aspects of the material world. The form of ignorance that is meant here (*avidyā*) is a fundamental misunderstanding and confusion concerning the nature of reality and our own nature. The only remedy for this kind of ignorance is transcendental wisdom (*prajñāpāramitā*). From this point of view, it is very important that the inner work involving holotropic states offers more than just increase of our knowledge about the universe. It is also a unique way of gaining insights about issues of transcendental relevance, as we have seen throughout this book.

Biographical, Perinatal, and Transpersonal Roots of Aggression

Let us now look from the same perspective at the second "poison," the human propensity to aggression. The nature and scope of human aggression cannot be explained simply by references to our animal origin. Seeing humans as "naked apes" whose aggression is the result of some factors that we share with animals, such as base instincts, genetic strategies of "selfish genes," or signals from the "reptilian brain," does not take into account the nature and degree of human violence. Animals exhibit aggression when they are hungry, defend their territory, or compete for sex. The violence exhibited by humans, which Erich Fromm called "malignant aggression" (Fromm 1973), has no parallels in the animal kingdom.

Mainstream psychologists and psychiatrists attribute the specifically human aggression to a history of frustrations, abuse, and lack of love in infancy and childhood. However, explanations of this kind fall painfully short of accounting for extreme forms of individual violence, such as serial murders of the Boston Strangler or Geoffrey Dahmer type, and particularly for mass societal phenomena like Nazism and Communism. Difficulties in the early histories of individuals are of little help in understanding psychological motives for bloody wars, revolutions, genocide, and concentration camps, phenomena that involve large numbers of people. Self-exploration using holotropic states throws an entirely new light on the problem of these forms of human violence. Probing the depth of our psyche, we discover that the roots of this problematic and dangerous aspect of human nature are much deeper and more formidable than academic psychologists have ever imagined.

There is no doubt that traumas and frustrations in childhood and infancy represent important sources of aggression. However, this connection barely scratches the surface of the problem. Deep systematic inner work sooner or later reveals additional significant roots of human violence in the trauma of biological birth. The vital emergency, pain, and suffocation experienced for many hours during our delivery generate enormous amounts of anxiety and murderous aggression that remain stored in our psyche and body. This repository of fundamental mistrust and hostility toward the world constitutes a significant aspect of the dark side of human personality that C. G. Jung called the Shadow.

As we saw earlier, the reliving of birth in holotropic states is typically accompanied by images of inconceivable violence, both individual and collective. This includes experiences of mutilation, murder, and rape, as well as scenes of bloody wars, revolutions, racial riots, and concentration camps. Lloyd deMause (1975), a pioneer in the field of psychohistory, a discipline that applies the methods of depth psychology to sociopolitical events, studied speeches of political and military leaders, as well as posters and caricatures from the time of wars and revolutions. He was struck by the extraordinary abundance of figures of speech, metaphors, and images related to biological birth that he found in this material.

Military leaders and politicians of all ages, referring to a critical situation or declaring war, typically use terms that describe various aspects of perinatal distress. They accuse the enemy of choking and strangling us, squeezing the last breath out of our lungs, or confining us, and not giving us enough space to live (Hitler's *Lebensraum*). Equally frequent are allusions to quicksand, dark caves, tunnels, and confusing labyrinths, dangerous abysses into which we might be pushed, and the threat of engulfment or drowning.

Similarly, the leaders' promises of victory tend to come in the form of perinatal images. They pledge that they will rescue us from the darkness of a treacherous labyrinth and guide us to the light on the other side of the tunnel. They vow that after the oppressor is overcome, everybody will again breathe freely. I have shown in another context the deep similarity between the paintings and drawings depicting perinatal experiences and the symbolism of posters and caricatures from the time of wars and revolutions (Grof 1996).

However, even explanations recognizing perinatal sources of aggression do not adequately account for the nature, scope, and depth of human violence. Its deepest roots reach far beyond the boundaries of the individual, into the transpersonal domain. In holotropic states, they take the form of wrathful deities, devils, and demons and of complex mythological themes, such as the Apocalypse or Ragnarok, the Twilight of the Gods. I have given earlier in this book several examples of these dark archetypal forces operating in the depth of our psyche. Additional potential repositories of aggression on the transpersonal level are past life memories and phylogenetic matrices reflecting our animal past.

As we have seen, the study of holotropic states discloses a very shattering and discouraging image of human nature and of the scope and depth of aggression that our flesh is heir to. However, while it reveals the enormity of the problem, it also offers entirely new perspectives and hopes. It shows that there are unusually powerful and effective ways of dealing with human violence. In deep experiential work that reaches the perinatal and transpersonal levels, enormous amounts of aggression can be safely expressed, worked through, and transformed in a relatively short time. This work also throws new light on the nature of aggression and its relation to the human psyche. According to these insights, aggression is not something that reflects our true nature, but rather a screen that separates us from it.

When we succeed in penetrating this dark veil of elemental instinctual forces, we discover that the innermost core of our being is divine rather than bestial. This revelation is in full agreement with the famous passage from the Indian Upanishads that I have quoted earlier. The message of these ancient scriptures is very clear: "Tat tvam asi" (Thou art That)—"in your deepest nature you are identical with the Divine." In my experience, responsible work with holotropic states can bring very encouraging practical results. Deep inner self-exploration leads regularly to a major reduction of aggression and of self-destructive tendencies, as well as an increase of tolerance and compassion. It also tends to foster reverence for life, empathy for other species, and ecological sensitivity.

Psychospiritual Sources of Insatiable Greed

This brings us to the third "poison" of Tibetan Buddhism, a powerful force that combines the qualities of lust, desire, and insatiable greed. Together with "malignant aggression," these qualities are certainly responsible for some of the darkest chapters in human history. Western psychologists link various aspects of this force to the libidinal drives described by Sigmund Freud. From this perspective, insatiable greed would be explained in terms of unresolved oral issues from the time of nursing. Similarly, excessive preoccupation with money would be associated with repressed anal impulses and sexual extremes would reflect a phallic fixation. The craving for power was most thoroughly described in the psychology of Freud's renegade disciple Alfred Adler, who saw it as a compensation for feelings of inferiority and inadequacy.

The insights from holotropic states considerably enrich this picture. They reveal additional deep sources of this aspect of human nature on the perinatal and transpersonal levels of the psyche. When our process of experiential self-exploration reaches the perinatal level, we typically discover that our existence up to that point has been largely inauthentic. We realize, to our surprise and astonishment, that our entire life strategy has been misdirected. It becomes clear to us that much of what we have been striving for has been strongly dictated by the unconscious emotions and driving energies that were imprinted in our psyche and body at the time of our birth.

The memory of the frightening and highly uncomfortable situation to which we were exposed at the time of our delivery stays alive in our system. It exerts a very powerful influence on us throughout our life, unless it is brought fully into consciousness and worked through in systematic experiential self-exploration. Much of what we do in life and how we do it can be understood in terms of belated efforts to cope with this incomplete gestalt of birth and the fear of death associated with it.

When this traumatic memory is close to the surface of our psyche, it causes feelings of dissatisfaction with our present situation. In and of itself, this discomfort is unspecific and amorphous, but it can be projected on a large spectrum of issues. We can attribute it to our unsatisfactory physical appearance or inadequate resources and lack of material possessions. It might seem to us that the reason for our dissatisfaction is our low social status and lack of influence in the world. We can feel that the source of our discontent is insufficient power and fame, inadequate knowledge or skills, and any number of other things.

Whatever might be the reality of the present circumstances, the situation never seems satisfactory and the solution always appears to lie in the future. Like the fetus stuck and struggling in the birth canal, we feel a strong need to get to a situation that is better than the present one. As a result of this compelling drive toward some future accomplishment, we never live fully in the present and our life feels like a preparation for something better to come.

Our fantasy reacts to this feeling of existential discomfort by creating an image of a future situation that would bring satisfaction and would correct the perceived deficiencies and shortcomings. The existentialists talk about this mechanism as "auto-projecting" into the future. Consistent application of this strategy results in a life pattern that people refer to as "treadmill" or "rat-race" type of existence—pursuing fantasized mirages of future happiness, while not being able to fully enjoy what is available in the present. This misguided, inauthentic, and unrewarding approach to existence can be practiced throughout the entire lifetime until death brings the "moment of truth" and mercilessly reveals its emptiness and futility.

Auto-projecting into the future as a means of correcting existential dissatisfaction is a "loser strategy" whether or not we achieve the desired goals. It is based on a fundamental misunderstanding and misperception of our needs. For this reason, it can never bring us the fulfillment we expect from it. When we are not able to reach the goals we envision, we attribute our continuing dissatisfaction to our failure to reach the alleged corrective measures. When we succeed in attaining these goals, this typically does not bring what we hoped for and our feelings of discomfort are not relieved. In addition, we are not able to correctly diagnose why we continue feeling dissatisfied. We do not realize that we are pursuing a fundamentally wrong strategy of existence, one that cannot bring us fulfillment no matter what its results are. We usually attribute the failure to the fact that the goal was not sufficiently ambitious or that the specific choice of the goal was wrong.

This pattern often leads to a reckless irrational pursuit of various grandiose goals that is responsible for many problems in our world and results in much human suffering. This strategy lacks any connection to the realities of life and can thus be acted out on many different levels. Since it never brings true fulfillment, it does not make much difference whether the protagonist is a pauper or a billionaire in the category of Aristotle Onassis or Howard Hughes. Once our basic survival needs are satisfied, the quality of our life experience has much more to do with our state of consciousness than with external circumstances.

Misguided efforts to achieve satisfaction by pursuit of external goals can actually bring paradoxical results. I have worked with people who after decades of hard work and struggle finally reached the goal, about which they had dreamed their entire life, and the next day became severely depressed. Joseph Campbell described this situation as "getting to the top of the ladder and finding out that it stands against the wrong wall." This frustrating pattern can be considerably weakened by bringing fully into consciousness the memory of birth, confronting the fear of death connected with it, and experiencing psychospiritual rebirth. By connecting experientially to the memory of the prenatal or post-natal situation rather than the imprint of the birth struggle, we significantly reduce the unrelenting preoccupation with future achievments and are able to draw much more satisfaction from the present.

However, the roots of our dissatisfaction and existential malaise reach even deeper than the perinatal level. In the last analysis, the insatiable craving that drives human life is transcendental in nature. In the words of Dante Alighieri (1989), the great Italian poet of the early Renaissance, "the desire for perfection is that desire which always makes every pleasure appear incomplete, for there is no joy or pleasure so great in this life that it can quench the thirst in our soul." In the most general sense, the deepest transpersonal roots of insatiable greed can best be understood in terms of Ken Wilber's concept of the Atman Project (Wilber 1980).

Wilber explored and described the specific consequences of the basic tenet of perennial philosophy, which asserts that our true nature is divine. This essence of our existence has been called by different names—God, the Cosmic Christ, Keter, Allah, Buddha, Brahman, the Tao, and many others. Although the process of creation separates and alienates us from our cosmic source, our divine identity, the awareness of this connection is never completely lost. The deepest motivating force in the human psyche on all the levels of our development is the craving to return to the experience of our divinity. However, the constraining conditions of the incarnate existence do not allow the experience of full spiritual liberation in and as God.

We can use here as an illustration a story about Alexander the Great, a person whose unique secular accomplishments would be difficult to match. He came as far in achieving a divine status in the material world as any human being can possibly hope for. This was actually expressed in one of the attributes that was commonly associated with his name—Divine Alexander. The story goes as follows:

After an unparalleled series of military victories through which he had aquired vast territories lying between his native Macedonia and India, Alexander finally reached India. There he heard about a yogi who had unusual powers, or siddhis, among others the ability to see the future. Alexander decided to pay him a visit. When he arrived to the yogi's cave, the sage was immersed in his regular spiritual practice. Alexander inpatiently interrupted his meditation, asking him if he indeed had the power to see the future. The yogi nodded in silence and returned to his meditation. Alexander interrupted him again with another urgent question: "Can you tell me if my conquest of India will be successful?" The yogi meditated for a while and then slowly opened his eyes. He gave Alexander a long gentle look and said compassionately: "What you will ultimately need is about six feet of ground."

It would be difficult to find a more poignant example for our human dilemma—our desperate effort to seek realization of our divinity through material means. The only way we can attain our full potential as divine beings is through an inner experience. This requires death and transcendence of our separate selves, dying to our identity as a "skin-encapsulated ego." Because of our fear of annihilation and because of our grasping onto the ego, we have to settle for Ātman substitutes or surrogates. These change as we go through life and are always specific for a particular stage.

For a fetus and the newborn, the Ātman substitute is the bliss experienced in a good womb and on a good breast. For an infant it is satisfaction of basic physiological drives and of the need for security. By the time we attain the adult age, the Ātman project reaches enormous complexity. The Ātman surrogates now cover a wide spectrum and include, besides food and sex, also money, fame, power, appearance, knowledge, and many other things. At the same time, we all have a deep sense that our true identity is the totality of cosmic creation and the creative principle itself. For this reason, substitutes of any degree and scope will always remain unsatisfactory. The ultimate solution for the insatiable greed is in the inner world, not in secular pursuits of any kind and scope. Only the experience of one's divinity in a non-ordinary state of consciousness can ever fulfill our deepest needs.

The Persian mystical poet Rūmī made it very clear: "All the hopes, desires, loves, and affections that people have for different things—fathers, mothers, friends, heavens, the earth, palaces, sciences, works, food, drink—the saint knows that these are desires for God and all those things are veils. When men leave this world and see the King without these veils, then they will know that all were veils and coverings, that the object of their desire was in reality that One Thing" (Hines 1996). Thomas Traherne, the seventeenth-century English poet and clergyman, who was an ardent exponent of the way of life he called "felicity," reached the same realization when he had a profound mystical experience. Here is an excerpt from his account describing this event:

The streets were mine, the temple was mine, the people were mine. The skies were mine, and so were the sun and moon and stars, and all the world was mine, and I the only spectator and enjoyer of it. I knew no churlish proprieties, nor bounds, nor divisions; but all proprieties and divisions were mine; all treasures and the possessors of them. So that with much ado I was corrupted, and made to learn the dirty devices of this world, which I now unlearn, and become, as it were, a little child again that I may enter into the kingdom of God.

Walking the Mystical Path with Practical Feet

If we accept that the material universe as we know it is not a mechanical system but a virtual reality created by Absolute Consciousness through an infinitely complex orchestration of experiences, what are the practical consequences of this insight? And what influence does the awareness that our being is commensurate with that of the cosmic creative principle have on our system of values and on the way we conduct our life? These are questions of great theoretical and practical relevance, not only for each of us as individuals, but for all humanity, and for the future of life on this planet. In trying to answer them, we will again look at the insights of people who have experienced holotropic states of consciousness.

For many religions, the recipe for dealing with the hardships of life is to play down the importance of the earthly plane and to focus on the transcendental realms. Some of these creeds recommend a shift in attention and emphasis from the material world to other realities. They suggest prayer and devotion as a way of communicating with various higher realms and superior beings. Others offer and underscore direct experiential access to transcendental realms by means of meditation and other forms of personal spiritual practice. The religious systems with this orientation portray the material world as an inferior domain that is imperfect, impure, and conducive to suffering and misery. From their point of view, reality appears to be a valley of tears and incarnate existence a curse or a quagmire of death and rebirth.

These creeds and their officials offer their dedicated followers the promise of a more desirable domain or a more fulfilling state of consciousness in the Beyond. In more primitive forms of popular beliefs, these are various forms of abodes of the blessed, paradises, or heavens. These become available after death for those who meet the necessary requirements defined by their respective theology. For more sophisticated and refined systems of this kind, heavens and paradises are only stages of the spiritual journey and its final destination is dissolution of personal boundaries and union with the divine, or extinguishing the fire of life and disappearance into the nothingness (*nirvāṇa*).

According to the Jain religion, we are in our deepest nature pristine monads of consciousness (*jīvas*) and are contaminated by our entanglement in the world of biology. The goal of the Jain practice is to drastically reduce our participation in the world of matter, free ourselves from its polluting influence, and regain our pristine status. Another example is the original form of Buddhism called Theravada or Hīnayāna (the Small Vehicle). This school of Buddhism is an austere monastic tradition that offers the teaching and spiritual discipline necessary for achieving personal enlightenment and liberation. Its ideal is the *arhat*, the saint or sage at the highest stage of development, living as a hermit in seclusion from the world. Similar emphasis on personal liberation (*mokṣa*) can also be found in the Hindu Vedanta.

However, other spiritual orientations embrace nature and the material world as containing or embodying the Divine. Thus the Tantric branches of Jainism, Hinduism, and Buddhism have a distinctly life-affirming and life-celebrating orientation. Similarly, the Buddhist Mahāyāna (the Great Vehicle) teaches that we can reach liberation in the middle of everyday life if we free ourselves from the three "poisons"—ignorance, aggression, and desire. When we succeed, *saṃsāra,* or the world of illusion, birth, and death, becomes *nirvāṇa.* Various Mahāyāna schools emphasize the crucial role of compassion as an important expression of spiritual realization. Their ideal is the Bodhisattva, who is interested not only in his own enlightenment, but also in the liberation of all other sentient beings.

Let us take a look at this dilemma using the insights from holotropic states. What can we gain from moving away from life and escaping from the material plane into transcendental realities? And, conversely, what is the value of embracing wholeheartedly the world of everyday reality? Many spiritual systems define the goal of the spiritual journey as dissolution of personal boundaries and reunion with the Divine. However, those people who have actually experienced in their inner explorations identification with Absolute Consciousness, realize that defining the final goal of the spiritual journey as the experience of oneness with the supreme principle of existence involves a serious problem.

They become aware of the fact that the undifferentiated Absolute Consciousness/Void represents not only the end of the spiritual journey, but also the source and the beginning of creation. The Divine is the principle offering reunion for the separated, but also the agent responsible for the division and separation of the original unity. If this principle were complete and self-fulfilling in itself, there would not be any reason for it to create and the other experiential realms would not exist. Since they do, the tendency of Absolute Consciousness to create clearly expresses a fundamental "need." The worlds of plurality thus represent an important complement to the undifferentiated state of the Divine. In the terminology of the Cabala, "people need God and God needs people."

The overall scheme of the cosmic drama involves a dynamic interplay of two fundamental forces, one of which is centrifugal (*hylotropic* or matter-oriented) and the other centripetal (*holotropic* or aiming for wholeness) in relation to the creative principle. The undifferentiated Cosmic Consciousness shows an elemental tendency to create worlds of plurality that contain countless separate beings. We have discussed earlier some of the possible "reasons" or "motives" for this propensity to generate virtual realities. And conversely, the individualized units of consciousness experience their separation and alienation as painful and manifest a strong need to return to the source and reunite with it. Identification with the embodied self is fraught, among others, with the problems of emotional and physical suffering, spatial and temporal limitations, impermanence, and death.

We can experience this dynamic conflict in its full form when our self-exploration in holotropic states takes us to the brink of the ego death. At this point, we oscillate and are torn between these two powerful forces. One part of us, the holotropic one, wishes to transcend the identification with the body-ego and experience dissolution and union with a larger whole. The other part, the hylotropic one, is driven by the fear of death and by the self-preservation instinct to hold onto our separate identity. This conflict is extremely difficult and can represent a serious obstacle in the process of psychospiritual transformation. It ultimately requires that we surrender and sacrifice our familiar identity without knowing what will replace it on the other side, if anything at all.

Even if our present way of being in the world is not particularly comfortable, we might anxiously hold onto it when the alternative is unknown. Yet we sense deep within ourselves that our existence as a separate embodied self in the material world is, in and of itself, inauthentic and cannot satisfy our innermost needs. We feel a strong pull to transcend our boundaries and reclaim our true identity. It helps to know intellectually, before we get involved in systematic inner work, that experiencing the ego death is a symbolic experience and does not entail real death and annihilation. However, the fear of dying and surrendering the ego is so overwhelming and convincing that, when we are experiencing it, it is difficult to trust this knowledge and find it comforting.

If it is true that our psyche is governed by these two powerful cosmic forces, the hylotropic and the holotropic, and that these two are in a fundamental conflict with each other, is there an approach to existence that can adequately cope with this situation? Since neither separate existence nor undifferentiated unity is fully satisfactory, what is the alternative? Is it at all possible under these circumstances to find a solution, a life strategy that would address this paradox? Can we find an eye in the hurricane of these conflicting cosmic tendencies where we can rest in peace? Can we find satisfaction in a universe whose fabric is woven by forces that oppose each other?

Clearly, the solution is not to reject embodied existence as inferior and worthless and try to escape from it. We have seen that experiential worlds, including the world of matter, represent not only an important and valuable, but absolutely necessary, complement to the undifferentiated state of the creative principle. At the same time, our efforts to reach fulfillment and peace of mind will necessarily fail, and possibly backfire, if they involve only objects and goals in the material realm. Any satisfactory solution will thus have to embrace both the earthly and the transcendental dimensions, both the world of forms and the Formless.

The material universe as we know it offers countless possibilities for extraordinary adventures in consciousness. As embodied selves, we can witness the spectacle of the heavens with its billions of galaxies, breathtaking sunrises and sunsets, waxing and waning of the moon, or the wonder of the lunar and solar eclipses. We can watch fantastic displays of clouds, the gentle beauty of the rainbows, and the shimmering luster of the aurora borealis. On the surface of the earth, nature has created an endless variety of landscapes, from great oceans, rivers and lakes to giant mountain ranges, silent deserts, and the cold beauty of the Arctic. Together with the astonishing variety of life forms in the animal and botanical kingdoms, these provide endless opportunities for unique experiences.

Only in the physical form and on the material plane can we fall in love, enjoy the ecstasy of sex, have children, listen to Beethoven's music, or admire Rembrandt's paintings. Where else than on earth can we listen to the song of a nightingale or taste baked Alaska? We could add to our list the joys of sports, traveling, playing musical instruments, painting, and countless others. The material world offers infinite possibilities for research of the organic and inorganic realms, of the surface of the earth, of the depth of the ocean, and of the far reaches of the cosmic space. The opportunities for the explorations of the micro- and the macroworld are virtually unlimited. In addition to the experiences of the present, there is also the adventure of probing the mysterious past, from the ancient civilizations and the antidiluvian world to the events during the first microseconds of the Big Bang.

Benefits from Self-Exploration and Spiritual Practice

To participate in the phenomenal world and to be able to experience this rich spectrum of adventures requires a certain degree of identification with the embodied self and acceptance of the world of matter. However, when our identification with the body-ego is absolute and our belief in the material world as the only reality unshatterable, it is impossible to fully enjoy our participation in creation. The specters of personal insignificance, impermanence, and death can completely overshadow the positive side of life and rob it of its zest. We also have to add to it our frustration associated with repeated futile attempts to realize our full divine potential within the constraints imposed on us by the limitations of our bodies and of the material world.

To find the solution to this dilemma, we have to turn within. Repeated experiences of holotropic states tend to loosen our belief that we are a "skin-encapsulated ego." We continue to identify with the body-ego for pragmatic purposes, but this identification becomes more tentative and playful. If we have sufficient experiential knowledge of the transpersonal aspects of existence, including our own true identity and cosmic status, everyday life becomes much easier and more rewarding. As our inner search continues, we also sooner or later discover the essential emptiness behind all forms. As the Buddhist teachings suggest, knowledge of the virtual nature of the phenomenal world and its voidness can help us achieve freedom from suffering. This includes the recognition that belief in any separate selves in our life, including our own, is ultimately an illusion. In Buddhist texts, the awareness of the essential emptiness of all forms and the ensuing realization that there are no separate selves is referred to as *anatta*, literally "no-self."

Jack Kornfield, a psychologist and Vipassana Buddhist teacher, describes his first encounter with the concept of *anatta* during his meeting with the late Tibetan spiritual teacher Kalu Rinpoche. Trying to get as much as possible from his encounter with this remarkable human being, Jack asked him with the eagerness of a zealous beginner: "Please, could you describe for me in a few sentences the very essence of the Buddhist teachings?" Kalu Rinpoche replied: "I could do it, but you would not believe me and it would take you many years to understand what I mean." Jack politely insisted: "Please, can you tell me anyway? I would like to know." Kalu Rinpoche's answer was brief and succinct: "You do not really exist."

Awareness of our divine nature and of the essential emptiness of all things that we discover in our transpersonal experiences, form the foundations of a metaframework that can help us considerably to cope with the complexity of everyday existence. We can fully embrace the experience of the material world and enjoy all that it has to offer—the beauty of nature, human relationships, love-making, family, works of art, sports, culinary delights, and countless other things.

However, no matter what we do, life will bring obstacles, challenges, painful experiences, and losses. When things get too difficult and devastating, we can call on the large cosmic perspective that we have discovered in our inner quest. The connection with higher realities and the liberating knowledge of *anatta* and the emptiness behind all forms makes it possible to tolerate what otherwise might be unbearable. With the help of this transcendental awareness we might be able to experience fully the entire spectrum of life or "the whole catastrophe," as Zorba the Greek called it.

Systematic self-exploration using holotropic experiences can also help us to enhance and refine our sensory perception of the world. This "cleansing of the doors of perception" as Aldous Huxley called it, referring to William Blake's poem, makes it possible to fully appreciate and enjoy all the possibilities of the adventures in consciousness associated with embodied existence. A general increase in zest is most dramatic during mystical states and during the hours or days immediately following them. Here it is often so intense that we can speak of an "afterglow." In a more mitigated form, this increase in zest and a generally enhanced

218   The Cosmic Game

quality of life represent lasting aftereffects of such mystical revelations.

A person whose experience of life is limited to the hylotropic mode of consciousness and who has not had experiential access to the transcendental and numinous dimensions of reality will find it very difficult to overcome deep-seated fear of death and find deeper meaning in life. Under these circumstances, much of the daily behavior is motivated by the needs of the false ego and significant aspects of life are reactive and inauthentic. For this reason, it is essential to complement everyday practical activities with some form of systematic spiritual practice that provides experiential access to the transcendental realms.

In pre-industrial societies, the opportunity for transcendental experiences existed in many different forms—from shamanic rituals, rites of passage, and healing ceremonies to ancient mysteries of death and rebirth, mystical schools, and the meditation practices of the great religions of the world. In recent decades, the Western world has seen a significant revival of various ancient spiritual practices. In addition, representatives of modern depth psychology have developed effective new approaches facilitating spiritual opening. These tools are available to all those who are interested in psychospiritual transformation and consciousness evolution.

C. G. Jung, the forefather of transpersonal psychology, described in his writings a life strategy that addresses both the secular and the cosmic dimensions of ourselves and of existence. He suggested that we should complement our everyday activities in the external world by systematic self-exploration, by an inner search reaching into the deepest hidden recesses of our psyche. By directing our attention inward, we can connect with the Self, a higher aspect of our being, and benefit from its guidance. In this way, we can draw on the immense resources of the collective unconscious that contain the wisdom of ages.

According to Jung, we should not orient ourselves in life only on the basis of the external aspects of the situations we are facing. Our decision-making should be based on a creative synthesis of our pragmatic knowledge of the material world and the profound wisdom drawn from the collective unconscious during systematic inner self-exploration. This suggestion of the great Swiss psychiatrist is in general agreement with the conclusions that many people with whom I have worked over the years have drawn from their holotropic explorations.

I have seen repeatedly that the pursuit of this strategy can lead to a more fulfilling, enjoyable, and creative way of life. It makes it possible to be fully in the world of everyday reality and yet be aware of the numinous dimensions of existence and of our own divine nature. The ability to reconcile and integrate these two aspects of life belongs to the loftiest aspirations of the mystical traditions. Thus Sheik Al-'Alawi describes the Supreme Station, the highest stage of spiritual development in the Sufi tradition, as the state of being inwardly drunk with the Divine Essence and yet outwardly sober.

Individual Transformation and Planetary Future

The potential benefits of this approach to existence transcend the narrow interests of the individuals who practice it. This strategy applied on a sufficiently large scale could have important implications for human society and our future. In the last few decades, it has become increasingly clear that humanity is facing a crisis of unprecedented proportions. Modern science has developed effective measures that could solve most of the urgent problems in today's world—combat the majority of diseases, eliminate hunger and poverty, reduce the amount of industrial waste, and replace destructive fossil fuels by renewable sources of clean energy.

The problems that stand in the way are not of an economical or technological nature. The deepest sources of the global crisis lie inside the human personality and reflect the level of consciousness evolution of our species. Because of the untamed forces in the human psyche, unimaginable resources are being wasted in the absurdity of the arms race, power struggle, and pursuit of "unlimited growth." These elements of human nature also prevent a more appropriate distribution of wealth among individuals and nations, as well as a reorientation from purely economic and political concerns to ecological priorities that are critical for survival of life on this planet.

Diplomatic negotiations, administrative and legal measures, economic and social sanctions, military interventions, and other similar efforts have so far had very little success. As a matter of fact, they have often produced more problems than they solved. It is becoming increasingly clear, why they had to fail. It is impossible to alleviate this crisis by application of the strategies rooted in the same ideology that created it in the first place. In the last analysis, the current global crisis is of a psychospiritual nature. It is therefore hard to imagine that it could be resolved without a radical inner transformation of humanity and its rise to a higher level of emotional maturity and spiritual awareness.

Considering the paramount role of violence and greed in human history, the possibility of transforming modern humanity into a species of individuals capable of peaceful coexistence with their fellow men and women regardless of race, color, and religious or political conviction, let alone with other species, certainly does not seem very plausible. We are facing the formidable challenge of instilling humanity with profound ethical values, sensitivity to the needs of others, voluntary simplicity, and a sharp awareness of ecological imperatives. At first glance, this task might appear too unrealistic and utopian to offer any real hope.

However, the situation is not as hopeless as it might appear. As we saw earlier, profound transformation of this kind is exactly what happens in the course of systematic inner work using holotropic states, whether it is meditational practice, powerful experiential forms of therapy, or responsible supervised work with psychedelic substances. Similar changes can also be observed in people who experience spontaneous psychospiritual crises and have the privilege of a good support system and sensitive guidance.

A strategy of existence integrating deep inner work with inspired action in the external world could thus become an important factor in resolving the global crisis, if it were practiced on a sufficiently large scale. Inner transformation and accelerated consciousness evolution could significantly improve our chances for survival and for peaceful coexistence. I have collected and systematically described the insights from the study of holotropic states hoping that those people who will choose this path or are walking it already will find them useful and helpful during their own journey.

A Recipe for Planetary Healing: Lessons from a Native American Ceremony

I would like to close this chapter by relating an experience of profound healing and transformation that occurred many years ago in a group of people with whom I shared a holotropic state of consciousness. Although it happened almost a quarter of a century ago, I still feel very moved and tearful whenever I think and talk about it. This event showed me the depth of the problems we are facing in our world where for many centuries hatred has been passed from one generation to another. However, it also gave me hope and trust in the possibility of lifting this curse and dissolving the barriers that separate us from each other.

After I came to the United States in 1967, I participated in government-sponsored research at the Maryland Psychiatric Research Center exploring the potential of psychedelic therapy. One of our projects at the center was a training program for mental health professionals. It made it possible to administer up to three high-dose LSD sessions to psychiatrists, psychologists, and social workers for educational purposes. One of our subjects in this program was Kenneth Godfrey, a psychiatrist from the Veterans Administration Hospital in Topeka, Kansas. I was the guide in his three psychedelic sessions and we became very close friends.

When I was still in Czechoslovakia, I read about the Native American Church, a syncretistic religion combining Indian and Christian elements and using as a sacrament the Mexican psychedelic cactus peyote. I became very interested in having a personal experience of a peyote ceremony that would make it possible for me to compare therapeutic use of psychedelics with their ritual use. After my arrival in the United States, I was looking for such an opportunity, but without success. It turned out that both Ken and his wife were of Native American origin and had good connections with their people. When we were parting after Ken's third session, I asked him if he could mediate for me participation in a peyote ceremony and he promised to try. Several days later, he called me on the phone and told me that a road chief, who was a good friend of his, had invited me and several other people from our staff to join a peyote ceremony of the Patawatome Indians.

The following weekend five of us flew from Baltimore to Topeka, Kansas. The group consisted of our music therapist Helen Bonny, her sister, psychedelic therapist Bob Leihy, professor of religion Walter Houston Clark, and myself. We rented a car at the Topeka airport and drove from there deep into the Kansas prairie. There, in the middle of nowhere, stood several teepees, the site of the sacred ceremony. The sun was setting and the ritual was about to begin. Before we could join the ceremony, we had to be accepted by the other participants, all of whom were Native Americans. We had to go through a process that resembled a dramatic encounter group.

With intense emotions, the native people brought up the painful history of the invasion and conquest of North America by white intruders—the genocide of American Indians and rapes of their women, the expropriation of their land, the senseless slaughter of the buffalo, and many other atrocities. After a couple of hours of dramatic exchange, the emotions quieted down and, one after the other, the Indians accepted us into their ceremony. Finally, there was only one person who had remained violently opposed to our presence—a tall, dark, and sullen man. His hatred toward white people was enormous. It took a long time before he finally reluctantly agreed that we could join the group. It happened only after much pressure from his own people, who were unhappy about further delays of the ceremony.

Finally everything was settled, at least on the surface, and we all gathered in a large teepee. The fire was started and the sacred ritual began. We ingested the peyote buttons and passed the staff and the drum. According to the Native American custom, whoever had the staff could sing a song or make a personal statement; there was also the option to pass. The man who was so reluctant to accept us sat directly across from me. It was clear that he did not really wholeheartedly participate in the ceremony. Every time the staff and drum made the circle and came to him, he very angrily passed them on. My perception of the environment was extremely sensitized by the influence of peyote. This man became a sore point in my world and I found looking at him increasingly painful. His hatred seemed to radiate from his eyes and fill the entire teepee.

The morning came and, shortly before sunrise, we were passing the staff and the drum for the last time. Everybody said a few words summing up his or her experiences and impressions from the night. Walter Houston Clark's speech was exceptionally long and very emotional. He expressed his deep appreciation for the generosity of our Native American friends, who had shared with us their beautiful ceremony. Walter specifically stressed the fact that they accepted us in spite of everything *we* had done to them—invaded and stolen their land, killed their people, raped their women, and slaughtered the buffalo. At one point of his speech, he referred to me—I do not remember exactly in what context—as "Stan, who is so far from his homeland, his native Czechoslovakia."

When Walter mentioned Czechoslovakia, the man who had resented our presence all through the night suddenly became strangely disturbed. He got up, ran across the teepee, and threw himself on the ground in front of me. He hid his head in my lap and held my body in a firm embrace, crying and sobbing loudly. After about twenty minutes, he quieted down, returned to his place, and was able to talk. He explained that the evening before the ceremony he had seen us all as "pale faces" and thus automatically enemies of Native Americans. After hearing Walter's remark, he realized that, being of Czechoslovakian origin, I had nothing to do with the tragedy of his people. He thus hated me throughout the sacred ceremony without justification.

The man seemed heart-broken and desolate. After his initial statement came a long silence during which he was going through an intense inner struggle. It was clear that there was more to come. Finally, he was able to share with us the rest of the story.

During World War II, he had been drafted into the U.S. Air Force and, several days before the end of the war, he personally participated in a rather capricious and unnecessary American air-raid on the Czech city of Pilsen, known for its beer and its automobile factory. Not only had his hatred toward me been unjustified, but our roles were actually reversed; he was the perpetrator and I was the victim. He invaded my country and killed my people. This was more than he could bear.

After I had reassured him that I did not harbor any hostile feelings toward him, something remarkable happened. He went to my remaining four friends from Baltimore, who were all Americans. He apologized for his behavior before and during the ceremony, embraced them, and asked them for forgiveness. He said that this episode had taught him that there would be no hope for the world if we all carried in us hatred for the deeds commited by our ancestors. And he realized that it was wrong to make generalized judgments about racial, national, and cultural groups. We should judge people on the basis of who they are, not as members of the group to which they belong.

His speech was a worthy sequel to the famous letter of Chief Seattle to European colonizers. He closed it with these words: "You are not my enemies, you are my brothers and sisters. You did not do anything to me or my people. All that happened a long time ago in the lives of our ancestors. And, at that time I might actually have been on the other side. We are all children of the Great Spirit, we all belong to Mother Earth. Our planet is in great trouble and if we keep carrying old grudges and do not work together, we will all die."

By this time, most people in the group were in tears. We all felt a sense of deep connection and belonging to the human family. As the sun was slowly rising in the sky, we partook in a ceremonial breakfast. We ate the food that throughout the night had been placed in the center of the teepee and was consacrated by the ritual. Then we all shared long hugs, reluc-tantly parted, and headed back home. We carried with us the memory of this invaluable lesson in interracial and international conflict resolution that will undoubtedly remain vivid in our minds for the rest of our lives. For me, this extraordinary synchronicity experienced in a holotropic state of consciousness generated hope that, sometime in the future, a similar healing will happen in the world on a global scale.

11
The Sacred and the Profane

We do not understand much of anything, from the "big bang" all the way down to the particles in the atoms of a bacterial cell. We have a wilderness of mystery to make our way through in the centuries ahead.

—Lewis Thomas

Not everything that counts can be counted. Not everything that can be counted counts.

—Albert Einstein

Spirituality and Religion in Modern Society

The understanding of human nature and of the cosmos shared by modern technological societies is significantly different from the worldviews found in the ancient and pre-industrial cultures. To some extent, this is a natural result of historical progress and should be expected. Over the centuries, scientists from different disciplines have systematically explored various aspects of the material world and accumulated an impressive amount of information that was not available in the past. They have vastly complemented, corrected, and replaced earlier concepts about nature and the universe. However, the most striking difference between the two worldviews is not in the amount and accuracy of data about material reality. It is a fundamental disagreement concerning the sacred or spiritual dimension of existence.

All the human groups of the pre-industrial era were in agreement that the material world which we perceive and in which we operate in our everyday life is not the only reality.

Their worldviews, although varying in details, described the cosmos as a complex system of hierarchically arranged levels of existence. In this understanding of reality, which Arthur Lovejoy (1964) called the Great Chain of Being, the world of gross matter was the last link. Higher domains of existence included in pre-industrial cosmologies harbored deities, demons, discarnate entities, ancestral spirits, and power animals. Ancient and pre-industrial cultures had a rich ritual and spiritual life that revolved around the possibility of achieving direct contact with these ordinarily hidden dimensions of reality and receiving from them important information, assistance, or even intervention in the course of material events.

The everyday activities of the societies sharing this worldview were based not only on the information received through the senses, but also on the input from these ordinarily invisible realms. Anthropologists with traditional Western education were often baffled by what they called the "double logic" of the aboriginal cultures that they studied. While the natives clearly showed great practical intelligence, possessed extraordinary skills, and were able to produce ingenious implements for survival and sustenance, they combined their pragmatic activities, such as hunting, fishing, and building shelters, with strange, often complex and elaborate rituals. In these they appealed to various entities and realities that for the anthropologists were imaginary and nonexistent.

These differences in the worldviews find their strongest expression in the area of death and dying. The cosmologies, philosophies, and mythologies, as well as spiritual and ritual life, of the pre-industrial societies, contain a very clear message that death is not the absolute and irrevocable end of everything, that life or existence in some form continues after the biological demise. The eschatological mythologies of these cultures are in general agreement that a spiritual principle, or soul, survives the death of the body and experiences a complex series of adventures in consciousness in other realities.

The posthumous journey of the soul is sometimes described as a travel through fantastic landscapes that bear some similarity to those on earth, other times as encounters with various archetypal

beings, or as a progression through a sequence of nonordinary
states of consciousness. In some cultures the soul reaches a
temporary realm in the Beyond, such as the Christian purgatory
or the *lokas* of Tibetan Buddhism, in others an eternal abode—
heaven, hell, paradise, or the sun realm. Many cultures have
independently developed a belief system in metempsychosis or
reincarnation that includes return of the unit of consciousness to
another physical lifetime on earth.

All pre-industrial societies seemed to agree that death was
not the ultimate defeat and end of everything, but a transition to
another form of existence. The experiences associated with death
were seen as visits to important dimensions of reality that de-
served to be experienced, studied, and carefully mapped. The
dying people were familiar with the eschatological cartographies
of their cultures, whether these were shamanic maps of the
funeral landscapes or sophisticated descriptions of the Eastern
spiritual systems, such as those found in the *Bardo Thödol, The
Tibetan Book of the Dead.*

Bardo Thödol deserves a special notice in this context. This
important text of Tibetan Buddhism represents an interesting
contrast to the exclusive pragmatic emphasis on productive life
and denial of death characterizing the Western industrial civilization. It describes the time of death as a unique opportunity for
spiritual liberation from the cycles of death and rebirth and a
period that determines our next incarnation, if we do not achieve
liberation. From this perspective, it is possible to see the experiences in the *bardos,* or intermediate states between lives, as
being in a way more important than incarnate existence. In view
of this fact, it is absolutely essential that we prepare ourselves for
this journey by systematic practice during our lifetime.

These descriptions of the sacred dimensions of reality and
the emphasis on spiritual life are in sharp conflict with the belief
system that dominates the industrial civilization. Our worldview
has been to a great extent shaped by materialistically oriented
science, which asserts that we live in a universe where only
matter is real. Theoreticians of various scientific disciplines
have formulated an image of reality according to which the
history of the universe is the history of developing matter. Life,

consciousness, and intelligence are seen as more or less accidental and insignificant epiphenomena of this development. They
appeared on the scene after billions of years of evolution of
passive and inert matter in a trivially small part of an immense
universe. Clearly, the understanding of human nature and of the
universe based on such premises is in principle incompatible
with any form of spiritual belief. When we subscribe to this
image of reality, spirituality appears to be an illusory, if not
delusional, approach to existence.

This seeming incompatibility of science and spirituality is
quite remarkable. Throughout history, spirituality and religion had
played a critical and vital role in human life, until their influence
was undermined by the scientific and industrial revolution. Science
and religion represent extremely important parts of human life,
each in its own way. Science is the most powerful tool for obtaining information about the world we live in and spirituality is
indispensable as a source of meaning in our life. The religious
impulse has certainly been one of the most compelling forces
driving human history and culture. It is hard to imagine that this
would be possible, if ritual and spiritual life were based on entirely unfounded fantasies and fallacies. To exert such a powerful
influence on the course of human affairs, religion has to reflect a
very fundamental aspect of human nature, in spite of the fact that
it has often been expressed in very problematic and distorted ways.

If the worldview created by materialistic science really were
a true, full, and accurate description of reality, then the only
group in the entire history of humanity that has ever had adequate understanding of the human psyche and of existence
would be the intelligentsia of technological societies subscribing
to philosophical materialism. All the other perspectives and
worldviews, including the great mystical traditions of the world
and the spiritual philosophies of the East, would by comparison
appear to be primitive, immature, and deluded systems of thought.
This would include the Vedanta, various schools of yoga, Taoism, Vajrayāna, Hīnayāna, and Mahāyāna Buddhism, Sufism,
Christian mysticism, the Cabala, and many other sophisticated
spiritual traditions that are products of centuries of in-depth
explorations of the human psyche and consciousness.

Naturally, since the ideas described in this book are in basic congruence with various schools of the perennial philosophy, they would fall into the same category. They could be dismissed as irrational, ungrounded, and unscientific and the evidence on which they are based would not even be seriously considered. It seems therefore important to clarify the relationship between religion and science and to find out if these two critical aspects of human life are truly incompatible. And if we find out that there is a way of bringing the two of them together, it would be essential to define the conditions under which they can be integrated.

The belief that religion and science have to be mutually incompatible reflects a fundamental misunderstanding of the nature of both. Correctly understood, true science and authentic religion are two important approaches to existence that are complementary and do not in any way compete with each other. As Ken Wilber very appropriately pointed out, there cannot really be a conflict between genuine religion and true science. If there seems to be such a conflict, we are very likely dealing with "bogus religion" and/or "bogus science" (Wilber 1983).

Much confusion in this area is based on serious misconceptions concerning the nature and function of science, resulting in improper use of scientific thinking. An additional source of unnecessary problems is a misunderstanding concerning the nature and function of religion. For the purpose of our discussion, it is essential to distinguish true science from scientism and to clearly differentiate between spirituality and organized religion.

Scientific Theory and Scientific Method

Modern philosophy of science has clarified the nature, function, and proper use of theories in the exploration of various aspects of the universe. It exposed the errors that allowed materialistic monism to dominate Western science and indirectly also the worldview of the industrial civilization. In retrospect, it is not difficult to see how this has happened. The Newtonian image of the physical world as a fully deterministic mechanical system was so successful in its practical applications that it became a model for all the other scientific disciplines. To be scientific became synonymous with thinking in mechanistic terms.

An important result of the technological triumphs of physics was strong support for philosophical materialism, a position that Newton himself did not hold. For him, the creation of the universe was inconceivable without divine intervention, without the superior intelligence of the Creator. Newton believed that God created the universe as a system governed by mechanical laws. For this reason, once it had been created, it could be studied and understood as such. Newton's followers kept the image of the universe as a deterministic supermachine, but disposed of the notion of an intelligent creative principle as an unnecessary and embarassing leftover from the irrational dark ages. Sensory data about material reality became the only permissible source of information in all branches of science.

In the history of modern science, the image of the material world based on Newtonian mechanics entirely dominated the thinking in biology, medicine, psychology, psychiatry, and all the other disciplines. This strategy reflected the basic metaphysical assumption of philosophical materialism and was its logical consequence. If the universe is essentially a material system and physics is a scientific discipline that studies matter, physicists are the ultimate experts concerning the nature of all things and the findings in other areas should not be allowed to be in conflict with the basic theories of physics. Determined application of this type of logic resulted in systematic suppression or misinterpretation of findings in many fields that could not be brought into consonance with the materialistic worldview.

This strategy was a serious violation of the basic principles of modern philosophy of science. Strictly speaking, scientific theories apply only to observations on which they are based and from which they were derived. They cannot be automatically extrapolated to other disciplines. Conceptual frameworks articulating the information available in a certain area cannot be used to determine what is and is not possible in some other domain and to dictate what can and cannot be observed in the corresponding scientific discipline. Theories about the human psyche should be based on observations of psychological processes, not on the theories that physicists have made about the material world. But this is exactly the way mainstrean scientists have used in the past the theoretical framework of seventeenth-century physics.

The practice of illicit generalization of the worldview of physicists to other fields has been only part of the problem. Another serious but common error that further complicates the situation is the tendency of many scientists not only to adhere to outdated theories and generalize them to other fields, but to mistake them for accurate and definitive descriptions of reality. As a result, they tend to reject any data that are incompatible with their theoretical framework, rather than seeing them as a reason to change their theories. This confusion of the map with the territory is an example of what is known in modern logic as "error in logical typing." Gregory Bateson, a brilliant generalist and seminal thinker who spent much time studying this phenomenon, once facetiously stated that when a scientist continues making errors of this type, he or she might one day eat in a restaurant the menu instead of the dinner.

A basic characteristic of a true scientist is not uncritical adherence to materialistic philosophy and unshakeable loyalty to the stories about the universe promulgated by mainstream science. What characterizes a true scientist is commitment to unbiased rigorous application of the scientific method of exploration to all the domains of reality. This means systematic collection of observations in specifically defined situations, repeated experimentation in any domain of existence that makes application of such a strategy possible, and comparing of the results with others working under similar circumstances.

The most important criterion of the adequacy of a particular theory is not whether it conforms with the views held by the academic establishment, pleases our common sense, or seems plausible, but whether it it congruent with the facts of systematic and structured observation. Theories are indispensable tools for scientific reasearch and progress. However, they should not be confused with an accurate and exhaustive description of how things are. A true scientist sees his or her theories as the best available conceptualization of the currently available data and is always open to adjusting or changing them if they cannot accommodate new evidence. From this perspective, the world view of materialistic science has become a straitjacket that inhibits further progress instead of facilitating it.

Science does not rest on a particular theory, no matter how convincing and self-evident it might appear. The image of the universe and scientific theories about it have changed many times in the history of humanity. What characterizes science is the method of obtaining information and of validating or disproving theories. Scientific research is impossible without theoretical formulations and hypotheses. Reality is too complex to be studied in its totality, and theories reduce the range of observable phenomena to a workable size. A true scientist uses theories, but is aware of their relative nature and is always ready to adjust them or abandon them when new evidence emerges. He or she does not exclude from rigorous scrutiny any phenomena that can be scientifically studied, including controversial and challenging ones, such as nonordinary states of consciousness and transpersonal experiences.

In the course of the twentieth century, physicists themselves have radically changed their understanding of the material world. Revolutionary discoveries in the subatomic and astrophysical realms have destroyed the image of the universe as an infinitely complex, fully deterministic mechanical system made of indestructible particles of matter. As the exploration of the universe shifted from the world of our everyday reality, or the "zone of the middle dimensions," to the microworld of subatomic particles and to the megaworld of distant galaxies, physicists discovered the limitations of the mechanistic worldview and transcended them.

The image of the universe that had dominated physics for almost three hundred years collapsed under the avalanche of the new observations and experimental evidence. The commonsense Newtonian understanding of matter, time, and space was replaced by the strange wonderland of quantum-relativistic physics full of baffling paradoxes. Matter in the everyday sense of "solid stuff" completely disappeared from the picture. The neatly separated dimensions of absolute space and time fused into Einstein's four-dimensional space-time continuum. And the consciousness of the observer had to be recognized as an element that plays an important role in creating what earlier appeared to be purely objective and impersonal reality.

Similar breakthroughs have also occurred in many other disciplines. Information and systems theories, Rupert Sheldrake's concept of morphogenetic fields, the holonomic thinking of David Bohm and Karl Pribram, Ilya Prigogine's explorations of dissipative structures, the chaos theory, and Ervin Laszlo's unified interactive dynamics are just a few salient examples of these new developments. These new theories show increasing convergence and compatibility with the mystical worldview and with the findings of transpersonal psychology. They also provide a new opening for the ancient wisdom that materialistic science rejected and ridiculed.

The narrowing of the gap between the worldview of hard sciences and that of transpersonal psychology is certainly a very exciting and encouraging phenomenon. However, it would be a serious mistake for psychologists, psychiatrists, and consciousness researchers to let their conceptual thinking be restricted and controlled by the theories of the new physics instead of the old one. As I mentioned earlier, each discipline has to base its theoretical constructs on the observations from its own field of inquiry. The criterion for the validity of the scientific findings and concepts in a certain area is not their compatibility with the theories in another field, but the rigor of the scientific method with which they were obtained.

The Worldview of Materialistic Science: Fact and Fiction

In general, Western science has been extremely successful in finding the laws governing the processes in the material world and in learning to control them. Its efforts to provide answers concerning some fundamental questions of existence, such as how the world came into being and developed into its present form, have been much less spectacular and impressive. To get a proper perspective on this situation, it is important to realize that what we know as the "scientific worldview" is an image of the universe that rests on a host of daring metaphysical assumptions. These are often presented and seen as facts that have been proven beyond any reasonable doubt, while in reality they stand on a very shaky ground, are controversial, or are inadequately supported by evidence.

In any case, the answers that materialistic science offers for the most basic metaphysical questions are not more logical or less fantastic than those found in perennial philosophy. Thus in regard to the origin of the universe, there are many competing cosmological theories. The most popular of them asserts that everything began some 15 billion years ago in the Big Bang when all the matter in the universe, as well as time and space, emerged into existence from a dimensionless point or *singularity*. The rival theory of continuous creation portrays an eternally existing universe without a beginning and an end, in which matter is continuously created out of nothing. Neither of these alternatives represents exactly a rational, logical, and easy to imagine solution to this fundamental question of existence.

Equally bold and problematic are the theories of materialistic scientists concerning the biological realm. The phenomenon of life, including the DNA and its capacity of self-reproduction, allegedly spontaneously emerged from random interactions of inorganic matter in the chemical ooze of the primordial ocean. The evolution from primitive unicellular organisms to the extraordinary variety of species constituting the animal and plant life on our planet then resulted from random mutations of the genes and natural selection. And probably the most fantastic assertion of materialistic science is that consciousness appeared sometime late in the evolutionary process as a product of neurophysiological processes in the central nervous system.

When we subject the above concepts to rigorous scrutiny based on modern philosophy of science, systematic application of the scientific method, and logical analysis of the data, we will discover that they are hardly sober facts and that in many instances they lack adequate support by the facts of observation. The theory suggesting that the material constituting the universe

with its billions of galaxies spontaneously exploded into existence from a dimensionless *singularity* certainly does not satisfy
our reason. We are left with many burning questions, such the
source of the material that emerged in the Big Bang, the cause
and trigger of the event, the origin of the laws governing it, and
many others. The idea of the eternally existing universe in which
matter is continuously created out of nothing is equally staggering in its own way. The same is true about the remaining scientific
theories describing the origin of our universe.

   We are told that the cosmos essentially created itself and that
its entire history from the hydrogen atoms to *Homo sapiens* did
not require guiding intelligence and can be adequately understood
as resulting from material processes governed by natural laws.
This is not a very believable assumption, as many physicists themselves realize. Stephen Hawking, considered by some the greatest
living physicist, admitted that "the odds against a universe like
ours emerging out of something like the Big Bang are enormous."
And Princeton physicist Freeman Dyson once commented: "The
more I examine the universe and the details of its architecture, the
more evidence I find that the universe in some sense must have
known we were coming" (Smoot and Davidson 1993).

   Reconstructive studies of the early processes during the first
few minutes of the existence of the universe have revealed an
extraordinary and astonishing fact. Had the initial conditions been
only somewhat different, for example, had one of the fundamental constants of physics been altered by a few percent in either
direction, the resulting universe would not have been able to
support life. In such a universe, humans would never have come
into being to function as its observers. These coincidences are so
numerous and unlikely that they inspired the formulation of the
so-called Anthropic Principle (Barrow and Tipler 1986). This
principle strongly suggests that the universe might have been
created with the specific intention or with the purpose of bringing forth life and human observers. This points to participation
of superior cosmic intelligence in the process of creation or at
least allows interpretation in those terms.

   The failure of the Darwinian theory to explain evolution
and the extraordinary richness of life forms simply as a result of

mechanically operating natural forces is becoming increasingly obvious. The problems and loopholes of Darwinism and neo-Darwinism have been summarized in Phillip Johnson's book *Darwin on Trial* (1993). While evolution itself is a well-established fact, it is highly unlikely that it could have occurred without the guidance of higher intelligence and that it has been—to borrow Richard Dawkins' famous term—the work of a "blind watchmaker" (Dawkins 1986). There are too many facts in evolution that are incompatible with such an understanding of nature.

Random mutations in the genes that represent the basic explanatory principle of the neo-Darwinian theory of evolution are known to be in most instances harmful and are an unlikely source of advantageous changes in the organism. Moreover, emergence of a new species would require a highly improbable combination of a number of very specific mutations. An example is the evolutionary transition from reptiles to birds that required, among other things, simultaneous development of feathers, light hollow bones, and a different skeletal structure. In many instances, the transitional forms leading to new organs would not offer evolutionary advantage (as exemplified by a partially developed eye), or would even represent a liability (such as an incompletely formed wing).

To make things even more complicated for Darwinians, nature has often supported the emergence of forms that clearly represent an evolutionary disadvantage. For example, the beautiful tail of the peacock clearly makes the male more vulnerable to predators. The Darwinians argue that this is outweighed by the fact that beautiful tail attracts the females and increases the opportunities for copulation and transmisssion of genes. This appears to be a desperate effort to save the materialistic perspective at the price of conceding that peahens might have quite extraordinary aesthetic and artistic sensibilities. As Phillip Johnson (1993) pointed out, this situation is certainly more compatible with the concept of intelligent divine creation than with the Darwinian theory that gives all credit to blind material forces: "It seems to me that the peacock and the peahen are just the kind of creatures a whimsical creator might favor, but that an 'uncaring mechanical process' like natural selection would never permit to develop."

Important challenges against the Darwinian interpretation of evolution can also be drawn from the analysis of paleontological findings. In spite of enormous investments of time and energy, the existing fossil record has so far failed to fill in the missing links between species. Its general profile has not as yet been able to support a single transition from one species to another. The "Cambrian explosion," a sudden appearance of new multicellular organisms with widely differing body plans within a geologically negligible period of 10 million years ("the biological Big Bang") clearly demands a mechanism other than natural selection for its explanation.

More importantly, all the above arguments against Darwinism and neo-Darwinism focus only on the level of anatomy and physiology. They are superficial and negligible as compared to the problems that have emerged from biochemical understanding of various life processes. Modern science has shown that the secret of life is on the molecular level. Until recently, evolutionary biologists could be unconcerned with the molecular details of life, because very little was known about them. The complexity and intricacy of the molecular arrangements responsible for the structures and mechanisms underlying life processes is so spectacular that it represents a mortal blow for the Darwinian theory. In his recent book *Darwin's Black Box: The Biochemical Challenge to Evolution,* Michael J. Behe (1996) clearly demonstrated the failure of Darwinian thinking to account for the molecular structure and dynamics of life. The power of his argument is so devastating that it makes the problem of anatomy and fossil records irrelevant to the question of evolution.

The statistical improbability of life emerging out of random chemical processes is astronomical, as was clearly demonstrated by scientists of the stature of the world-famous astrophysicist Fred Hoyle and Francis Crick, the co-discoverer of the structure of DNA. The existence of over 200,000 proteins that have highly specialized biochemical and physiological functions in living organisms represents, in and of itself, an insurmountable problem. Fred Hoyle (1983) found the solution to this dilemma in embracing the theory of *panspermia,* according to which microorganisms are distributed throughout the universe and were brought to our planet by interstellar travel, possibly in the tail of a comet. Hoyle concluded that life is "a cosmological phenomenon, perhaps the most fundamental aspect of the universe itself."

Francis Crick (1981) went even farther. According to him, to avoid damage by the extreme interstellar conditions, the microorganisms must have traveled in the head of a spaceship sent to earth by a higher civilization that had developed elsewhere some billions of years ago. Life on our planet started when these organisms began to multiply. Hoyle's and Crick's approach does not, of course, solve the mystery of the origin of life; it simply defers it to another time and location. Both of them avoid the problem how life came into existence in the first place.

Information theorist H. Yockey (1992), who had attempted to assess the mathematical probability of the spontaneous origin of life, concluded that the information needed to begin life could not have developed by chance. He suggested that life be considered a given, like matter or energy. On the basis of the existing scientific evidence, it is highly implausible that the origin of life on our planet and the development of the rich plethora of species are the result of random mechanical forces. It is hard to imagine that they occurred without the intervention and participation of superior cosmic intelligence.

This brings us to the most critical point of our discussion, the claim of materialistic science that matter is the only reality and that consciousness is its product. This thesis has often been presented with great authority as a scientific fact that has been proven beyond any reasonable doubt. However, when it is subjected to closer scrutiny, it becomes obvious that it is not and never was a serious scientific statement, but a metaphysical assumption masquerading as one. It is an assertion that cannot be proved and thus lacks the basic requirement for a scientific hypothesis, namely testability.

Consciousness and Matter

The gap between matter and consciousness is so radical and profound that it is hard to imagine that consciousness could simply emerge as an epiphenomenon out of the complexity of material processes in the central nervous system. We have ample clinical and experimental evidence showing deep correlations between the anatomy, physiology, and biochemistry of the brain, on the one hand, and conscious processes, on the other. However, none of these findings proves unequivocally that consciousness is actually generated by the brain. The origin of consciousness from matter is simply assumed as an obvious and self-evident fact based on the belief in the primacy of matter in the universe. In the entire history of science, nobody has ever offered a plausible explanation how consciousness could be generated by material processes, or even suggested a viable approach to the problem.

The attitude that Western science has adopted in regard to this issue resembles the famous Sufi story. On a dark night, a man is crawling on his knees under a candelabra lamp. Another man sees him and asks: "What are you doing? Are you looking for something? " The man answers that he is searching for a lost key and the newcomer offers to help. After some time of unsuccessful joint effort, the helper is confused and feels the need for clarification. "I don't see anything! Where did you lose it?" he asks. The response is very surprising; the owner of the key points his finger to a dark area outside of the circle illuminated by the lamp and mumbles: "Over there!" The helper is puzzled and inquires further: "So why are you looking for it here and not over there?" "Because it is light here and I can see. Over there, I would not have a chance!"

In a similar way, materialistic scientists have systematically avoided the problem of the origin of consciousness, because this riddle cannot be solved within the context of their conceptual framework. There have been instances where some researchers claimed to have found the answer to the brain-consciousness problem, but these efforts do not withstand a closer scrutiny. The most recent example of this kind is the widely publicized book *The Astonishing Hypothesis* by the British physicist and biochemist Francis Crick (1994), Nobel laureate and co-discoverer with James Watson of the chemical structure of the DNA. As we read his book, "the astonishing hypothesis" turns out to be nothing more than a restatement of the basic metaphysical assumption of materialistic science: "You, your joys and your sorrows, your memories and ambitions, your sense of personal identity and free will, are in fact no more than the behavior of a vast assembly of nerve cells and their associated molecules."

In the specific treatment of the problem, Crick first simplifies the problem of consciousness by reducing it to the process of visual perception. He then proceeds to review a long list of experiments showing that the act of visual perception is associated with the activities in the retina and in the neurons that belong to the optical system. This is nothing new; it has long been known that seeing an object involves chemical and electric changes in the retina, in the optical tract, and in the suboccipital cortex. More refined and detailed study and analysis of these processes do not contribute anything to the solution of the basic mystery: What is it that is capable of transforming chemical and electric changes in the cerebral cortex into a conscious experience of a reasonable facsimile of the observed object?

What materialistic science wants us to believe is that it is possible that the brain itself has the capacity to somehow translate these chemical and electric changes into a conscious subjective perception of the observed material object. The nature of the process and mechanism capable of carrying out this operation eludes any scientific analysis. The assertion that something like this is possible is a wild and unsubstantiated conjecture based on a metaphysical bias rather than a scientific statement supported by solid evidence. Crick's book lists impressive experimental evidence of correlations between consciousness and the neurophysiological processes, but it avoids the central and critical issue. We are back to the Sufi story mentioned earlier.

The idea that consciousness is a product of the brain naturally is not completely arbitrary. Like Crick, its proponents usually refer to the results of many neurological and psychiatric experiments and to a vast body of very specific clinical observations from neurology, neurosurgery, and psychiatry, to support their position. When we challenge this deeply ingrained belief, does it mean that we doubt the correctness of these observations? The evidence for a close connection between the anatomy of the brain, neurophysiology, and consciousness is unquestionable and overwhelming. What is problematic is not the nature of the presented evidence but the interpretation of the results, the logic of the argument, and the conclusions that are drawn from these observations.

While these experiments clearly show that consciousness is closely connected with the neurophysiological and biochemical processes in the brain, they have very little bearing on the nature and origin of consciousness. There actually exists ample evidence suggesting exactly the opposite, namely that consciousness can under certain circumstances operate independently of its material substrate and can perform functions that reach far beyond the capacities of the brain. This is most clearly illustrated by the existence of out-of-body experiences (OOBEs). These can occur spontaneously, or in a variety of facilitating situations that include shamanic trance, psychedelic sessions, hypnosis, experiential psychotherapy, and particularly near-death situations.

In all these situations consciousness can separate from the body and maintain its sensory capacity, while moving freely to various close and remote locations. Of particular interest are "veridical OOBEs," where independent verification proves the accuracy of perception of the environment under these circumstances. There are many other types of transpersonal phenomena that can mediate accurate information about various aspects of the universe that had not been previously received and recorded in the brain.

Let us now take a closer look at the relevant clinical observations and laboratory experiments, as well as the interpretations of the evidence provided by traditional science. There is no doubt that various processes in the brain are closely associated and correlated with specific changes in consciousness. A blow on the head leading to brain concussion or compression of the carotid arteries limiting the oxygen supply to the brain can cause loss of consciousness. A lesion or tumor in the temporal lobe of the brain is often associated with very characteristic changes of consciousness that are strikingly different from those observed in persons with a pathological process in the prefrontal lobe. The differences are so distinct that they can help the neurologist to identify the area of the brain afflicted by the pathological process. Sometimes a successful neurosurgical intervention can correct the problem and the conscious experience returns to normal.

These facts are usually presented as conclusive evidence that the brain is the source of human consciousness. At first glance, these observations might appear impressive and convincing. However, they do not hold up when we subject them to closer scrutiny. Strictly speaking, all that these data unequivocally demonstrate is that changes in the brain function are closely and quite specifically connected with changes in consciousness. They say very little about the nature of consciousness and about its origin; they leave these problems wide open. It is certainly possible to think about an alternative interpretation that would use the same data, but come to very different conclusions.

This can be illustrated by looking at the relationship between the TV set and the TV program. The situation here is much clearer, since it involves a system that is human-made and incomparably simpler. The final reception of the TV program, the quality of the picture and of the sound, depends in a very critical way on proper functioning of the TV set and on the integrity of its components. Malfunctions of its various parts result in very distinct and specific changes of the quality of the program. Some of them lead to distortions of form, color, or sound, others to interference between the channels. Like the neurologist who uses changes in consciousness as a diagnostic tool, a television mechanic can infer from the nature of these anomalies which parts of the set and which specific components are malfunctioning. When the problem is identified, repairing or replacing these elements will correct the distortions.

Since we know the basic principles of the television technology, it is clear to us that the set simply mediates the program and that it does not generate it or contribute anything to it. We would laugh at somebody who would try to examine and scrutinize all the transistors, relays, and circuits of the TV set and analyze all its wires in an attempt to figure out how it creates the programs. Even if we carry this misguided effort to the molecular, atomic, or subatomic level, we will have absolutely no clue why, at a particular time, a Mickey Mouse cartoon, a Star

Trek sequence, or a Hollywood classic appear on the screen. The fact that there is such a close correlation between the functioning of the TV set and the quality of the program does not necessarily mean that the entire secret of the program is in the set itself. Yet this is exactly the kind of conclusion that traditional materialistic science drew from comparable data about the brain and its relation to consciousness.

Western materialistic science has thus not been able to produce any convincing evidence that consciousness is a product of the neurophysiological processes in the brain. It has been able to maintain its present position only by resisting, censoring, and even ridiculing a vast body of observations indicating that consciousness can exist and function independently of the body and of the physical senses. This evidence comes from parapsychology, anthropology, LSD research, experiential psychotherapy, thanatology, and the study of spontaneously occurring nonordinary states of consciousness. All these disciplines have amassed impressive data demonstrating clearly that human consciousness is capable of doing many things that the brain (as understood by mainstream science) could not possibly do.

Science and Religion

The authority that materialistic science enjoys in modern society has made atheism the most influential ideology in the industrial world. Although in the last decades this trend seems to be reversing, the number of people who seriously practice religion and think of themselves as "believers" has certainly decreased considerably with scientific progress. Because of the spell that materialistic science exerts on industrial societies, even believers often find it difficult to avoid the undermining and discrediting influence that Western science has had on religion. It is very common for people with religious upbringing to reject religion of any kind when they receive scientific education, because they start seeing any spiritual inclination as primitive and undefendable.

Organized religion, bereft of its experiential component, has largely lost the connection to its deep spiritual source and as a result has become empty, meaningless, and increasingly irrelevant in our life. In many instances, live and lived spirituality based on profound personal experience has been replaced by dogmatism, ritualism, and moralism. The most belligerent partisans of mainstream religion insist on literal belief in the exoteric versions of spiritual texts that appear childish and blatantly irrational to the educated modern mind. This is further confounded by the untenable positions that religious authorities maintain in regard to some important issues of modern life. For example, denying women the right of ministry violates democratic values and dwelling on the prohibition of contraception in face of such dangers as AIDS and overpopulation is absurd and highly irresponsible.

If we consider the descriptions of the universe, nature, and human beings developed by materialistic science, it is clear that they are in sharp contrast with the accounts offered by the scriptures of the great religions of the world. Taken literally and judged by the criteria of various scientific disciplines, the stories of the creation of the world, origin of humanity, immaculate conception, death and rebirth of divine personages, temptation by demonic forces, and judgment of the dead belong to the realm of fairy tales or handbooks of psychiatry. And it would be very difficult to reconcile such concepts as Cosmic Consciousness, reincarnation, or spiritual enlightenment with the basic tenets of materialistic science. However, it is not impossible to bridge the gap between science and religion if both are correctly understood.

As we have seen, much confusion in this area is caused by serious misconceptions concerning the nature and function of science and scientific theories. What is presented as a scientific refutation of spiritual realities is often based on scientistic argumentation rather than science. An additional source of unnecessary problems concerning religion is a serious misunderstanding and misinterpretation of the spiritual symbolism in sacred scriptures. This approach is characteristic of fundamentalist movements in mainstream religions.

When scientism and fundamentalism collide, neither side seems to realize that many of the passages in spiritual scriptures around which the controversy revolves should not be understood as references to concrete personages, geographical places, and historical events, but as accounts of transpersonal experiences. Scientific descriptions of the universe and the stories in religious texts do not relate to the same realities, they do not compete for the same terrain. As mythologist Joseph Campbell pointed out in his inimitable style, "the immaculate conception is not a problem for gynecologists and the promised land is not a piece of real estate."

The fact that modern astronomers have not found the images of God and angels on the photographs made by even the best of telescopes is not a scientific proof that they do not exist. Similarly, our knowledge that the inside of the earth consists of liquid iron and nickel does not in any way disprove the existence of the underworld and hell. Spiritual symbolism accurately portrays events and realities that we experience in holotropic states of consciousness and does not refer to occurrences in the material world of our everyday reality. Aldous Huxley made this very clear in his excellent essay "Heaven and Hell" (Huxley 1959). The only field that is capable of approaching the problem of spirituality scientifically is thus consciousness research focusing on systematic and unbiased exploration of nonordinary states of consciousness.

Many scientists use the conceptual framework of contemporary science in a way that resembles a fundamentalist religion more than it does science. They mistake it for a definitive description of reality and authoritatively implement it to censor and suppress all observations that challenge its basic assumptions. The worldview of materialistic science is clearly incompatible with the theologies of organized religions and the authority that science enjoys in our society certainly works in favor of its position. Since most people in our culture are not aware of the difference between religion and spirituality, the destructive influence of this kind of "science" affects not only religion, but extends to spiritual activity of any kind. If we want to achieve clarity concerning the basic issues involved in this conflict, it is essential to make a clear distinction not only between science and scientism, but also between religion and spirituality.

Spirituality and Religion

The failure to differentiate between spirituality and religion is probably the most important source of misunderstanding concerning the relationship between science and religion. Spirituality is based on direct experiences of nonordinary dimensions of reality and does not necessarily require a special place or an officially appointed person mediating contact with the Divine. It involves a special kind of relationship between the individual and the cosmos and is, in its essence, a personal and private affair. The mystics base their convictions on experiential evidence. They do not need churches or temples; the context in which they experience the sacred dimensions of reality, including their own divinity, are their bodies and nature. And instead of officiating priests, they need a supportive group of fellow seekers or the guidance of a teacher who is more advanced on the inner journey than they are themselves.

At the cradle of all great religions were visionary experiences of their founders, prophets, saints, and even ordinary followers. All major spiritual scriptures—the Vedas, the Upanishads, the Buddhist Pali canon, the Bible, the Koran, the Book of Mormon, and many others are based on direct personal revelations. Once religion becomes organized, it often completely loses the connection with its spiritual source and becomes a secular institution exploiting the human spiritual needs without satisfying them. Instead, it creates a hierarchical system focusing on the pursuit of power, control, politics, money, possessions, and other secular concerns.

Organized religion is institutionalized group activity that takes place in a designated location—a temple or a church—and involves a system of appointed officials who may or may not have had personal experiences of spiritual realities. Religious hierarchy tends to actively discourage and suppress direct spiritual experiences in its members, because they foster independence and cannot be effectively controlled. When this happens, genuine spiritual life continues only in the mystical branches, monastic orders, and ecstatic sects of the religions involved.

There is no doubt that the dogmas of organized religions are generally in fundamental conflict with science, whether this science uses the Newtonian-Cartesian model or is anchored in the emerging paradigm. However, the situation is very different in regard to spiritual experiences. In the last twenty-five years, systematic study of these experiences has become the main focus of a special discipline called transpersonal psychology. Spiritual experiences, like any other aspect of reality, can be studied scientifically; they can be subjected to careful, open-minded research. There is nothing unscientific about unbiased and rigorous study of these phenomena and of the challenges they represent for a materialistic understanding of the world. The critical question in this regard is the nature and the ontological status of mystical experiences. Do they reveal deep truths about some basic aspects of existence or are they products of superstition, fantasy, or mental disease?

The main obstacle in the study of spiritual experiences is the fact that traditional psychology and psychiatry are dominated by a materialistic philosophy and lack genuine understanding of religion and spirituality. In their emphatic rejection of religion, they do not make a distinction between primitive folk beliefs or the fundamentalists' literal interpretations of sacred scriptures, on the one hand, and sophisticated mystical traditions or Eastern spiritual philosophies, on the other. Western materialistic science has indiscriminately rejected any spiritual concepts and activities, including those based on centuries of systematic introspective exploration of the psyche. Many of the great mystical traditions developed specific technologies for inducing spiritual experiences and combined observation and theoretical speculation in a way that resembled modern science.

An extreme example of this lack of discrimination is Western science's rejection of Tantra, a system that offers an extraordinary spiritual vision of existence in the context of a comprehensive and sophisticated scientific worldview. Tantric scholars developed a profound understanding of the universe that has been in many ways validated by modern science. It included sophisticated models of space and time, the concept of the Big Bang, and such elements as a heliocentric system, interplanetary attraction, spherical shape of the earth and planets, and entropy.

Additional achievments of Tantra included advanced mathematics and the invention of the decimal count with a zero. Tantra also had a profound psychological theory and experiential method, based on maps of the subtle or energy body involving psychic centers (*çhakras*) and conduits (*nāḍīs*). It has developed highly refined abstract and figurative spiritual art and a complex ritual (Mookerjee and Khanna 1977).

Psychiatric Perspective on Religion

From the point of view of Western academic scientists, the material world represents the only reality and any form of spiritual belief reflects lack of education, primitive superstition, magical thinking, or regression to infantile patterns of functioning. The belief in any form of existence after death is not only refuted, but often ridiculed. From a materialistic perspective, it seems absolutely clear and unquestionable that the death of the body, particularly the brain, is the end of any form of conscious activity. Belief in the posthumous journey of the soul, an afterlife, or reincarnation is nothing but a product of wishful thinking of people who are unable to accept the obvious biological imperative of death.

People who have direct experiences of spiritual realities are in our culture seen as mentally ill. Mainstream psychiatrists make no distinction between mystical experiences and psychotic experiences and see both categories as manifestations of psychosis. The kindest judgment about mysticism that has so far come from official academic circles was the statement of the Committee on Psychiatry and Religion of the Group for the Advancement of Psychiatry entitled "Mysticism: Spiritual Quest or Psychic Disorder?" This document published in 1976 conceded that mysticism might be a phenomenon that lies between normalcy and psychosis.

In the present climate, even the suggestion that spiritual experiences deserve systematic study and should be critically examined appears absurd to conventionally trained scientists. Showing serious interest in this area, in and of itself, can be considered a sign of poor judgment and blemishes the researcher's professional reputation. In actuality, there exists no scientific "proof" that the spiritual dimension does not exist. The refutation of its existence is essentially a metaphysical assumption of Western science, based on an incorrect application of an outdated paradigm. As a matter of fact, the study of holotropic states, in general, and transpersonal experiences, in particular, provides more than enough data suggesting that postulating such a dimension makes good sense (Grof 1985, 1988).

At the cradle of all great religions of the world were powerful personal experiences of the visionaries who initiated and sustained these creeds—the divine epiphanies of the prophets, mystics, and saints. These experiences, revealing the existence of sacred dimensions of reality, were the inspiration and vital source of all religious movements. Gautama Buddha, meditating under the Bo tree, had a dramatic visionary experience of Kama Mara, the master of the world illusion, of his three seductive daughters trying to distract him from his spiritual quest, and of his menacing army attempting to intimidate him and prevent him from reaching enlightenment. He successfully overcame all these obstacles and achieved illumination and spiritual awakening. On another occasion, the Buddha also envisioned a long chain of his previous incarnations and experienced a profound liberation from karmic bonds.

Mohammed's "miraculous journey," a powerful visionary state during which archangel Gabriel escorted Mohammed through the seven Moslem heavens, Paradise, and Hell, was the inspiration for the Koran and for the Islamic religion. In the Judeo-Christian tradition, the Old Testament offers a dramatic account of Moses' experience of Yahwe in the burning bush and the New Testament describes Jesus' temptation by the devil during his stay in the desert. Similarly, Saul's blinding vision of Christ on the way to Damascus, St. John's apocalyptic revelation in his cave on the island Patmos, Ezechiel's observation of the flaming chariot, and many other episodes clearly are transcendental experiences in nonordinary states of consciousness. The Bible describes many additional instances of direct communication with God and the angels. The descriptions of the temptations of St. Anthony and of the visionary experiences of other saints and Desert Fathers are well-documented parts of Christian history.

Western psychiatrists interpret such visionary experiences as manifestations of serious mental diseases, although they lack adequate medical explanation and the laboratory data supporting this position. Mainstream psychiatric literature contains articles and books that discuss what would be the most appropriate clinical diagnoses for the great figures of spiritual history. St. John of the Cross has been called a "hereditary degenerate," St. Teresa of Avila dismissed as a hysterical psychotic, and Mohammed's mystical experiences have been attributed to epilepsy.

Many other religious and spiritual personages, such as the Buddha, Jesus, Ramakrishna, and Śri Ramana Maharshi have been seen as suffering from psychoses, because of their visionary experiences and "delusions." Similarly, some traditionally trained anthropologists have argued whether shamans should be diagnosed as schizophrenics, ambulant psychotics, epileptics, or hysterics. The famous psychoanalyst Franz Alexander, known as one of the founders of psychosomatic medicine, wrote a paper in which even Buddhist meditation is described in psychopathological terms and referred to as "artificial catatonia" (Alexander 1931).

Religion and spirituality have been extremely important forces in the history of humanity and civilization. Had the visionary experiences of the founders of religions been nothing more than products of brain pathology, it would be difficult to explain the profound impact they have had on millions of people over the centuries and the glorious architecture, paintings, sculptures, and literature they have inspired. There does not exist a single ancient or pre-industrial culture in which ritual and spiritual life did not play a pivotal role. The current approach of Western psychiatry and psychology thus pathologizes not only the spiritual but also the cultural life of all human groups throughout centuries except the educated elite of the Western industrial civilization that shares the materialistic worldview.

The official position of psychiatry in regard to spiritual experiences also creates a remarkable split in our own society. In the United States, religion is officially tolerated, legally protected, and even righteously promoted by certain circles. There is a Bible in every motel room, politicians pay lipservice to God in their speeches, and collective prayer is a standard part of the presidential inauguration ceremony. However, in the light of materialistic science, people who take seriously religious beliefs of any kind appear to be uneducated, suffering from shared delusions, or emotionally immature.

And if somebody in our culture has a spiritual experience of the kind that inspired every major religion in the world, an average minister will very likely send him or her to a psychiatrist. It has happened on many occasions that people who had been brought to psychiatric facilities because of intense spiritual experiences were hospitalized, subjected to tranquilizing medication or even shock treatments, and received psychopathological diagnostic labels that stigmatized them for the rest of their lives.

Holotropic States of Consciousness and the Image of Reality

The differences between the understanding of the universe, nature, human beings, and consciousness developed by Western science and that found in the ancient and pre-industrial societies is usually explained in terms of superiority of materialistic science over superstition and primitive magical thinking of native cultures. Careful analysis of this situation reveals that the reason for this difference is not the superiority of Western science, but the ignorance and naïvité of industrial societies in regard to holotropic states of consciousness.

All pre-industrial cultures held these states in high esteem and spent much time and energy trying to develop effective and safe ways of inducing them. They possessed deep knowledge of these states, systematically cultivated them, and used them as the major vehicle of their ritual and spiritual life. The worldviews of these cultures reflected not only the experiences and observations made in the everyday state of consciousness, but also those from deep visionary states. Modern consciousness research and transpersonal psychology have shown that many of these experiences are authentic disclosures of ordinarily hidden dimensions of reality and cannot be dismissed as pathological distortions.

In visionary states, the experiences of other realities or of new perspectives on our everyday reality are so convincing and compelling that the individuals who have had them have no other choice than to incorporate them into their worldview. It is thus systematic experiential exposure to nonordinary states of consciousness, on the one side, and the absence thereof, on the other, that sets the technological societies and pre-industrial cultures ideologically so far apart. I have not yet met a single individual who has had a deep experience of the transcendental realms and continues to subscribe to the worldview of Western materialistic science. This development is quite independent of the level of intelligence, type and degree of education, and professional credentials of the individuals involved.

Holotropic States of Consciousness and Human History

In this book, we have explored in some detail holotropic states of consciousness, their nature, content, and profound effect on the worldview, hierarchy of values, and strategy of existence. What we have learned from the study of holotropic experiences throws an entirely new light on the spiritual history of humanity. It shows that spirituality is a critical dimension of the human psyche and existence and takes authentic religion based on direct experience out of the context of pathology, where it has been relegated by materialistic science.

All the cultures in human history except the Western industrial civilization have held holotropic states of consciousness in great esteem. They induced them whenever they wanted to connect with their deities, other dimensions of reality, and with the forces of nature. They also used them for diagnosing and healing, cultivation of extrasensory perception, and artistic inspiration. They spent much time and energy trying to develop safe and effective ways of inducing them. As I described in the introduction to this book, these "technologies of the sacred," mind-altering techniques developed in ancient and aboriginal cultures for ritual and spiritual purposes, ranged from shamanic trance-inducing methods of various indigenous cultures to sophisticated practices of various mystical traditions and Eastern spiritual philosophies.

The practice of holotropic states can be traced back to the dawn of human history. It is the most important characteristic feature of shamanism, the oldest religion and healing art of humanity. Holotropic states are intimately connected with shamanism in several important ways. The career of many shamans begins with spontaneous episodes of visionary states, or psychospiritual crises, that the anthropologists call, with a typical Western bias, "shamanic illness." Others are initiated into the shamanic profession by practicing shamans through similar experiences induced by powerful mind-altering procedures, particularly drumming, rattling, chanting, dancing, or psychedelic plants. Accomplished shamans are able to enter holotropic states at will and in a controlled way. They use them for healing, extrasensory perception, exploration of alternate dimensions of reality, and other purposes. They can also induce them in other members of their tribes and provide for them the necessary guidance.

Shamanism is quite ancient, probably at least thirty to forty thousand years old; its deepest roots can be traced far back into the Paleolithic era. The walls of the famous caves in southern France and northern Spain, such as Lascaux, Font de Gaume, Les Trois Frères, Altamira, and others, are decorated with beautiful images of animals. Most of them represent species that actually roamed the Stone Age landscape—bisons, wild horses, stags, ibexes, mammoths, wolves, rhinos, and reindeer. However, others like the "Wizard Beast" in Lascaux are mythical creatures that clearly have magical and ritual significance. And in several of these caves are paintings and carvings of strange figures combining human and animal features, who undoubtedly represent ancient shamans.

The best known of these images is the "Sorcerer of Les Trois Frères," a mysterious composite figure combining various male symbols. He has the antlers of a stag, eyes of an owl, tail of a wild horse or wolf, human beard and penis, and paws of a lion. Another famous carving of a shaman in the same cave complex is the "Beast Master" presiding over the Happy Hunting Grounds teeming with beautiful animals. Also well known is the hunting

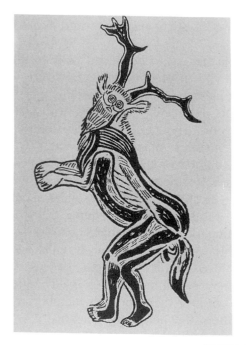

Figure 6. The Sorcerer of Les Trois Frères. A composite figure combining various male symbols—the antlers of a stag, the eyes of an owl, the tail of a wild horse or wolf, a human beard, and the paws of a lion.

Source: Reprinted from The Way of the Animal Powers *by Joseph Campbell. Used by permission of HarperCollins Publishers, Inc. © Copyright 1989 by Harper and Row.*

Figure 7. Beast Master. An engraved figure from Les Trois Frères cave representing the "Animal Master," a half-animal, half-human shamanic figure standing in the middle of the "Happy Hunting Ground" surrounded by wild animals.

Source: Reprinted from The Way of the Animal Powers *by Joseph Campbell. Used by permission of HarperCollins Publishers, Inc. © Copyright 1989 by Harper and Row.*

Figure 8. Hunting Scene (Lascaux). A hunting scene from the Lascaux cave representing an eventrated bison bull and a man with bird-like features and an erect penis, very likely a shaman in a trance. Near him is a bird perched on a staff.

Source: Reprinted from The Way of the Animal Powers *by Joseph Campbell. Used by permission of HarperCollins Publishers, Inc. © Copyright 1989 by Harper and Row.*

Figure 9. The Dancer. A dynamic shamanic figure from the cave called La Gabillou.

Source: Reprinted from The Way of the Animal Powers *by Joseph Campbell. Used by permission of HarperCollins Publishers, Inc. © Copyright 1989 by Harper and Row.*

scene on the wall in Lascaux. It shows a wounded bison and a lying figure of a shaman with an erect penis. The grotto known as La Gabillou harbors a carving of a shamanic figure in dynamic movement whom the archeologists call "The Dancer." In addition, on the clay floor of one of the caves, the discoverers found footprints in circular arrangement suggesting that its inhabitants conducted dances, similar to those that are still being performed by many aboriginal cultures for the induction of trance states.

Shamanism is not only ancient, it is also universal; it can be found in North and South America, in Europe, Africa, Asia, Australia, Micronesia, and Polynesia. The fact that so many different cultures throughout human history have found shamanic techniques useful and relevant suggests that the holotropic states engage what the anthropologists call the "primal mind"— a basic and primordial aspect of the human psyche that transcends race, sex, culture, and historical time. Shamanic techniques and procedures have survived until this very day in cultures that have escaped the profound influence of the Western industrial civilization.

The ritual and spiritual life in most native societies is practically synonymous with inducing holotropic states of consciousness in the context of healing rituals and various other sacred ceremonies held for a variety of purposes and occasions. Of special importance are the so-called rites of passage, first defined and described by the Dutch anthropologist Arnold van Gennep (1960). These are powerful rituals that have been performed in various pre-industrial cultures at the time of important biological and social transitions, such as circumcision, puberty, marriage, birth of a child, menopause, and dying.

Like the shamanic procedures, the rites of passage use powerful mind-altering technologies. The initiates have profound holotropic experiences that revolve around psychospiritual death and rebirth. This is then interpreted as dying in the old role and being born into the new one. Thus, for example, in one of the most important of such ceremonies, the puberty rite, the psychological death and rebirth of the adolescents is understood as death of boys and girls and birth of adult men and women. An important function of similar rituals is also to provide experiential access to the transcendental realm, validate the group's cosmology and mythology, and establish or maintain the individual's connection with other realities.

Holotropic states of consciousness also played a critical role in the ancient mysteries of death and rebirth, sacred and secret procedures in which initiates experienced powerful psychospiritual transformation. These mysteries were based on mythological stories about deities symbolizing death and transfiguration. In ancient Sumer, it was Inanna and Tammuz, in Egypt Isis and Osiris, and in Greece the deities Attis, Adonis, Bacchus, and Persephone. Their Mesoamerican counterparts were the Aztec Quetzalcoatl, or the Plumed Serpent, and the Hero Twins of the Mayan Popol Vuh. These mysteries were particularly popular in the Mediterranean area and in the Middle East, as exemplified by the Sumerian and Egyptian temple initiations, the Mithraic mysteries, or the Greek Korybantic rites, Bacchanalia, and the mysteries of Eleusis.

An impressive testimony for the power and impact of the experiences involved is the fact that the Eleusinian mysteries were conducted regularly and without interruption for a period of almost two thousand years and kept attracting prominent people from the entire ancient world. The cultural importance of the mysteries for the ancient world becomes evident when we realize that among their initiates were many famous and illustrious figures of antiquity. The list of neophytes included the philosophers Plato, Aristotle, and Epictetus, the military leader Alcibiades, the playwrights Euripides and Sophocles, and the poet Pindaros. The famous statesman Cicero, who participated in these mysteries, wrote a exalted report about their effects and their impact on the ancient civilization in his book *De Legibus* (Cicero 1987).

In the telestrion, the giant initiation hall in Eleusis, three thousand neophytes at a time experienced profound psychospiritual transformation. The exposure of such large numbers of people, including prominent philosophers, artists, and statesmen, to powerful holotropic states had to have an extraordinary impact on Greek culture and thus on the history of European culture in general. It is truly astonishing that this important aspect of the ancient world has remained largely unrecognized and unacknowledged by historians.

The specifics of the mind-altering procedures involved in these secret rites have remained for the most part unknown, although it is likely that the sacred potion *kykeon* that played a critical role in the Eleusinian mysteries was a concoction containing alkaloids of ergot similar to LSD (Wasson, Hofmann, and Ruck 1978) and that psychedelic materials were also involved in the Bacchanalia and other types of rites. Whatever "technologies of the sacred" were used in Eleusis, their effects on the psyche of the initiates had to be profound to keep the interest and attention of the ancient world alive for a period of almost two millennia.

Holotropic states have also played an important role in the great religions of the world. I mentioned earlier the visionary experiences of the founders that served as the vital source and inspiration for all the major religions. While these initial experiences were more or less spontaneous and elemental, many of these religions developed in the course of their history sophisticated procedures specifically designed to induce mystical experiences. Here belong, for example, different techniques of yoga, meditations used in Vipassanā, Zen, and Tibetan Buddhism, as well as spiritual exercises of the Taoist tradition and complex Tantric rituals. We could also add various elaborate approaches used by the Sufis, the mystics of Islam. They regularly used in their sacred ceremonies, or zikers, intense breathing, devotional chants, and trance-inducing whirling dance.

From the Judeo-Christian tradition, we can mention here the breathing exercises of the Essenes and their baptism involving half-drowning, the Christian Jesus prayer (hesychasm), the exercises of Ignatius of Loyola, and various Cabalistic and Hassidic procedures. Approaches designed to induce or facilitate direct spiritual experiences are characteristic of the mystical branches of the great religions and of their monastic orders.

Ritual use of psychedelic plants and substances has been a particularly effective technology for inducing holotropic states of consciousness. The knowledge of these powerful tools reaches far back, to the dawn of human history. In Chinese medicine, reports about psychedelic plants can be traced back more than 3,000 years. The legendary divine potion referred to as *haoma* in the ancient Persian Zend Avesta and as *soma* in India was used by the Indo-Iranian tribes several millennia ago and was probably the most important source of the Vedic religion and philosophy.

Preparations from different varieties of hemp have been smoked and ingested under various names (hashish, *charas, bhang, ganja, kif,* marijuana) in the Oriental countries, in Africa, and in the Caribbean area for recreation, pleasure, and during religious ceremonies. They have represented an important sacrament for such diverse groups as the Brahmans, certain Sufi orders, ancient Scythians, and the Jamaican Rastafarians.

Ceremonial use of various psychedelic materials also has a long history in Central America. Highly effective mind-altering plants were well known in several Pre-Hispanic Indian cultures—among the Aztecs, Mayans, Olmecs, and Mazatecs. The most famous of these are the Mexican cactus *peyote* (*Lophophora williamsii*), the sacred mushroom *teonanacatl* (*Psilocybe mexicana*), and *ololiuqui,* seeds of different varieties of the morning glory plant (*Ipomoea violacea* and *Turbina corymbosa*). These materials have been used as sacraments until this day by the Huichol, Mazatec, Chichimeca, Cora, and other Mexican Indian tribes, as well as the Native American Church.

The famous South American *yajé* or *ayahuasca* is a decoction from a jungle liana (*Banisteriopsis caapi*) and various other plant additives. The Amazon area is also known for a variety of psychedelic snuffs. Aboriginal tribes in Africa ingest and inhale preparations from the bark of the eboga shrub (*Tabernanthe iboga*). They use them in small quantities as stimulants and in larger dosages in initiation rituals for men and women. The above list represents only a small fraction of psychedelic compounds that have been used over many centuries in ritual and spiritual life of various human groups all over the world.

Holotropic States in the History of Psychiatry

Holotropic states of consciousness played a very important role in the development of depth psychology and psychotherapy. Most books describing the early history of this movement trace its beginnings to the Austrian physician and mystic Franz Anton Mesmer. Although Mesmer himself attributed the changes in consciousness experienced by his patients to "animal magne- tism," his famous Paris experiments were forerunners of the extensive psychological work with clinical hypnosis. Jean-Martin Charcot's hypnotic sessions with hysterical patients conducted in the Paris Salpetrière and the research in hypnosis carried out in Nancy by Hippolyte Bernheim and Ambroise Auguste Liébault played an important role in the professional development of Sigmund Freud.

During his study journey to France, Freud visited both Charcot and the Nancy group and learned to use hypnosis. He employed this skill in his initial explorations of the unconscious of his patients. But holotropic states had a critical role in the history of psychoanalysis in yet another way. Freud's early analytical specu- lations were inspired by his work with a hysterical patient whom he treated jointly with his friend Joseph Breuer. This client, to whom Freud refers in his writings as Miss Anna O., experienced spontaneous episodes of holotropic states in which she repeat- edly psychologically regressed into her childhood. The opportu- nity to witness the reliving of traumatic memories that occurred in these states and the therapeutic effects of this process had a deep influence on Freud's thinking.

For a variety of reasons, Freud later radically changed his strategies. He abandoned the use of hypnosis and shifted his emphasis from direct experience to free association, from actual trauma to Oedipal fantasies, and from conscious reliving and emotional abreaction of unconscious material to transference dynamics. In retrospect, these changes were unfortunate; they limited and misdirected Western psychotherapy for the next fifty years (Ross 1989). As a consequence of this development, psy- chotherapy in the first half of this century was practically synony- mous with talking—face to face interviews, free associations on the couch, and the behaviorist deconditioning.

As psychoanalysis and other forms of verbal psychotherapy gained momentum and reputation, the status of direct experien- tial access to the unconscious changed dramatically. Holotropic states that had been earlier seen as being potentially therapeutic and capable of providing valuable information about the human psyche became associated with pathology. Since that time, the prevailing practice in the treatment of these states, when they occur spontanously, has been to suppress them with all available means. It took many years before professionals began to rediscover the value of holotropic states and of direct emotional experience.

Holotropic States and Modern Consciousness Research

The renaissance of professional interest in holotropic states began in the early 1950s, shortly after the discovery of LSD-25, with the advent of psychedelic therapy. It continued few years later with new revolutionary developments in psychology and psychotherapy. A group of American psychologists and psychiatrists who were deeply dissatisfied with behaviorism and Freudian psychoanalysis felt and expressed the need for a new orientation in their fields. Abraham Maslow and Anthony Sutich responded to this call and launched a new branch of psychology that they called humanistic psychology. Within a short time, this movement became very popular.

Humanistic psychology provided the context for the development of a broad spectrum of innovative therapies. While traditional psychotherapies used primarily verbal means and intellectual analysis, these new so-called experiential therapies emphasized direct experience and expression of emotions. They also used various forms of body work as an integral part of the process. The best known among them, Fritz Perls' Gestalt therapy (Perls 1976), has since become very popular and is widely used, particularly outside the academic circles.

In spite of these radical departures from mainstream therapeutic strategies, most of the experiential therapies still relied to a great degree on verbal communication and required that the client stay in the ordinary state of consciousness. However, some of the new approaches were so powerful that they were able to profoundly change the state of consciousness of the clients. Besides psychedelic therapy, this included some of the neo-Reichian techniques, primal therapy, rebirthing, holotropic breathwork, and a few others.

Although these new experiential methods have not yet been accepted by mainstream academic circles, their development and use started a new chapter in the history of psychotherapy. They are closely related to ancient and aboriginal psychospiritual technologies that have played a critical role in the ritual, spiritual, and cultural history of humanity. If, in the future, they are accepted and their value recognized, they certainly have the potential to revolutionize the theory and practice of psychiatry.

In the second half of this century, significant contributions to the technology of inducing holotropic states have come not only from clinical work, but also from laboratory research. Biochemists have been able to identify the active alkaloids of many psychedelic plants and produce them in the laboratory. The most famous among them are *mescaline* from peyote, *psilocybine* from the Mexican magic mushrooms, and *ibogaine* from the African eboga shrub. Less known but important are *harmaline* from ayahuasca, *tetra-hydro-cannabinol* (THC) from hashish, and the *tryptamine derivatives* found in the South American snuffs and in the skin secretions of certain toads.

Chemical research has also added to this already rich psychedelic armamentarium the extremely potent semisynthetic LSD-25 and a large number of synthetic substances, particularly MDA, MDMA (Ecstacy or Adam), 2-CB, and other amphetamine derivatives. This made it possible to conduct systematic clinical and laboratory research of the effects of these compounds on a large scale and to study the physiological, biochemical, and psychological processes involved.

A very effective way of inducing holotropic states is sensory isolation or deprivation, which involves a significant reduction of meaningful sensory stimuli. Its extreme form involves total immersion in a large, completely dark, and acoustically isolated tank and a custom-made waterproof mask with an airpipe. Similarly, sleep deprivation and even dream deprivation can profoundly change consciousness. Dream deprivation without sleep deprivation can be achieved by waking experimental subjects every time their rapid eye movements (REM) indicate they are dreaming. There also exist laboratory devices that make it possible to learn lucid dreaming.

Another well-known mind-altering laboratory procedure is biofeedback, a method that allows to guide the individual by electronic signals into specific experiential realms characterized by preponderance of certain frequencies of brainwaves. A rapidly growing market now offers a rich spectrum of mind-altering devices that can induce holotropic states of consciousness by combining in various ways acoustic, optical, and kinesthetic stimulation. The account of new avenues in consciousness research would not be complete without mentioning thanatology, a discipline focusing on the study of near-death experiences (NDEs). Thanatological research has been the source of some of the most remarkable observations in the entire transpersonal field.

The renaissance of interest in holotropic states that we have witnessed in the last few decades has generated an extraordinary amount of revolutionary data. Researchers of different areas of consciousness research have amassed impressive evidence that seriously challenges the theories of materialistic science concerning the nature of consciousness. It leaves little doubt that the current scientific worldview that assumes primacy of matter and sees consciousness as its derivative cannot be adequately supported by facts of observation.

As a matter of fact, the observations from transpersonal psychology directly contradict the current image of consciousness as a byproduct of neurophysiological processes in the brain. The existence of the "veridical out-of-body experiences" in near-death situations would alone be sufficient to topple this leading myth of materialistic science. These experiences show that disembodied consciousness is capable under certain circumstances of accurately perceiving the environment without the mediation of senses.

What is probably most remarkable in the present situation is the degree to which academic circles have managed to ignore and suppress all the new evidence that shatters the most fundamental metaphysical assumptions of materialistic science. The recognition of the limitations of the existing conceptual frameworks to assimilate the new revolutionary data prompted Abraham

Maslow and Anthony Sutich, the two founders of humanistic psychology, to launch yet another psychological discipline that has become known as transpersonal psychology. This field studies the entire spectrum of human experience including the holotropic states and represents a serious attempt to integrate science and spirituality.

Conclusions

The main purpose for writing this final chapter was to establish that the cosmology described in this book is not incompatible with the findings of science, but with the philosophical conclusions that were inappropriately drawn from these findings. What the experiences and observations described in this book challenge is not science, but materialistic monism. I hope that I have been able to show that the materialistic worldview rests on a number of questionable metaphysical assumptions that are not adequately supported by facts and scientific evidence.

What characterizes true science is open-minded and open-ended application of the scientific method of inquiry to any domain of reality that allows it, no matter how absurd this undertaking might appear from a traditional perspective. I believe that pioneers in various areas of modern consciousness research have done exactly that. They have studied with great courage a wide spectrum of holotropic experiences and amassed in the process vast amounts of fascinating data. Many of the phenomena they have observed represent a crucial challenge to deeply ingrained beliefs that have long been falsely considered to be established scientific facts.

The more than four decades that I have spent in consciousness research have convinced me that the only way the proponents of materialistic science can maintain their present worldview is by systematically censoring and misinterpreting all the data concerning holotropic states. They have certainly successfully used this strategy in the past, whether the source of the challenging data was historical study, comparative religion, anthropology, or various areas of modern consciousness research. This certainly is true about parapsychology, psychedelic therapy, and experiential psychotherapies. Thanatology and the work with laboratory mind-altering techniques are additional examples.

I am convinced that this strategy cannot be continued indefinitely. It is becoming increasingly evident that the basic assumptions that represent the cornerstones of materialistic monism are at present not adequately supported by scientific data. In addition, the amount of evidence from consciousness research that has to be suppressed and ignored is rapidly growing. It is not enough to show that the claims of transpersonal psychology are incompatible with the worldview of materialistic science. To silence the conceptual challenges, it would be necessary to demonstrate that the observations from transpersonal psychology and consciousness research, including those described in this book, can be adequately accounted for and explained in the context of the materialistic paradigm.

I seriously doubt that mainstream materialistic critics would be more successful in accomplishing this task than the researchers in the transpersonal field have been themselves. I have the privilege of knowing most of them personally. They all have traditional academic backgrounds and had exerted great effort to find conventional explanations for their findings before they decided to seek a radical alternative. I know from my own experience that it was the disturbing and painful inadequacy of the old paradigm to account for the data and not iconoclastic zeal and delight that was responsible for the origins of transpersonal psychology.

It is important to emphasize that the cosmology described in this book is not in conflict with the facts and observations of any scientific discipline. What is being questioned and challenged is the appropriateness of the philosophical conclusions drawn from these observations. The ideas in this book do not change any of the specifics described by materialistic science. They simply provide an overarching metaframework for the phenomena constituting consensus reality. According to the materialistic worldview, the universe is a mechanical system that essentially created itself and consciousness is an epiphenomenon of material processes. The findings of transpersonal psychology and consciousness research strongly suggest that the universe might be a creation of superior cosmic intelligence and consciousness an essential aspect of existence.

There exist no scientific findings that demonstrate the priority of matter over consciousness and the absence of creative intelligence in the universal scheme of things. Adding the insights from consciousness research to the findings of materialistic science provides a more complete understanding of many important aspects of the cosmos for which we currently have unsatisfactory and unconvincing explanations. These include such fundamental questions as the creation of the universe, the origin of life on our planet, the evolution of species, and the nature and function of consciousness.

In addition, this new perspective on reality includes as its integral part the rich spectrum of holotropic experiences and related phenomena. This is a large and important domain of existence for which materialistic science has failed to provide reasonable and convincing rational explanations. After repeated frustrating attempts, I have myself given up hope that I would be able to explain my experiences and observations in the context of the conceptual framework that I received during my academic training. If any of the critics of transpersonal psychology succeed in presenting a convincing, sober, and down-to-earth materialistic explanation of the extraordinary world of holotropic experiences, I will be the first one to welcome it and congratulate them.

Bibliography

Alexander, F. 1931. "Buddhist Training as Artificial Catatonia." *Psychoanalyt. Rev.* 18: 129.

Ash, S. 1967. *The Nazarene.* New York: Carroll and Graf.

Aurobindo, Sri. 1976. *The Synthesis of Yoga.* Pondicherry, India: Sri Aurobindo Ashram, Publication Department.

Aurobindo, Sri. 1977. *The Life Divine.* Pondicherry, India: Sri Aurobindo Ashram, Publication Department.

Bache, C. M. 1980. *Lifecycles: Reincarnation and the Web of Life.* New York: Paragon House.

———. 1996. "Expanding Grof's Concept of the Perinatal." *Journal of Near-Death Studies* 15: 115.

———. 1997. *Dark Night, Early Dawn: Death–Rebirth and the Field Dynamics* (unpublished manuscript).

Barrow, J. D. and Tipler, F. J. 1986. *The Anthropic Cosmological Principle.* Oxford: Clarendon Press.

Behe, M. 1996. *Darwin's Black Box: The Molecular Challenge to Evolution.* New York: The Free Press.

269

Bohm, D. 1980. *Wholeness and the Implicate Order*. London: Routledge & Kegan Paul.

Bolen, J. S. 1984. *Goddesses in Everywoman. A New Psychology of Women*. San Francisco: Harper & Row.

———. 1989. *Gods in Everyman: A New Psychology of Men's Lives and Loves*. San Francisco: Harper & Row.

Campbell, J. 1968. *The Hero with a Thousand Faces*. Princeton, NJ: Princeton University Press.

———. 1972. *Myths to Live By*. New York: Bantam.

Chittick, W. 1983. *The Sufi Path of Love*. Albany: State University of New York Press.

Cicero: *De Legibus*. Newburyport, MA.: Focus Information Group, Inc.

Crick, F. 1981. *Life Itself, Its Origin, and Nature*. New York: Simon & Schuster.

———. 1994. *The Astonishing Hypothesis: The Scientific Search for the Soul*. New York: Scribner.

Dante, A. 1989. *The Banquet* (C. Ryan, trans.). Saratoga, CA: Amma Libri & Co.

Dawkins, 1986. *The Blind Watchmaker*. Harlow, UK: Longman.

deMause, L. 1975. "The Independence of Psychohistory." In *The New Psychohistory* (L. deMause, ed.). New York: The Psychohistory Press.

Einstein, A. 1962. *Mein Weltbild*. Berlin: Ullstein Verlag.

Fromm, E. 1973. *Anatomy of Human Destructiveness*. New York: Holt, Rinehart & Winson.

Gennep, A. van. 1960. *The Rites of Passage*. Chicago: University of Chicago Press.

Goleman, D. 1995. *Emotional Intelligence: Why It Can Matter More Than IQ*. New York: Bantam Books.

Grof, S. 1975. *Realms of the Human Unconscious: Observations from LSD Research*. New York: Viking Press.

———. 1980. *LSD Psychotherapy*. Pomona, CA: Hunter House.

———. 1985. *Beyond the Brain: Birth, Death, and Transcendence in Psychotherapy*. Albany: State University of New York Press.

———. 1988. *The Adventure of Self-Discovery*. Albany: State University of New York Press.

———. 1994. *Books of the Dead: Manuals for Living and Dying*. London: Thames & Hudson.

———. 1996. "Planetary Survival and Consciousness Evolution: Psychological Roots of Human Violence and Greed." *World Futures* 47: 243.

Grof, S. and Bennett, Z. 1992. *The Holotropic Mind: The Three Levels of Human Consciousness and How They Shape Our Lives*. San Francisco: Harper Publications.

Grof, S. and Grof, C. 1980. *Beyond Death: The Gates of Consciousness*. London: Thames & Hudson.

Grof, C. and Grof, S. 1990. *The Stormy Search for the Self*. Los Angeles: J. P. Tarcher.

Hahn, T. N. 1993. "Please Call Me by My True Names." In *Collected Poems*. Berkeley, CA: Parallax Press.

Harman, W. 1984. *Higher Creativity: Liberating the Unconscious for Breakthrough Insights*. Los Angeles: J. P. Tarcher.

Hines, B. 1996. God's *Whisper, Creation's Thunder: Echoes of Ultimate Reality in the New Physics*. Brattleboro, VT: Threshold Books.

Hoyle, F. 1983. *The Intelligent Universe*. London: Michael Joseph.

Huxley, A. 1945. *Perennial Philosophy*. New York and London: Harper and Brothers.

———. 1959. *The Doors of Perception* and *Heaven and Hell*. Harmondsworth, UK: Penguin Books.

Johnson, P. E. 1993. *Darwin on Trial*. Downer's Grove, IL: InterVarsity Press.

Jung, C. G. 1956. *Symbols of Transformation*. Collected Works, vol. 5, Bollingen Series XX. Princeton, NJ: Princeton University Press.

———. 1959. *The Archetypes and the Collective Unconscious*. Collected Works, vol. 9,1. Bollingen Series XX. Princeton, NJ: Princeton University Press.

———. 1960. *Synchronicity: An Acausal Connecting Principle*. Collected Works, vol. 8, Bollingen Series XX. Princeton, NJ: Princeton University Press.

————. 1973. Letter to Carl Selig, February 25, 1953. *C. G. Jung's Letters,* vol. 2, Bollingen Series XCV. Princeton, NJ: Princeton University Press.

Koestler, A. 1978. *Janus.* New York: Random House.

Lao-tzu. 1988. *Tao Te Ching* (Stephen Mitchell trans.). New York: Harper & Row.

Laszlo, E. 1993. *The Creative Cosmos.* Edinburgh: Floris Books.

Leibniz, G. W. von. 1951. *Monadology.* In *Leibniz: Selection* (P. P. Wiener, ed.). New York: Scribner.

Lovejoy, A. O. 1964. *The Great Chain of Being: A Study of the History of an Idea.* Cambridge, MA: Harvard University Press.

Maslow, A. 1964. *Religions, Values, and Peak Experiences.* Columbus, OH: Ohio State University Press.

Monroe, R., 1994. *The Ultimate Journey.* New York: Garden City, NY. Doubleday.

Mookerjee, A. and Khanna, M. 1977. *The Tantric Way.* London: Thames & Hudson.

Murphy, M. and White, R. A. 1978. *The Psychic Side of Sports.* Menlo Park, CA: Addison-Wesley.

Odent, M. 1995. "Prevention of Violence or Genesis of Love? Which Perspective?" Presentation at the Fourteenth International Transpersonal Conference in Santa Clara, California, June.

O'Neill, E. 1956. *Long Day's Journey into Night.* New Haven, CT: Yale University Press.

Origenes Adamantius (Origen). 1973. *De Principiis (On First Principles).* (G. T. Butterworth, transl.). Gloucester, MA: Peter Smith.

Pagels, H. 1990. *The Cosmic Code.* New York: Bantam Books.

Perls, F. 1976. *The Gestalt Approach and Eye-Witness to Therapy.* New York: Bantam.

Pistis Sophia. 1921. (G. R. S. Mead, trans.). London: John M. Watkins.

Plato. 1961a. *Laws. The Collected Dialogues of Plato.* Bollingen Series LXXI. Princeton, NJ: Princeton University Press.

————. 1961b. *The Republic. The Collected Dialogues of Plato.* Bollingen Series LXXI. Princeton, NJ: Princeton University Press.

Plotinus. 1991. *The Enneads*. London: Penguin Books.

Ring, K. 1982. *Life at Death: A Scientific Investigation of the Near-Death Experience*. New York: Quill.

———. 1985. *Heading toward Omega: In Search of the Meaning of the Near-Death Experience*. New York: Quill.

Ring, K. and Cooper, S. 1996. "Seeing with the Senses of the Soul (Sehen mit den Sinnen der Seele)." *Esotera* 12: 16–21.

Roberts, J. 1973. *The Education of Oversoul—7*. Englewood Cliffs, NJ: Prentice Hall.

Ross, C. *Multiple Personality Disorder: Diagnosis, Clinical Features, and Treatment*. New York: John Wiley.

Sartre, J.-P. 1960. *The Devil and the Good Lord*. New York: Alfred A. Knopf.

Schuon, F. 1969. *Spiritual Perspectives and Human Facts*. London: Perennial Books.

Smith, H. 1976. *The Forgotten Truth: The Common Vision of the World's Religions*. San Francisco: Harper & Row.

Smoot, G. and Davidson, K. 1993. *Wrinkles in Time*. New York: W. Morrow.

Stevenson, I. 1966. *Twenty Cases Suggestive of Reincarnation*. Charlottesville, VA: University of Virginia Press.

———. 1984. *Unlearned Languages*. Charlottesville, VA: University of Virginia Press.

———. 1987. *Children Who Remember Previous Lives*. Charlottesville, VA: University of Virginia Press.

———. 1997. *Reincarnation and Biology: A Contribution to the Etiology of Birthmarks and Birth Defects*. Westport, CT: Praeger.

Tarnas, R. (In press). *Cosmos and Psyche: Intimations of a New World View*. New York: Random House.

Thorne, K. 1994. *Black Holes and Time Warps: Einstein's Outrageous Legacy*. New York: W. W. Norton.

Traherne, T. 1986. *Centuries of Meditation*. Ridgefield, CT: Morehouse Publishers.

Wambach, H. 1979. *Life before Life.* New York: Bantam.

Wasson, R. G., Hofmann, A., and Ruck, C. A. P. 1978. *The Road to Eleusis: Unveiling the Secret of the Mysteries.* New York: Harcourt, Brace, Jovanovich.

Watson, B. (trans.). 1968. *Complete Works of Chuang Tzu.* University of Colorado Press.

Watts, A. 1966. *The Book about the Taboo against Knowing Who You Are.* New York: Vintage Books.

———. 1969. "Murder in the Kitchen." *Playboy,* December 1969. Also in *Does It Matter: Essays on Man's Relation to Materiality.* New York: Vintage Books, 1968.

Whitehead, A. N. 1929. *Process and Reality.* New York: Macmillan.

———. 1967. *Science and the Modern World.* New York: Free Press.

Wilber, K. 1980. *The Atman Project: A Transpersonal View of Human Development.* Wheaton, IL: The Theosophical Publishing House.

———. 1983. *A Sociable God: Brief Introduction to a Transcendental Sociology.* New York: McGraw-Hill.

———. 1995. *Sex, Ecology, and Spirituality: The Spirit of Evolution.* Boston: Shambhala Publications.

———. 1996. *A Brief History of Everything.* Boston: Shambhala Publications.

———. 1997. *The Eye of Spirit: An Integral Vision for a World Gone Slightly Mad.* Boston: Shambhala Publications.

Williams, G. C. 1966. *Adaptation and Natural Selection.* Princeton, NJ: Princeton University Press.

Yockey, H. 1992. *Information Theory and Molecular Biology.* Cambridge: Cambridge University Press.

Index

A

Absolute, the. *See* Consciousness, Absolute

absolute nothingness. *See* Void

Adler, Alfred, 206

aesthetic appreciation

enhanced in holotropic states, 46, 66

aggression, destruction and violence. *See also* murder; violence

malignant, 107, 203

perinatal experience and, 204

roots of, 203–5

birth trauma and, 106, 143–44

separates people from their true nature, 204

Al-ʿAlawi, Sheik, 219

Alexander, Franz, 252

Alexander the Great, 209–10

Alighieri, Dante, 208–9

animal past lives, persons with, 178

animals, identification with, 37, 63, 64, 185

annihilation, experiences of. *See also* death

during moment of birth, 145–46

anthropocentrism, 42

anxiety. *See* fear

archetypes, 86–87. *See also* collective unconscious; *specific archetypes*

as bridging material and spiritual worlds, 86–87

in holotropic breathwork, 23–24, 68–73

in holotropic states, 21–24, 37–38, 68–72

perinatal access to, 141

Arrien, Angeles, ix

art. *See also* drama

creation and, 66–68

Asch, Sholem, 162, 163

astral projection, experiment in, 194–96

astrology, 181

atheists' dilemma as seen in holotropic states, 56–57

Aurobindo, Śri, 56, 78, 79

275